An Immigrant's Quest

AMERICAN DREAM

Angelo Pellegrini

1986

NORTH POINT PRESS

San Francisco

This book is for Robert Mondavi, Italian immigrant and winegrower of distinction. His American Dream, gradually formulated from the time he graduated from Stanford University, was to prove that some of the world's great vintages could be grown on American soil. With the aid of his family, all active in the winery, and as a former president of the California Wine Institute, he has been largely instrumental in making wine drinkers of the four continents aware of the excellence of American wine. I respectfully salute the realization of his dream.

CONTENTS

AMERICAN DREAM

CHAPTER I

The Initial Challenge

What is the American dream? Is it to rise from log cabin origins to the White House? From a clerk to the president of the corporation? From poverty to wealth? From obscurity to professional distinction? Or is it a more modest dream—to have congenial employment, a happy family, and own one's own home? By the end of the recently celebrated bicentennial, many of these goals had been achieved by the millions who had come to America during the two preceding centuries. Since most had been drawn hither by the promise implicit in America's fabulous natural endowment, it was inevitable that they should conceive the American dream in economic terms. But economic gain has no more than marginal relevance to my vision of the dream.

Anyone who has more than an elementary knowledge of American history will agree that there are two American dreams: the collective and the individual. The collective dream was, initially, the enduring hope that the nation would progress in accordance with the "truths, ends, and purposes" set forth in the Declaration of Independence and the Constitution, especially its preamble and the Bill of Rights. I shall have something to say later on how this dream has fared.

As for the individual dream: its content—that which one dreams of and seeks to gain—is highly personal; the right to the dream, with the realistic hope of gaining what one seeks, is the supreme heritage, transmitted from generation to generation, of every American citizen. This legacy is structured in our democracy. When Jefferson, in writing the Declaration of Independence, substituted "the pursuit of happiness" for Locke's word "property" in listing a person's inalienable rights, the right to the dream became a part of the fundamental law.

During the first two centuries after the founding fathers had established the new nation, the dream, as one of economic gain, was realized with relative ease by those who were shrewd, aggressive, and richly endowed with the acquisitive instinct; and it was during these decades that the nation's endowment—land—was up for grabs. Thereafter, when what was left of the total natural endowment was largely in the domain of private enterprise and when the growth of monopolies had reduced the effectiveness of competition and the plenitude of general opportunities, there was a tendency, for the first time in our history, to become skeptical about the American dream as one of economic gain. It was no longer possible, for example, to do what Rockefeller had done. At sixteen years of age he began work as a clerk. At age twenty-four he invested three thousand dollars in an oil refinery; and at age forty he owned ninety percent of the nation's oil refineries. This was symbolic of what could be dreamed of and achieved during that period in our economic history when so much was available to anyone whose talent and temperament were congenial to that sort of quest.

Similarly, about six decades later, when my generation graduated from college in the middle twenties, opportunities for employment or for venturing into one's own enterprise were virtually unlimited. When the agents of higher education had come to urge our high school senior class to go to college, they sought to persuade us by a single argument: the more education you have, the greater will be your income. Commencement speakers made the same promise, along with certain pieties that no one took seriously. The sequel proved them prophetic. For while we worked toward a college degree, we had the assurance that our studies were an apprenticeship in the real life course we would follow thereafter. Nor were we disappointed; when we graduated, and had had a much needed rest after years of laborious study, each one of us proceeded to the workplace that the logic of the times had made available to us. Those who had chosen to continue their studies in graduate school were welcomed by the dean with no questions asked—an undergraduate degree was the only requirement. Not so today.

Forty years later, when my son graduated from the university, employment opportunities were severely limited. He, with a degree in romance languages, and one of his friends, with a degree in philosophy, could find no employment, so they did what had probably never been done before. Using their backgrounds in humanistic studies to lure salmon into their nets, they earned their bread as commercial fishermen in Bristol Bay. It was rumored that their extraordinary success prompted others in the fishing fleet seeking to increase their catch to return to school and earn a degree in liberal arts.

What, then, of the dream in our and future generations? Is it myth or reality? Such dreams as Rockefeller indulged in are now out of the question. Considering the continuing depletion of the planet's major resource systems, wisdom requires us to dream of ways of conserving rather than exploiting what remains of our natural endowment. This is not only a matter of declared national policy, but it ought also to be the concern of every individual. One who, in his personal design for living, avoids waste, extravagance, conspicuous consumption—quite independently of what the community may require—is a true conservationist. One who owns a plot of ground, adds to its natural fertility, and keeps it productive, helps to maintain, even by ever so little, the nation's cornucopia. One who plants a tree of a rare variety, or who gathers seeds of certain flora and provides for their germination and development is reducing the number of species that are in danger of extinction. These are dreams that increase self-respect because they embody what is right and proper and, though they require little of the dreamer, they add enormously to the general welfare.

There is current evidence, for those whose goal it is to rise from the log cabin (that is, from humble origins) to political or other eminence, that such opportunities are still a reality. The governors of our two most populous states, several senators, a score or more congressmen, and hundreds of others who have achieved eminence in business and the professions are children of immigrants who had little or no education and who began life as common laborers. Their gift to the new land was the talent and intelligence lodged in their genes, and those who were capable of dreaming, and who lived long enough, would see the dream realized in their children. Imagine, for example, the felicity that must grace the golden years of the parents of Mario Cuomo, governor of New York.

As I said above, economic gain is of no more than marginal relevance to my conception of the dream. The opportunity to earn one's bread, yes. That is a condition precedent to all else. Beyond that, the American Dream, properly conceived, is the inalienable right to seek happiness in self-realization. A just society, the overall goal of which is to promote the general welfare, says, in effect, to each of its members: Know thyself. Discover as early as possible your talent, your highest potential and within the framework of that self-knowledge, set a course, pursue it with vigor and imagination so that you may realize what was latent in your inborn physical and spiritual endowments. Where you need legitimate aid in your quest, society will provide it. And always remember that in your design for living the welfare of others is no less important than your own.

Bearing this in mind, I suggest that we forget about economic gain and concentrate on becoming something—the best that is latent in us. The dream, thus conceived, is and always has been a reality. The more we insist on the dream as an inalienable right and pursue it with determination, the more likely it will be to remain a live option available to all. For ultimately it derives from us, the people, and, as a community working together and intent on the same ends, we are, at any moment in our history, more likely to be what we had intended to become than to be something else. With that vision always in focus, every advance we make may very well lead to another and every realization of the dream will engender another.

However, some individuals, in pursuing their dream with the conviction that the end they seek is consistent with promoting the general welfare, may have to pay a price for their quest. Here I write from personal experience. What follows is an account of my own response to our society's imperative. Having defined my conception of the dream as achieving happiness through self-realization, I shall elaborate on my quest, the labor it has entailed, and the measure of self-realization I have achieved thus far. By its very nature, the quest is coextensive with life, and, even though I am now in my early eighties, the process continues. It began when I was ten years of age, reached a crisis when I was forty-five, and entered its most productive decades immediately thereafter. As I noted above, one who takes the American dream seriously and who strives with passion and determination to achieve its promise, always with the compelling awareness that the welfare of others is as important as one's own, may have to pay a price. My crisis was the price I had to pay.

What was this crisis? In the early thirties I joined the Communist party and soon thereafter, unhappy with what it had to offer, I left it. In the summer of

1948, nearly twenty years later, I was summoned to appear before a committee of the legislature that had been organized to investigate radical activities at the university. The penalty for refusing to cooperate with this committee was prosecution for contempt of the legislature. I shall give an account of the entire event later, in its proper place.

In order to understand fully my behavior and that of the committee and to place the sad interlude in its historical perspective, I must review the entire course of my general and political education as an immigrant to the "new land." There is a logic in it, an inevitability, that I am sure my contemporaries will understand; such is my hope. Except for this one flaw, my story is a happy one. Furthermore, one who reads with care and shares my passionate belief in the immutable and humane principles on which our democracy was founded will agree that this story must not go unrecorded. Poetry has been defined as emotion remembered in tranquility. Since mine was an intellectual experience charged with emotion, I have waited this long to record it so that I might reflect on it with the calm tranquility that is the blessing of the final years of a life lived in the warmth and glow of continuous, congenial labor and that approaches the ineluctable end with no major regrets.

I was not born with a silver spoon in my mouth, but a kind destiny attended my nativity. My parents were of sound peasant stock. They had no formal education, but they were intelligent, industrious, happily married, and dedicated to the welfare of their five children, of whom I was the firstborn son. We, including our parents, were born in Casabianca, a small community in the region of Italy known as Tuscany. The region itself, with Florence at its center, is the justly celebrated garden spot of sunny Italy. In addition to its art treasures, it has a certain natural endowment: the temperate climate, the soil, the olive groves, the Chianti hills noted for their vinifera grapes. Of the peasants who lived there, those who owned enough unencumbered land managed to keep bread on the table; others not so fortunate inherited a marginal existence from their parents. Of these, the ones who had the courage and managed to secure the necessary funds left the region. Some sought employment elsewhere in Europe. The more bold and imaginative (my parents among them), sustained by the hope of more and better bread, went to America. Father went first, to find employment and establish a home. Mother and the children joined him two years later in the fall of 1913.

The place where my father settled was McCleary, Grays Harbor county, in the state of Washington. The distance from Casabianca by ship and by rail was approximately seven thousand miles. In 1913, the amount of time required for an immigrant, traveling in agonizing discomfort, to journey from the one place to the other was thirty-one days. Such was our journey. The hope that sustained us from the day we left our native landscape—throughout the wretched days at sea, the fear and uncertainty that weighed heavily on us while we were detained at Ellis Island, the interminable days with scant food and nights without sleep while crossing the vast continent—was that we were on the way to live with our father in a land that he had described as a terrestrial paradise.

And such it was. In less than a year after our arrival we were rich. The land we needed was ours for the asking. Firewood littered the landscape. There was game in the hills and fish in the waters. The internal organs of beef cattle—liver, heart, kidney, tripe—were given freely to us who were barbarian enough to eat them. Father had a job. Mother, with the aid of the children, took in boarders. We had cows in the barn, pigs in the sty, rabbits in hutches, chickens in the henhouse. On rich land that had never been cultivated we grew all our vegetables and some of our fruit.

These resources were ours at no cost other than the sweat of our brows. As intended citizens we had a proprietary interest in the great cornucopia of a land that, according to Charles Beard (who wrote at about the same time as our arrival), was blessed with the greatest natural endowment of any nation in the world—an endowment, material and spiritual, that had been celebrated by Walt Whitman some half a century before:

> Fecund America!
> Thou envy of the globe! thou miracle!
> Thou, bathed, choked, swimming in plenty,
> Thou lucky Mistress of the tranquil barns . . .
> Thou mental, moral orb . . . !
> As a strong bird on pinions free,
> Joyous, the amplest spaces heavenward cleaving,
> Such be the thought I'd think of thee, America!

I have said that within a year after our arrival in father's earthly paradise we were rich, in the manner to which peasants traditionally aspired—bread on the table, clothes on the back, a roof over the head. To amass what we needed of this fabulous abundance was the family's initial challenge.

McCleary was a thriving community on the western frontier, a company town founded in the middle nineties by Henry McCleary and his two brothers. The only industry was a combined logging and milling operation. The use of the several acres we cultivated was given to us at no cost by the brothers. Father could have had title to the land for a few hundred dollars, but he believed that the value of the land was in its produce not in a legal document. And, since we were privileged to cultivate as many acres of it as we needed and at no cost, why pay for a deed? When the trees on the hillside had been felled, the stump land was available for two dollars an acre. Had father invested the first few hundred dollars we saved in such land, I would now be a fat cat instead of a retired schoolteacher. A German immigrant did precisely that, and half a century later his heirs sold it for several million dollars.

I do not record this in criticism of my father, for I do not regret what to others may seem in him a lack of vision. His dream was fully realized when he had settled his family in that richly endowed area of the opulent Pacific Northwest, and my dream, though a different sort and not then formulated, was latent in his. His labor and his careful husbandry brought me to the new land and to a properly nurtured manhood. That was enough. Under the circumstances, no father could have done more for his firstborn son. Furthermore, life is attended by certain evils, and, as Doctor Johnson noted two centuries ago, wealth eliminates only one of them—poverty.

I have attributed this achievement to father, for, in accordance with the patriarchy of the Old World, he was the head of the family. But in our household, mother was his equal and partner. Whatever of importance was ventured, whether proposed by one or the other, was always the result of their joint decision. My tribute to her was published in the *Pacific Spectator*, Autumn 1949, shortly after her death.

I have given a full account of our immigration to America and its consequences in my several books. In writing this story I shall repeat only certain matters that are relevant to my theme: the search for the meaning of America—its political, economic, and judicial history—as entailed by my pursuit of the American dream.

CHAPTER II

A World of Labor and Learning

Since I was ten years of age and had known labor as a peasant boy in the Old World (labor that had yielded no more than the daily crust of bread), what impressed me initially above all else was America's material fecundity. What use I have made of this is reflected in my current status: well fed, in good health, father and husband of a happy family in our own home, and securely provided for, for the rest of my life. Later, and by slow degrees, I discovered what I had not known or expected: the "mental, moral orb," America's spiritual endowment. What I have absorbed of that endowment is the subject of this chronicle.

When father summoned us to join him and gave an account of the resources he had found in McCleary, he said nothing about educational opportunities for us children. When, after our arrival, he took us on a tour of the landscape that would be our home, noting several times with the pride of a benefactor that all we saw was essentially our own, he did not direct our attention to the schoolhouse, plainly visible on a hill at the edge of the forest. Why the omission?

There are two reasons. We had come to America in search of bread, and not of anything else implied in the word "opportunity." The word, so current in the American way of life, was not in the vocabulary of the peasant; the options to which it referred were unknown in his world. Furthermore, in our heritage there was no tradition of culture as formal education. Father had one year of formal education; mother had none. Since education had not been their expectation, they did not particularly regret the lack of it. For these reasons father had not directed our attention to the schoolhouse, and none of us had really noticed the omission.

Had father known what his firstborn son would eventually learn, he would have realized that the school was a part of the structure and plan of the new land and a central element in its pragmatic philosophy. America, with its commerce and industry expanding on the eve of World War I, needed educated workers. Thus, when we arrived on the scene, the concept of education for all, gratis for the lower grades and at a minimum cost in college, was already current in American society. It was uniquely American. Had father known this, he would have realized that an adequate appraisal of the new land's resources must include education for the children, that there could be no way of avoiding the little school at the top of the hill.

The new land was strange in many ways; the strangest of these was that it required children to go to school until they were sixteen years of age. We were informed of this fact by the principal of the McCleary school. He came into our home as one who bears good news, not in the least aware that we might find it incomprehensible. There are two laws, he told us: Children must attend school until they are sixteen or have completed the eighth grade; and their employment in industry is prohibited until they reach that age. He welcomed us warmly into the community, and told us that the teachers were excellent and anxious to help us in all possible ways.

So that was the law! Incredible! Father reacted to its requirement with his habitual prudence. He granted that such a law might seem strange and absurd, but, he noted, there was no alternative but obedience. What he privately thought, not so much about the merits of the law as about his firstborn son going to school for another six years, I never did know. The merits of educational policy were not discussed in a peasant's home. However, we were ancestrally conditioned to obedience to authority, so what the state required, wisely or otherwise, must be obeyed. What would be my father's attitude toward my continuing school beyond what the law required? Would he readily agree to my going to the university in the big city, miles and miles away? When I returned to school in January, 1914, this question was not yet within the range of our imagination. However, in a few years I would press the issue, and father would have to commit himself.

When I began a new life in this blessed land of labor and learning, my parents planned the daily labor. There was much to do in order to maintain and add to the standard of living we had achieved by the end of the first year. Land to cultivate, animals to tend to, fuel for the wood burning stove to cut and fetch home from the forest; it was all labor that we were skilled in and did with a certain zest because it was immediately remunerative in a way and a degree hitherto unknown to us. It made us rich in the basics of life.

The kind destiny that attended my nativity provided me with a succession of wise, affectionate teachers of archetypal competence. In the world of learning, these would be my surrogate parents and would affect the course of my education. Within six months, the first of these had taught me enough of the English language so that I could enter the fourth grade, where I properly belonged at ten years of age. She immediately accepted the challenge I posed: I was a young boy willing to learn who must learn the language as quickly as possible. To that end, she devised an inspired strategy.

She explained it to me about fifty years later, when I discovered her quite by chance in a retirement home. Her name was Ivah Dobbs. She taught the first four grades. According to her plan, the first grade children would actually do the preliminary teaching, and I would learn to read precisely as they had learned at the start of the school term. (I joined the class three months after the start of the year.)

This is what she told me: "You were a strange appearance in our schoolroom and the center of attention for the first few days. You were dark and they were blond. The clothes you wore were unlike theirs. Since you knew no word of English, you never spoke. When someone asked your name, you shrugged your shoulders. You were a few years older than they and you never smiled. So I told them your name and something of what they should know about you in order to make them comfortable in your presence. This relieved them of their anxiety and made them eager to assist me in teaching you the language."

Her plan was flawless and produced immediate results. She told the class that for my benefit they would repeat the beginning reading exercises. The first grade reader was actually a book of drawings and pictures and, written in large letters under each, was the identifying legend. Thus on page one was the picture of a dog, and under it was the simple declarative, "This is a dog." There followed other pictures similarly identified. Standing in front of the class with reader in hand, each child in turn would read aloud, clearly and slowly, beginning on page one. The teacher would sit by me and point with her finger at each word as it was pronounced. Some of the words she pronounced herself, showing me how to produce the sound by proper placement of the lips and tongue.

The first to read for me was a little lad whose hair was parted in the middle. His complexion was the fairest of the fair, his face was narrow, and his mouth small with lips slightly pursed, but his voice was strong and he read well. Holding the reader firmly in both hands, he stood before the class looking intently at the page, anxious, no doubt, to avoid making a mistake in his first performance as a teacher. When he felt sure of himself, he raised his head, looked straight at me and pronounced the historic declarative, "This is a dog." The teacher, showing me how to pronounce the, to me, unfamiliar "th" sound, repeated, "This is a dog." And I understood every single word! In my great excitement, the built-in frown vanished and I smiled.

Putting words and pictures together, I immediately inferred the meaning of the brief declarative and translated it into Italian: *Questo e un cane*. The same number of words. This is a dog must mean *Questo e un cane*. Making similar inferences I translated other simple declaratives read to me. Thus by the end of that day I knew for certain the English pronoun "this," the indefinite article "a," the verb "is," and the nouns "dog," "cat," "rat," "boy," "girl." In the same manner, during the next few days, I learned the indefinite article "an," the definite article "the," and other nouns. From this sound beginning I quickly progressed to other forms: "these," "that," "those," "am," "are."

In learning so much that was fundamental in so little time, my knowledge of Italian was a considerable aid. Here I must make a relevant observation. The study discipline in an Italian school was imposed without mercy, especially in reading, writing, and arithmetic. No time was lost in pleasant diversions such as I found in the American schoolroom. The pace was swift, the standards high. Those who could not keep abreast were left behind. The

Darwinian hypothesis was at work in the classroom. The practical result was that a graduate of the third grade knew as much about reading, writing, and arithmetic as a sixth grader in the American school. Being such a graduate, I knew what my little teachers did not know—the elements of grammar and sentence structure. Since these are essentially similar in the two languages, my knowledge of Italian greatly facilitated my learning to read and write English. But learning to speak the language, to articulate it as a native, was more difficult. There were sounds, such as "th," that were unfamiliar. It would take time to learn to produce such sounds perfectly. And then there were words such as "tough" and "dough" that one simply had to accept on faith.

Thus, after one week of such exercises that the teacher devised, what had been completely dark was now clear. I no longer despaired. I felt confident that I would soon know the written language as well as my peers. What a relief to know that the language could be learned! What a thrill to hear "This is a dog" and understand what was heard! How exciting to cease being totally dumb! O this learning, what a thing it is!

And here I must give due credit to the teacher. She was as determined as I that I should learn the language in the shortest possible time. She became my friend, my tutor, and my guide. Had she been unsympathetic, or less skilled, I should have fared differently. She worked with me during the recess period, the lunch hour, and after school. She brought me into her home and, relentlessly pursuing the same method—"this is a chair," "this is a table," "that is the floor"—she enlarged my vocabulary and gradually taught me to see, to hear, to think, and to articulate in English. She drilled me in the elements of English grammar, especially in the conjugation of basic verbs, and after each session with her I religiously practiced what I had learned. Given her skill and devotion as a teacher and my own determination and self-discipline, at the end of six months in school I had learned enough of the language to be advanced to the fourth grade.

While thus learning the language, I continued to be an amused and fascinated spectator. Here I make no claim to having had an acuteness of observation beyond my years. During the time that I was effecting a transition from the Old to the New World, there were certain comparisons that even one so young as I could not fail to note. Between McCleary and Casabianca there was a dramatic difference in what I may call the ethics, conventions, and code of behavior that prevailed in the school. In the one, the necessary discipline was tempered by friendliness and informality; in the other, it was aggravated by the severe formality of the guardhouse. The code was sensibly permissive in the one, rigidly authoritarian in the other. When the teacher entered the schoolroom in Casabianca, the students stood at attention by their benches and sat when ordered to do so; the least infraction of the code was severely punished.

Here it was altogether different. The teacher was at her desk when the young ones drifted into the room. She greeted each one by name, caressed them, asked questions, commented on their apparel, graciously accepted what little gifts the students might offer, usually fruit or a flower. And the little ones themselves approached the teacher each morning as they would a doting grandmother. There was no cleavage between pupil and teacher, and unbecoming behavior was gently reprimanded: "Now Johnny, you mustn't pull Betty's hair! You wouldn't want someone to do that to you, would you?"

I noted in the classroom what I had also observed among the people in the town, namely that there were no visible class distinctions. No one appeared privileged, the teacher dealt with each one with amiable impartiality. The children of the McCleary brothers and of the company executives were in that school, but it was not possible to distinguish them from those of the loggers and mill hands. They all dressed pretty much alike and mingled freely. (In Casabianca, the daughter of the schoolteacher had, so to speak, a reserved seat in the room. Since she had caused certain amorous stirrings in me, I wrote her a letter from McCleary. She did not reply. My impertinence in writing to her must have offended her.)

There was also a marked difference in the general approach to education. As I have already noted, the study discipline in Casabianca was imposed without mercy. It was all work and no play. In McCleary the learning process was casual and relaxed. Work and play were nicely balanced so that the transition from the one to the other was scarcely noticed. The day was begun with a singing session—a strange though pleasant way to begin the school day! Each day the teacher read a short story or an episode of a long one to the class. There were mid-morning and mid-afternoon recesses and friendly

competitions in spelling and arithmetic. There were reports on activities—
who had an interesting experience to share with the class? The intent seemed
to be to make the day at school as pleasant as possible.

I had known none of these amenities in the school in Casabianca. In the
third grade we had begun the day with a rigorous exercise in composition.
The teacher chose the subject and she required from each pupil, with no
questions permitted, an acceptable essay on any phase of the subject. She
accepted nothing short of perfection, nor was she unique in this requirement.
The principal emphasis in the Italian school was on mastery of the language,
Dante's *dolce stil nuovo*; the language that had so fascinated a great English
poet that he had referred to it as:

> That soft bastard Latin
> Which melts like kisses from a female mouth
> And sounds as if it should be writ on satin.

Granted! The teacher's objective was commendable, but to require children
of peasants who had no cultural heritage whatever to do justice to such a
language in a daily composition was to impose on them a duty that made
them sweat with the fear of failure. I myself had done rather well in such exercises, but I must confess that beginning the day with a burst of song was much
more fun.

I have recorded these observations for their relevance to my theme, especially those that reflect the egalitarian ideal of the new land, an ideal that I
was in the process of discovering without knowing it; for without being
aware of it at the time, I was recording on the tabula rasa of my mind significant data for later interpretation. I remember, for example, the excitement
with which I read a certain section of Lord Macaulay's celebrated essay on
Milton in a graduate seminar in English literature. Defending Milton's role
in the rebellion against Charles the First, Macaulay wrote, "That great battle
was fought for no single generation, for no single land. The destinies of the
human race were staked on the same cast with the freedom of the English
people. Then were first proclaimed those mighty principles which have since
worked their way into the depths of the American forests . . . ."

Into the depths of the American forests! I had the strange sensation that
Macaulay was asking me to remember that, what I had observed in that
community and in that school at the center of one of those forests, I had later

interpreted in terms of those mighty principles. Magna Carta! The great rebellion! The glorious revolution! The consequences of those great victories
on the achievement of the rights of man were all implicit in the simple fact of
social equality—the lack of visible distinctions between the children of the
mill owners and those of the mill hands!

No visible distinctions! There was a philosophical basis for that phenomenon, a new and revolutionary concept of government, but it would be several years before I had the necessary knowledge of American history to understand that concept and to integrate it into all that I was learning about the
new land. Meanwhile the divinity that shapes our ends had ordained that I
should have my first lesson in American history near the end of my second
year in the McCleary school. It was an elementary beginning, but very sound
and very significant.

I was now in the fifth grade and in the custody of another teacher. The first
one had taught me with skill and affection, bless her! I could now read and
write and speak well enough to continue learning with my peers. The second
was Christine Edwards, no less skilled than the first, but a veritable dynamo
who was endowed with irrepressible enthusiasm. She was a matron with a
commanding maternal bosom who had expunged the word "impossible"
from her vocabulary. Her full round face was a galaxy of freckles, her head
was a thicket of bright red hair, and her blue eyes twinkled star like in their
deep sockets. There was no severity whatever in her happy face, but it
was aglow with confidence and jovial determination. When Henry Adams
assumed his professorship of history at Harvard, he noted that a teacher
affects eternity. Ivah Dobbs, Christine Edwards, and others of my teachers
certainly affected this mortal.

When I was placed in the custody of Christine Edwards, she announced
that she had planned the course of my education: "In three more years you
shall have completed the elementary grades; in the fall of 1919 you will go on
to high school, from which you will easily graduate in three years. Then you
will go on to college in the fall of 1922." She delivered the announcement
firmly and with a smile of confidence. The course was set. There were no
alternatives.

Christine Edwards, of Scottish ancestry, was then in her middle fifties, profoundly maternal (though unmarried), and I was her boy. Her ethical orien-

tation was that of a determined, ambitious, middle class Victorian mother who was planning the course of her son's education. From the course she set there would be no deviations, and, as shall be seen, there were none.

Drilled as I had been in strict obedience to parents, elders, teachers, and the ordinances of God, I listened to her and nodded affirmatively without really understanding the substance of what the freckled dynamo was saying. I knew the words "high" and "school," but did not know precisely what a high school was. Furthermore, whatever it was, there was none such in McCleary. And of college I knew absolutely nothing. I was in school in obedience to the law, and, being obedient by training, I would proceed along the course she prescribed without knowing precisely what the course was.

Later during that school year, Christine Edwards taught me what I needed to know in order to have some idea of what she had planned for me. Some idea, I say, for at that age, and given my peasant background, I could not possibly have grasped its total meaning. Thus I learned that high school is a four year course intermediate between the eight elementary years and college, but I could not conceive the possibility, the reality, of my going to school another four years beyond the six the law required. And as for going to the university! Christine Edwards explained that the university was an institution of higher learning where one prepared oneself for a career in the arts, the sciences, and the various professions—such as law. "Would you like to be a lawyer?" she asked. I laughed and shrugged my shoulders. I had never known a lawyer and hadn't the slightest notion of what a lawyer might be, as I certainly had of what a miller was, or a mason, or a baker. Her suggestion that I might go to college and become a lawyer was, in the context of my limited experience, without any really intelligible meaning. Had she suggested that I might go to paradise and become an angel, I would have understood her much better.

However, Christine Edwards had been wise in planning the course of my education. As a native American, the very embodiment of America's opulence, self-confidence, and boundless optimism, she had expected that her plan would set me on fire. Would it not have had that effect on an American boy as eager as I? But when I failed to respond in a more positive manner than a shrug of the shoulders, she must have realized that my bewildered acquiescence—not to say indifference—meant that I had found it impossible to grasp the reality of what she had proposed. The seed, however, had been dropped, and she was confident that time would bring it to fruition.

Meanwhile there was much to be done that was of immediate concern: The language barrier must be completely overcome, and Angelo Pellegrini must become an American boy perfectly at ease with his peers. Toward the achievement of that end Christine Edwards worked with passion. She lived in a cottage near our home, and every day whenever we could manage to be together she drilled me in grammar, spelling, and vocabulary. She urged me to mingle with the boys on the playfield and to play their games so that I might learn from them the ways of American boys. I did all she suggested, though the laborious routine that father prescribed for me at home left little time for play. But I learned readily and was pleased with what I learned. Not once did I feel discouraged or unequal to what Christine Edwards expected of me, and I learned so well that in the contests in spelling and arithmetic I was invariably among the winners. However, I must admit that my knowledge of the Italian language gave me somewhat of an advantage over my peers in spelling. Big words such as "materialistic," "indivisible," "agriculture," difficult for them because of their bigness, were easy for me because they were so nearly like their Italian equivalents that I knew so well. It was words such as "dough" and "tough" and "laughter" that puzzled me. But with Christine Edwards' aid and my increasing determination to learn, I was able to overcome the vagaries of the new language that I found so fascinating.

Then came the lesson in American history. It had not been included in Christine Edwards' plan for my education. Why not? Perhaps it had not occurred to her that as an immigrant to the new land I should learn immediately something of its history and its form of government, that I should become aware of the duties and rights of citizenship. Her motive in planning for me had been strictly academic. She was a teacher, and fate had placed in her custody an immigrant boy who could be taught and was eager to learn. Thus she had planned his course of education, and in her total design a knowledge of American history would be no more important than a knowledge of the history of Greece and Rome. But she gave me that first lesson. It was basic, elementary, and impressive. The occasion for it was the celebration of Thanksgiving Day in the McCleary school.

It was customary in those days, particularly in rural America for the schools to present an appropriate program on the eve of certain national holidays, an entertainment in which the entire school participated. After weeks of rehearsing skits, songs, and recitations, the program was presented in the school auditorium or, as in McCleary, in the village church, on the day preceding the holiday vacation. Such a program was planned in the McCleary school in celebration of Thanksgiving Day near the end of my second year in school. Christine Edwards was chosen to direct it and she decided that I should have a leading role in the festivities. Would I like that? Very good, for I never questioned what she required of me.

In preparation for the celebration, huge yellow pumpkins and ears of corn were brought into the room. On the walls there were pictures of Pilgrims and large paper cutouts of turkey gobblers. What was the meaning of all this? Who were the Pilgrims? Would Christine Edwards explain the meaning of Thanksgiving Day? She did that evening in her cottage, and she did it with characteristic thoroughness. Thus it was that I learned about the Pilgrim fathers, the settling of New England, the Declaration of Independence, the Revolution, George Washington, the Constitution. This was all very elementary and brief, but Christine Edwards assured me that in time I would learn the entire history. There were certain elements in that first lesson that were very significant.

She read to me the text of the Mayflower Compact: "We do by these present, solemnly and mutually . . . covenant and combine ourselves together into a civil body politic, for our better ordering and preservation; and by virtue hereof to enact equal laws . . . ." That simple compact, signed on November 11, 1620, she said was expanded into the Constitution of the United States of America, adopted September 17, 1787. She read to me the preamble: "We the people of the United States, in order to form a more perfect union, establish justice, insure domestic tranquility, provide for the common defense, promote the general welfare, and secure the blessings of liberty to ourselves and our posterity, do ordain and establish this constitution for the United States of America." Then she explained to me what is meant by self-government, democracy, and government by consent of the governed. I did not understand it all, but I did get the drift of what she was saying and more data was recorded on that tabula rasa for later interpretation.

She explained to me the meaning of the word "pilgrim"—a religious devotee who travels to a shrine, goes on a pilgrimage, or simply travels from land to land. Did I know the Italian equivalents of pilgrim and pilgrimage? Yes, I did: *pellegrino* and *pellegrinaggio*. And thereupon I discovered something that hadn't occurred to me before—that our family name was actually the plural form of *pellegrino*. So we, too, were pilgrims, she told me, and, significantly, as the Pilgrim fathers had landed at Cape Cod on November 11, 1620, so had we arrived in McCleary on November 11, 1913. We were, indeed, pilgrims, and there was comfort in that fact. The Pilgrim fathers had come in pursuit of religious freedom; we had come in pursuit of more and better bread. And to add to my comfort and make me feel less strange in the new land, Christine Edwards told me that her grandparents had been pilgrims from Scotland, and that the whole of America had been settled by *pellegrinis* from various lands. America differed in that respect from other nations, she said; we are a congregation of races. The children in the school were of English, Irish, German, and Scandinavian ancestry. The only difference between them and me was simply that their parents and grandparents had arrived in the new land somewhat sooner than my family. So you must not feel that you are an intruder, she said; in America we are all *pellegrinis* or descendants of *pellegrinis*. When you have completed your education you shall have forgotten all about Italy; you will then be an American.

I left her cottage that evening in a state of happy excitement. I had learned so much in so brief a time and understood so little, but I was immensely pleased by the little that I had understood. I had no precise idea of the meaning of the Mayflower Compact or of what she had said about democracy and government by consent of the governed, but I did understand that in America we were all *pellegrini* or descendants of *pellegrini*. The idea fascinated me so much and I was so pleased with Christine Edwards' use of my name, that I trotted home to the tune of *In America siamo tutti pellegrini*.

Thus briefed in the beginnings of American history, I was now ready to assume a leading role in the Thanksgiving Day program. And here, too, Christine Edwards had planned very wisely for me. A prominent role in the program would give me a bit of much needed status and quicken the process of my becoming a regular fellow among my peers. Unfortunately, the role she had chosen for me was not one I could perform in any very impressive manner. I was to sing the lead in a skit called "The Turkey Gobbler's Lament." I had not been asked whether I was a talented warbler. Since I had come from the land of opera stars, Christine Edwards had assumed that I could sing; if she thought I could, I would. What saved the day for me was that I was expected to sing like a turkey, and that I did without the slightest effort. What I remember of the song goes something like this:

> The turkey gobbler says, says he,
> At last what will become of me,
> Thanksgiving Day is here once more
> I feel my days are o'er.

There was a burst of applause and requests for an encore, whereupon I gobbled once more and all agreed that a real turkey could have done no better. Indeed, he could not!

I was now well on the way toward overcoming the language barrier, a formidable obstacle to becoming an American boy. To become such, indistinguishable from my peers, was a goal toward which I labored with determination.

Why so? For the very good reason that at that time there was no comfort whatever in the fact of being an Italian. This was not so much because of discrimination against us, but for the reason that we were crude, untutored peasants from the old country who had come to this marvelous new world, not as tourists on a grand vacation, but as virtual beggars seeking bread in exchange for the labor of our peasant hands. There was no prestige in being such, so I sought admiration by becoming something other, something better than I was—an American instead of an Italian boy.

Naturally I could not possibly change my physical self—I was the dark one among the fair—but I could become completely American in speech, in manners, in performance on the playfield, and in the general preoccupations of the young. I would also court admiration by superior performance in the classroom and on the playfield. My solo performance in the Thanksgiving holiday program had given me a measure of distinction. For a few precious moments I had been the center of attention: a peasant boy fresh from Italy singing the lead in a skit in celebration of a great American holiday! I would seek more such moments. Thus motivated, and always with the skilled and generous assistance of my teachers, I bent all my efforts toward the achievement of these desires.

My efforts were not in vain. I became an American boy—in school. It was no great achievement. After all, I was a young boy, well fed, in perfect health, strong, agile, alert, well taught, spilling over with normality, and armed with an effective weapon my peers generally lacked—a willingness to work to capacity to attain well-defined goals. Under the circumstances, the achievement of those goals, modest as they were, was in the very logic of my being.

In the classroom I had no difficulty at all in keeping abreast of the superior students; on the playfield I did rather well in baseball. But I could have done much better. In the classroom I had overcome the language barrier to excellent performance; on the playfield there was a barrier to stardom that I could not overcome—my father's indomitable will. He was determined to achieve security by the sweat of his brow—and of ours. Even before we arrived in McCleary he had planned to put us all to work. When we were settled, the work schedule he designed for me left no time for the practice necessary to excel in baseball and other games. It was not brutal and it was not unreasonable; it simply left no time to play the games. And since father could not understand the relevance of such games to education, I petitioned without success for a relaxation of the rule that required me to come home immediately after school. I knew I could become a star pitcher. I felt it in the very marrow of my bones. All I needed was time to practice, to practice as the other boys did, before and after school. Lacking that, I failed to achieve stardom, and the big leagues lost a potential Babe—a frowning, black-haired Babe from the "cesspool of Europe." What a pity that father's domestic economy should have had so regrettable a consequence!

I achieved, instead, undisputed supremacy in milking cows, keeping the wood bins full, tilling the soil, scrubbing floors, and kneading bread for mother. Not for these or other such irrelevancies in the education of an American boy, does one achieve immortality in the Hall of Fame.

In other ways the strategy worked. Having completed the fifth grade by the end of May, 1916 (after two and a half terms in school), my proficiency in the language now equal to that of my brightest classmates, I took the sixth and seventh grades in stride. Except for my physical appearance, even the most perceptive observer would not have seen that I was in any way different from my Nordic peers. When in September, 1918, I began the eighth, the last of the elementary grades, I was what I had planned to become—an American boy.

I was now in my fifteenth year. By the end of the term, In May, 1919, I would be sixteen and no longer required by law to attend school. Would that be my last year, the end of my formal education? In my home it was tacitly assumed that such would be the case. I was now approaching manhood. Physically more mature than my age would indicate, strong and healthy, and well trained in physical labor, I was ready to work as a man in the mill or on the railroad. And father, with his carefully planned domestic economy, was no doubt looking forward to the day when I would join the labor force and, in accordance with ancestral traditions, turn over to him the paycheck at the end of the month.

But I had other plans, the ones outlined for me by Christine Edwards. These I kept to myself, wisely waiting to cross those bridges when I came to them. Why raise issues prematurely? I would proceed without unnecessarily troubling the waters and hope that the logic of events would make my plans prevail. In this frame of mind I began the eighth grade. At this time, the same time World War I came to an end and that my family had our fifth anniversary in McCleary, I made a daring move: I instigated and led a revolt against the eighth grade teacher.

It was a bold move and perhaps somewhat impertinent, but it was justified. The teacher, a man in his middle years, was incompetent. How he had gained certification as a teacher remained a mystery. He was not a bad man; he simply lacked the necessary knowledge to teach the eighth grade. We soon found that in conducting the class he relied on the brighter students to answer the difficult questions. At first we thought that in doing this he was merely flattering us and putting the rest of the class to shame. But we became suspicious. Could he himself answer the difficult questions and solve the difficult problems? Consulting with two of the other bright students, I suggested that henceforth we should feign ignorance and leave the questions and the problems to the teacher. The strategy worked. Questions remained unanswered and problems unsolved. The daily embarrassment was pervasive, and the entire class became aware of the teacher's incompetence. A problem in arithmetic put it beyond doubt. One of the exercises in the text required each student to determine the amount of wallpaper necessary to paper the walls in his home. It was a tough assignment and students wanted to know how they should proceed. Would I explain the procedure to the class? I did not know.

Charles did not know. Martha did not know. The text itself suggested the procedure, but the teacher was incapable of making the necessary inferences to explain the text. Thus the problem was never solved. The resulting embarrassment, as on many previous occasions, was very distressing. The time had come for me to make my move.

Once again I consulted with some of the better students and proposed that we rebel—withdraw from school and register in the school at Summit, a few miles from the village. The eighth grade teacher there, a young and handsome lady, had assured me that we would be accepted. They agreed to what I proposed, and we sealed the agreement with a firm handshake. Our first move was to secure the consent of our parents.

This I had already done and with as much difficulty as I had expected. The move was especially daring for me for the reason that in Casabianca it would have been inconceivable. Father, whose consent was necessary, was still of Casabianca. In the Old World, a peasant, much less a peasant boy, did not question the authority or judge the competence of a teacher. Had a similar situation arisen there, two words would have been the allowable degree of protest: *pazienza* and *speriamo*. We must be patient. Let us hope. The storm has destroyed half the wheat crop. *Pazienza*. Will there be enough sun to ripen the grapes? *Speriamo*. Since the crop is a short one, will the landlord accept a third rather than a half? *Speriamo*. These expressions of resignation and a sense of futility were the peasant's perennial and only consolation in the presence of evil and injustice. The social order in which he lived, essentially hierarchical, denied him the right to take the initiative. Hence the alternatives: *pazienza, speriamo*.

Such had been father's attitude when I presented my plan. "Pazienza!" But I was no longer of Casabianca. I did not feel at all its burden of medievalism that still weighed so heavily on father. I kept insisting to him that we were now in America and that in America all was different, although I was not sure what "all" included. In the end I prevailed, but the clincher in my impassioned rhetoric was the assurance that we were not revolting, we were merely leaving one school to attend a better one. The teacher in the better school, sensitive to our distress, had tacitly approved my proposal and accepted us in her class. Father was also aware of the fact that I was a serious, determined student who had a record of consistently excellent performance, since each term he signed my report card, which I took pains to explain to him. For these reasons he gave his consent. My own view, however, was the heroic one: I had successfully led a revolt against authority as an American boy in the new land:

> A land of settled government,
> A land of just and old renown,
> Where Freedom slowly broadens down
> From precedent to precedent,

I no longer needed such consolation as was to be found in *pazienza* and *speriamo*.

CHAPTER III

There Is a Tide in the Affairs of Man . . .

In the context of a relatively non-permissive society and in view of my training in unquestioning obedience to authority, my move had been daring though carefully planned. The measure of its success exceeded my expectations. Knowing nothing about the metaphorical tide in the affairs of man, I had taken full advantage of this opportunity and ridden it to good fortune. The success of my rebel act—I preferred to consider it such—proved to be an important move toward attaining the goals Christine Edwards had set for me. Meanwhile, reactions came from other quarters: my father and the school board.

My departure from the school with three of my associates had left the eighth grade class completely demoralized—no discipline, slack attendance, and little instruction. There were rumors that the upstart "wop kid" had instigated the disrupting "strike," and I was summoned to appear before the school board. This consequence I had not anticipated, and I now needed a measure of daring that I lacked. Had I unwittingly broken the law? What punishment must I endure? Present fears were compounded by horrible imaginings: The reformatory; my family disgraced; my future ruined. I needed the aid of Christine Edwards, but she was no longer at McCleary School. What was the mettle of American authority? I knew very well what it was in Casabianca! I consulted with Laura Gibson, the teacher at Summit School. She assured me that I had not transgressed a law. I must go before the board without fear and tell them why I had organized the "revolt." "You are in school as the law requires," she said. "Have no fear, the board will understand."

But when I appeared before the board, I was unsteady with apprehension. With my heart drumming in my ears, I stated our case: We were not mischievous boys seeking to avoid going to school. We were serious students who wanted to study and to learn, but the teacher was incompetent. Questions remained unanswered and problems unsolved. So we had sought and been granted admission to the eighth grade class at Summit. We hadn't missed a single day of school, and so on.

The members of the board, much to my surprise and great relief, were very friendly. They promised an investigation. If the teacher were found to be incompetent, he would be dismissed and another would be hired to take his place. Meanwhile I and my associates were allowed to continue attending the Summit school. What a relief! I had the impression that some of the board members had already suspected the teacher's incompetence. In any case I was certain that an investigation would support the charge, and I felt completely vindicated. This could be an instance of government by the consent of the governed.

When I received the summons to appear before the board—an alarmingly formal letter—father was no less fearful than I. Peasants normally regard a formal written document with respect and suspicion, for the contents of such documents are seldom in their interest. Thus, when I gave father an account of the interview with the board, exaggerating a bit by telling him that they had promised to dismiss the teacher, he was incredulous. A peasant boy fresh from Italy had successfully questioned the authority and judged the competence of an American teacher. Impossible! I must be mistaken! Not at all, father. You forget what I told you—in America *all* is different. And I crowed a little.

Then he made his move. We had just finished an exceptionally fine dinner, and father, normally sober and understated, was invariably euphoric after he had had his measure of wine and a good dinner. "How far is the Summit school?" he asked. "About four miles," I answered. "And how long does it take you to walk there and back?" "Two hours," I said. "Then we must buy you a bicycle."

It was now my turn to be incredulous. I had wanted a bicycle for some time and knew that we could not afford it. A bicycle, such as many of the boys in school had, just for the pleasure of riding it, of enjoying the sense of speed in those early days before the advent of the automobile. What normal boy had not dreamed of such a luxury? On several occasions, when he was in an expansive mood after a fine dinner, I had been on the verge of pressing a request for a bicycle, but I had refrained, knowing too well that father's domestic economy precluded the purchase of anything that was not strictly necessary. His purchasing policy was to buy the best we could afford; there was no compromising on quality. However, absolute necessity must be established and ready cash must be in hand to pay the price. So the next day, with cash in hand and necessity established to father's satisfaction, we bought the best bicycle available in the village. A gleaming red bicycle!

It did not occur to me at the time, for I was too excited and pleased with the unexpected consequences of an act that but a few hours before I had feared might put me in the reformatory and bring disgrace upon our family. I often wondered later whether father's purchase of the bicycle was actually in conformity with his domestic economy. The walk to and from school in McCleary required half an hour, but the walk to and from the Summit school required two. The result was that I had an hour and a half less to devote to my many labors at home. Had father taken that into consideration? Having inherited some of his prudence in managing a household, I have since considered that when he bought me that bicycle he was thinking more about his domestic economy than my pleasure. But perhaps I do him wrong. Perhaps he, too, was beginning to realize that in America all *is* different.

In anticipating a favorable decision by the board, I had not been unreasonably optimistic. The investigation convinced the board that the teacher was incompetent and he was accordingly dismissed. Another, and a very good teacher, was engaged to replace him. After the Christmas and New Year's holidays, I was required by the board to return to the school where I properly belonged, and there I completed the eighth grade with high marks.

The Summit school interlude was all too brief, for it was a significant and utterly happy experience. My brief encounter with Laura, the Summit schoolteacher, had intensified my determination to proceed with the plans for my education set forth by Christine Edwards. My contact with her also made me aware of the charms of English poetry.

Laura had graduated from the university the preceding spring with a major in English literature. She was only six years older than I, and, since I was older than my years would indicate, we were practically contemporaries and very congenial. She taught with authority and contagious enthusiasm, particularly for her major subject, and she was intrigued that one of her students was an immigrant lad from Italy who was now quite fluent in both languages. She was fond of poetry and one day she asked if I would mind reading or reciting an Italian poem to the class. I didn't mind at all, and, on the morrow, I brought to class a book of poems by Leopardi and read "Amore e Morte."

> Fratelli, a un tempo stesso, Amore e Morte
> Ingenero la sorte . . .

She then read several poems to us, and it was from her lovely lips and in her melodious voice that I heard "Ode to the West Wind" for the first time, and years later memorized:

> O wild West Wind, thou breath of Autumn's being,
> Thou, from whose unseen presence the leaves dead
> Are driven, like ghosts from an enchanter fleeing . . .
> Wild Spirit, which art moving everywhere;
> Destroyer and preserver; hear, oh, hear!

Largely for my benefit she told the class that Shelley had lived his last years in Italy where he did his greatest work and where he died and was buried in the Protestant cemetery in Rome. A great English poet had written his classics in Italy and was buried in my native land! Glowing with pride I looked around the room.

Laura, who wrote verse herself, was strangely fascinated by the sound of the Italian language, and she asked me to read some more. "You are very fortunate," she said, "in being able to read that beautiful language so well. Do you realize that you are the only one in the entire school, the teachers included, who is fluent in two languages? Never forget it. Add to your knowledge of it. You are a child of two cultures, a rare privilege. In becoming an American, it is not necessary that you should forget your Italian heritage. As you continue your education, include in it further study of Italian culture." Since I had vaguely been aware of the advantage I had over my peers in knowing two languages, I took her advice. What follows will prove this young woman's wisdom, for, in formulating my dream as the pursuit of happiness through self-realization, remembering and enhancing my native heritage became a central element in the quest.

Laura quite naturally took it for granted that I would go on to high school and she also looked beyond high school and talked to me about going to college. Her memories fresh, she described college life in such vivid and concrete terms that the university ceased being an awesome institution of higher learning and became just another school where the students were a little older, the faculty a bit more sophisticated, and the study discipline proportionately more exacting. She told me about fraternity life, athletics, school politics, literary clubs, and the abiding friendships one established. She told me about the real possibility of working one's way through college. She herself had done it, working in the school cafeteria. In these ways she made real to me the carefree happy days of college, the days one would relive in memory and never forget. I listened fascinated to her account, thinking all the while about Christine Edwards' plans for my education that now seemed more real.

The summer of 1919 was a time of decision. Five years and six months had passed since I had begun the journey that would eventually lead to the goal of full membership in American society. Having learned the language and completed eight elementary grades, I had proved to my complete satisfaction that I was capable of reaching that coveted goal. I was now sixteen years of age. The legal requirement of school attendance had been fulfilled. The fairly straight and unencumbered course I had followed up to now had led to a crossroads. The one road led to the mill, the other to high school, college, and a professional career as yet vaguely perceived but full of promise. Which course would I take? I had already decided to follow the course outlined for me by Christine Edwards, and that decision was now strengthened by what Laura had told me about college. She had given me a vivid account of college life, made it irresistibly attractive, and convinced me that it was easily within my abilities. She had urged me to grasp the opportunity, and I had promised her that I would not fail to do so.

But I had not consulted father, and, in the world of Casabianca, which I still lived in at home, father was a man to be reckoned with. He had assumed that when the law's requirements had been fulfilled, I would leave school and go to work in the mill. If I raised the issue now, would he give his consent? The matter was complicated by the fact that the nearest high school was eight miles away. There would be the expense of daily bus fare and the further expense of time lost in travel. Under the circumstances, could father be persuaded that his firstborn son, now virtually a man, should remain in school? Had he yet realized that in America all is different? If he refused, would it be possible for me to proceed against his will? Fearing horrible consequences, I put off the confrontation. The bridge I must cross had not yet been reached.

It was the beginning of summer, and I had a full three months to plan my strategy before the fall term. Sustained by my unwavering faith in a benign destiny, I went to work in the mill. The pay for common labor in the summer of 1919 was three and a half dollars a day for men and two and a quarter for women (who, since the start of the war, had been hired by the company for the first time). What was the pay for boys who had come of age and were employed during the summer months? No one knew. Some took it for granted that they would be paid the lesser wage but, since I now considered myself a man, I expected to be paid a man's wages.

Why the uncertainty? Why not ask what I was being paid? When I accepted employment, did I not have the right to know what I was getting in exchange for my labor? Fair enough questions today when minimum wages are established by law, pay scales determined at the bargaining table, and civil and economic rights are realities rather than distant goals to be achieved. But these were the economic and industrial realities six decades ago. At that time, some of the inalienable rights of the Declaration and the Constitution were still largely theoretical and had to be realized later by bitter, often bloody, and always costly struggle.

We immigrants knew absolutely nothing of such rights, and I doubt that the natives themselves were any more aware of them. In any event, no one claimed them, and Henry McCleary's laissez-faire was never challenged. He operated his enterprise on the assumption that what was best for himself was good enough for his employees. He paid what he pleased, or what he couldn't avoid paying; he set the pace and hired and fired as he pleased. He deducted from his employees' wages an arbitrary sum to cover the cost of a totally inadequate medical service that provided only a minimum protection against injuries in the mill and logging camp. In brief, he had it all his way and no one questioned his authority. We immigrants, obsequious by tradition, were especially subservient to his will, for to question authority was an impertinence that might cost us our jobs.

For these reasons I hesitated to assert my right to know what I was being paid for my labor. But I was six years removed from Casabianca, I knew the language, I had persuaded myself (as I had tried to persuade father) that in America all was different, and I had already asserted my rights and successfully challenged authority. Differing in these ways from my immigrant elders, I decided to inquire about my wages and take the risk of being fired. Thus, after I had worked about a week, I summoned the appropriate degree of impertinence and put the question to my boss.

His name was Johnson, a short, chunky, corpulent Scandinavian who had a reputation for driving his men relentlessly—a reputation well deserved. Several times a day he made the rounds of his little kingdom to make sure that everyone was on the job. He would stare at a man at work with calculated ambiguity and then move on to observe someone else. Since he did not stop and observe everyone, his surveillance caused a great deal of fear and embarrassment. Was he observing in admiration of work well done? Was his surveillance a form of silent reproach, the preliminary to dismissal? No one knew; everyone, especially the immigrants, were fearful, and no one dared ask whether his performance was inadequate or whether he had done something wrong. Whatever his motives, Johnson's mode of supervision was a form of gratuitous cruelty.

It was on one of these occasions, when he stopped to fix me in his ambiguous stare, that I summoned the necessary courage and impertinence to ask my question. The answer was both a shock and a surprise. With a burst of unexpected joviality, as if he were kidding me and meant not a word of what he said, he raised his two chins from his chest, folded his hands on his ample belly, leaned slightly backward and delivered his answer: "I am paying you a dollar a day, all in change." Smiling ambiguously, eyes wide open, and lips slightly apart, he looked at me imperially as if he expected a bow and scrape. Before I could gather my wits, he became very stern and added, "If you are not satisfied, call at the office for your time." Then he moved on, leaving me to ponder my good fortune.

One dollar a day for doing the work of a man when the current pay was three dollars and a half. Incredible! The least I had expected was what women were paid. When I told father and the family what I was being paid, everyone was surprised, but no one was rebellious. Once again I heard those familiar words of resignation: *Pazienza. Speriamo*. The immigrants hadn't yet been sufficiently Americanized to stand up to a boss such as Johnson and tell him to stick his job up his ass. My eldest sister, happily employed in the factory, had been asked by one of the McCleary brothers to work in his home as a domestic. Her compensation would be what she was earning in the factory, which at that time was about thirty-five dollars a month. Had she been free to choose, she would have remained in the factory, but father had "persuaded" her to accept the offer. What the boss requires, one must not deny. *Pazienza!*

At sixteen years of age and six years removed from Casabianca, was I ready to stand up to Johnson and tell him to shove it? Not quite. The measure of my boldness had been in asking the impertinent question, but it fell short of asserting what I felt. I was disarmed by Johnson's awful presence. Also, to incur the ill will of a boss such as Johnson would do little to advance the interests of my family. This was a company town; another sister was working in the factory and a younger brother would soon be seeking employment there. *Pazienza*.

So I accepted Johnson's ultimatum to take it or leave it and continued working for a dollar a day in change. Since there was no alternative, a dollar a day was better than nothing. But once again the divinity that shapes our ends was looking out for me and provided the alternative I needed. During the second week of my employment, a maternal uncle whom I had never seen came unexpectedly to our home. When he left, after a brief and happy reunion with mother and the family, he took me with him.

He was employed by the Northern Pacific railroad as assistant foreman in an all-Italian extra gang of eighty men. I would be paid a man's wages, three dollars and seventy-five cents a day. Father readily gave his consent, since I would be in the custody of my uncle and the pay was nearly four times what I was earning in McCleary. Furthermore, the men of that gang were all Tuscans, people like ourselves; several of them were from Casabianca and adjacent communities. Among these were the head foreman and his wife whom father and mother had known in Italy, so there was no difficulty in securing parental permission to leave home. I would be in good company and earning good money; it was understood, of course, that at the end of the month I would send my pay home to father. He was keeper of the family purse and this was the solid basis of his domestic economy; no one questioned the inviolability of that tradition.

Railroad extra gangs were mobile and supplementary to section gangs, which were stationary. Uncle's gang was in Moclips, Washington, on the coast about seventy-five miles north of McCleary. When the job there was finished, the gang would move to Chehalis, a small city about forty miles south of McCleary. The men were quartered free of charge in converted boxcars, eight men to a car. The cook, the foreman's wife, and an assistant were paid by the railroad. Coal was provided by the railroad. The only expense was for food, which uncle said seldom exceeded seventy-five cents a day. Thus my contribution to the family's tidy reserve would be about three dollars a day. I was now a man, father's firstborn son and worthy successor. His first job in America had been as a section hand with the Northern Pacific, and so was mine. I would learn what he and uncle knew so well—the technique of railroad construction and maintenance. Since I knew the language so well, was it not reasonable to expect that in a few years I would become a division supervisor for the Northern Pacific? When this was discussed, father and uncle exchanged significant winks with a toss of the head toward me. They seemed to think that this was very reasonable to expect.

However, I had other plans. With these plans in mind, I mended my fences before leaving McCleary. Mr. Johnson must not think that I was quitting my job in defiance, for I might need employment in the factory in summers to come. Accordingly, I told him that I was going away to spend the summer with an uncle, and, thanking him for the work he had given me, I told him that I was looking forward to working for him again upon my return. He seemed pleased with my expression of gratitude. Before I left, father gave me the customary advice, which I assured him I would observe to the letter: Obey your uncle; avoid women and cards; do your work well; be a credit to your good family.

Thus admonished, I took my leave. The journey was short, but its consequences would be extensive. Some years later I remembered my departure from McCleary as a symbolic ritual, a belated bar mitzvah in a Catholic home. Leaving home for the first time to go to work as a man at a man's wages, I had cut the umbilical cord. Thereafter I would be on my own—completely on my own.

This was now a reality and I felt it on the first day that, with pick and shovel, I took my place among the men of the gang. Until then I had been a working member of the family and, as such, I had largely earned my keep.

But the bread I had eaten, the clothes I had worn, and such comforts as I had known had all been provided by my parents. In leaving home I had established my complete identity as an individual in the community of men. The bread I now ate and the clothes I now wore were paid for with my own earnings; for the first time in my life I made my own bed and washed my own clothes. I was now free to go at any time without asking anyone's permission and return when I pleased without fear of reproach. Living with men a decade or more older than I, doing the same work they did, receiving the same pay, participating in their discussions, serving as scrivener to some of my illiterate companions, and enjoying their admiration for my achievements in school, I now felt that I was a complete man. If, at the end of the summer, father refused to give me permission to continue my education, I would proceed without it.

I worked on the gang two months and three weeks, a brief time but rich in consequences. The work was heavy; by its very nature pick and shovel work cannot be otherwise. But I took it in stride, for I was a muscular young lion with energy to burn. Furthermore, the summer sun was tempered by the ocean breezes; the roar of the Pacific was in my ears and I was certain that in a couple of months my career as a section hand would end. Under such circumstances, I could well afford to take such laboring in stride, swing the pick and sledgehammer with a merry heart, and thrust the shovel harder than was necessary. I was on a lark, so to speak, getting in shape for the ball games at school and an alluring future, whereas my fellows on the job, amused at my reckless expenditure of energy, conserved theirs, knowing that there would be no end, except the very end itself, to their days with the pick and shovel.

There is much that I could write about my brief sojourn in Moclips at sixteen years of age, living in close quarters with eighty Italian immigrants whose only amusement and relaxation was with each other, but I must limit myself to what is relevant to my story. Father had asked me to avoid women and cards. In Moclips there were no women to avoid and cards were no temptation then and never have been. So I had plenty of time to read and to think and to write frequent letters to my family.

Remembering Laura's advice that I should add to my knowledge of the Italian language, I had taken with me Manzoni's *I Promessi Sposi,* an Italian classic of the same class as *War and Peace* or *Vanity Fair.* It was long and difficult. Reading it with studied care, a few pages each evening, I finished it by

the end of summer. I also read the Italian newspaper to which the gang foreman subscribed. Since I was the only one in the gang blessed with an education, I also read it for those who were illiterate and also assisted them with
whatever reading and writing needs they had. Thus, instead of trafficking in
women and cards, a peril against which father had wisely but needlessly
warned me, I devoted my leisure time to reading and thinking about my future as planned for me by Christine Edwards and Laura.

If my father refused his consent that I continue my education, should I defy
him? That was the sensitive question. He had done so much for me. We were
on good terms and I must not risk alienation. I hoped that I might be able to
persuade him. After much agonized reflection I decided that, if necessary, I
would go to high school and college without his consent. Laura had assured
me that I could earn my way. I was now netting three dollars a day. I would
put my earnings in a postal savings account and tell father that at the end of
summer I would bring it all to him in a lump sum. I would not, of course, tell
him that if he withheld his consent I would declare my independence, keep
the money, and continue working until I had saved enough money to proceed
with my education. My spirited and adventurous uncle applauded my plan
and assured me not only continuing employment but also whatever financial
aid I might need that he could provide.

Thus resolved, I wrote father a carefully thought out letter two weeks before I left the gang. Because of his judicious and persuasive temper, father was
known as l'Avvocato—the lawyer. In writing the letter I kept this in mind. I
dealt at some length with my dedication to study and my willingness to work
to capacity using brain and brawn, and I solemnly promised that if I were
permitted to continue with my education I would become a lawyer and bring
honor to the family: "You are a lawyer in name; your firstborn son will be a
lawyer in fact." I concluded the letter on a melodramatic note. Borrowing the
mood from the unhappy poet Leopardi, I vaguely hinted that if my request
were not granted, something terrible would happen to me—I might become
a vegetable and waste away in a profound melancholia.

Father's reply was prompt and brief. He gave me his blessings and promised such aid as the family could afford. Once again he warned against the
dangers of women and cards.

CHAPTER IV

Fear No More the Frown of the Great

What I have written thus far has focused on my learning process, at first as required by law, and later as motivated by my own need to understand this new land. In seeking to satisfy this need, the learning process itself and the further study of the language and culture of my native land became the very essence of the dream as I would eventually formulate it: the pursuit of happiness in self-realization. As I continue to recount my education, I will focus on the relevance of what I learned of the economic, political, and judicial history of America. Once again, my tutors and spiritual guides were a succession of teachers of exemplary competence.

Elma High School was an exceptionally good school. Compared to the little frame schoolhouse in McCleary with its two smelly outhouses, the physical layout of Elma High School was impressive: a three-story brick building, a gymnasium, and an athletic field. The main building had central heating, inside plumbing, an auditorium with an ample stage, a library (the first I had ever seen), and an adequately equipped laboratory. Clean, spacious, airy, and conducive to pleasant study, it was very definitely a *high* school.

It had an enrollment of about one hundred and thirty students and a faculty of ten—four men and six women. Many of the students came from surrounding communities: Whites, Garden City, Satsop, Brady, Oakville, Summit. I was the only one from McCleary during my first year. The curriculum was primarily designed to prepare one for college: history, languages, English, mathematics, and science. The standards were high, the discipline exacting, and the teachers uniformly competent. In its emphasis on the liberal arts and insistence on study and good behavior, the school was commendably late Victorian.

Such was the little world, friendly, congenial, and, to me, inspiring in which I would pursue my higher education. I give this brief profile because the school, the community, and some citizens provided me an opportunity to explore my resources, discover certain of my aptitudes, and test my abilities. Once again, that divinity that shapes our ends provided a benign guidance; and again in the person of a most extraordinary teacher.

Her name was Bess Evans and her home was in Vandalia, Missouri. She taught English, she had a degree in science, and she coached debate and dramatics. As a teacher she was more than merely competent—she was a wise, moral presence in the classroom. She communicated the material with precision and clarity, but her interest was in molding character:

> Delightful task! to rear the tender thought,
> And teach the young idea how to shoot.

Such was my impression and dear memory of Bess Evans.

On the very first day in her class I knew that I was in the presence of a great teacher. She gave me reason to believe that she regarded me with particular interest. For when she called the roll, she lingered over my name, pronounced it as if Italian were her native language, and with a quiet smile made me feel that she was pleased to have me in her class.

I have often wondered in recalling our happy association, whether I was, in my boyish way, in love with Bess Evans. I cannot be sure that I was not; I had a depth, honesty, admiration, respect, and warm intensity of feeling for her that, in a lad on the threshold of manhood, is very near a romantic attachment. Yet she was not as young or as good-looking as Laura nor as bubbly and maternal as Christine. Tall and slender, with a narrow face, nicely balanced features, and pince-nez glasses clipped to the bridge of her nose, she gave one the impression that she was a plain and proper lady. Her dress added something to the general impression of propriety: ankle-length skirt, bosom severely restrained under a fitted blouse with a narrow collar buttoned high on the throat and adorned with a narrow, pointed, plaid bowtie. As a female figure, she was not in the least seductive, but she had poise, dignity, and a moral cleanliness that inspired in me adoration if not love.

I cannot be sure that, as we worked together as student and teacher, she did not have something of the same feeling for me. She was in her middle thirties and unmarried. Was it by choice? Did she long for what she apparently did not have—the companionship of a man worthy of her? She had passed, though not by many years, that fullness of youth that I was approaching. Did my coming into her life, physically developed as I was and of a rather serious nature, make her keenly aware of what she longed for and did not have? Did that incline her to love me in a way that was close to the requirements of nature? Or was her feeling toward me no more than that of a dedicated teacher for a willing, capable, and respectful student? I was never sure whether it was the one or the other. However, I have always fancied that we were in love, she in her proper, and I in my boyish way. Given what we were, it could not have been anything more than that. But whatever its precise nature, the reciprocal affection enriched our student-teacher relationship. She gave more than duty required, more of her time and of her gifts, and I worked more diligently to be worthy of what she had to give.

An incident that occurred three and a half decades after I had graduated from high school dramatized in a most unusual way the depth and enduring character of that reciprocal affection. The occasion was a dinner in her honor at our home. She was then in her seventies; I was in my fifties, married, and the father of three children. Since she had left Elma and I had gone on to college in the fall of 1922, I had had no contact whatever with Bess Evans.

The reunion came about in a most unexpected way. By that time I had published four books and several essays; one of these was a tribute to my mother. Bess Evans, then living in retirement in Missouri, had read the essay and written me a letter to tell me, among other news of herself, that she was coming to the Pacific Northwest to attend a church conference. Would it be convenient for me to see her? I answered her letter immediately and asked her to have dinner with us.

I must confess that there were romantic overtones in my excitement as I anticipated her arrival, for my memory of Bess Evans had always been vivid, and there had been no diminution in that tenderness of feeling that I had had for her. When I called for her at her hotel, I was pleased to note that she was essentially what she had been thirty-five years before—a slender figure with the same poise, dignity, quiet smile, soft voice, and slow, precise articulation.

That evening at dinner I did something that, as I realized later, could have caused some embarrassment: I asked Bess Evans to join me in a toast. "Miss Evans," I said, "you probably know that Italians drink wine with their dinner. What you may not know is that grace at the table of an Italian family frequently assumes the form of a toast, and that all dear occasions are celebrated with the ritual pouring of the finest wine. For such occasions, bottles of great vintages are reserved in the cellar. I am now an American, but I have chosen to observe certain traditions of my Italian ancestry and I propose to celebrate our reunion in such a manner. If the occasion is as dear to you as it is to me, will you join me in consecrating it with the holy blood of the grape. It is the finest in our cellar."

"Yes, Angelo," she said, "the occasion certainly is as dear to me as it is to you. I have been a strict prohibitionist all my life. I have never knowingly taken a drop of anything alcoholic, but I do so now. And if this is a first step along the primrose path, may the Lord have mercy on me and forgive the transgression." We klinked glasses and drank. Such was the full measure of the lady who had taught me so much and so well.

Before I give an account of the way Bess Evans taught me and what I learned, I must explain what made her an extraordinary teacher. As I have already stated, her speech was precise and clear. Hence, her communication in the classroom was effective, and, in this respect, she was a good teacher. But she was much more than just a good teacher; her goal was to mold character by educating the intellect. She took the "high" in high school quite literally and sought to pursue education on a higher level. In the elementary grades the student required knowledge; in high school the student should begin to view knowledge in relation to learning. I don't remember if she ever referred to Cardinal Newman, but she certainly shared his view that the cultivation of the mind was an end in itself. In his discourses on *The Idea of a University*, he had said that the university's "function is intellectual culture. . . . It educates the intellect to reason well in all matters, to reach out towards the truth, and to grasp it." Bess Evans was anxious to begin this process in high school, and such was her goal as a teacher.

She was also a social and creative person, and, as such, had a social philosophy that was a rare blend of political liberalism and moral absolutism. This philosophy was reflected in her instruction and in her ability to reason well in all matters. Years later I came to regard her as an enlightened Whig and a Puritan. But there wasn't a trace of hypocrisy in her piety. Her living in accordance with the moral standards of the Victorian era and her trust in the absolutism of the decalogue did not blind her to the political and social realities of the world in which she lived. Had she lived in England at the time, she would have supported the three reform bills of 1832, 1867, and 1884 as she supported the fourth in 1918, and also as she supported the extension of the franchise to American women in 1920. One could be a proper lady and a good Christian and at the same time work toward a world in which a proper lady might live with dignity. She admired President Wilson's liberalism, supported the League of Nations, the establishment of the eight-hour workday, and the unionization of labor. For Bess Evans, a dedication to the achievement of these social ends was a natural extension of her belief in elementary Christianity.

Such was her liberal philosophy and I became acquainted with it as she coached me in debate and taught me how to reason well. Had I not, at her suggestion, joined the debate team, I might not have learned the meaning of what she called creative citizenship. It was during the three years that I was a member of the debate team that I became aware of current social problems, and the duty of the citizens of a self-governing society to work together toward rational solutions. It was something of which I had been hitherto totally unaware, and the discovery was timely and congenial to my serious temperament.

I credit Bess Evans' exceptional talents as a teacher and the special interest she took in me for my new awareness, my added interest in learning, and for my pursuit of education on a still higher level. For she was more a mentor and guide to me than a classroom teacher. In this respect she was very much like Christine Edwards, but where Christine had tutored me privately in the language and set me on a course to keep abreast of my peers, Bess Evans helped educate me and helped me discover whatever talents I had. That she liked me in a special way was never in doubt. Perhaps she felt that, since I was eager to learn and capable of learning, I was a student with whom she could work experimentally in accordance with her philosophy of teaching, a philosophy that was enriched by her political liberalism and moral absolutism. For whatever reason, she gave me much more than duty required.

Soon after the term began, I faced what appeared to be an insuperable difficulty. The principal had approved my plan to complete high school in three years. Having reviewed my school record, he arranged my schedule and encouraged me to make the attempt. I was confident that I could manage and do excellent work. I also wanted to participate in certain of the school activities, particularly football and debate, both for pleasure and as a means of achieving a much coveted status in the new school. Status! That was very important. I wanted to be noted, admired by my fellows; toward that end I would strive for excellence in the classroom and in all else that I ventured.

The difficulty was in finding time for football and other activities. The bus from McCleary arrived barely in time for the first morning class and departed promptly after the last session. Having no other means of getting home later, I could not go out for football. Nor could I participate in debate, since all practice sessions were held after school. I had never felt so frustrated. This difficulty could only be resolved if I arranged to live in Elma, and that was out of the question. Father would never consent to paying for my board and room. Since Albert Kirk, the football coach, had asked me to go out for the team and Bess Evans had asked me to participate in debate, I brought my difficulty to them. Within twenty-four hours what had seemed insuperable was overcome. They found employment for me in the village cafe. I would work in the evenings and early mornings. The pay would be board and room and a cash pittance! When I reported this to father, I presented it as a fait accompli, and I did it with such an air of personal triumph that he was mystified. He pressed his lips and raised his eyebrows. Was it his way of saying that he was beginning to understand that in America all *is* different? He gave his consent without speaking a word, and I knew that henceforth father would be with me all the way.

I was now on my way to being completely on my own, free and independent to pursue my studies and to work toward the goals I had set for myself. If I should fail, I could blame no one but myself. But I would not fail. Christine

Edwards had convinced me that the word "impossible" did not exist. In high school I achieved my first full measure of success. I completed the high school course in three years as planned, and I won high marks and participated in such school activities as football, dramatics, school politics, the school paper, and debate. By my involvement in these, I achieved the status and the ego satisfaction I sought. I was a big frog in a little pond.

The progress I made in high school was not so much in the acquisition of knowledge as in self-discovery and the education of the mind. Before I give an account of how this was achieved, I must, for the record, express my gratitude to the entire Elma community for its friendliness, kindness, and generosity. Even though I was the only foreigner in the school and in the village, I was made to feel perfectly at home. The ladies for whom I worked in the restaurant, and who taught me the rudiments of American cuisine, were understanding mothers rather than stern employers. The attorney, the photographer, the pharmacist, the editor of the Elma *Chronicle,* the members of the school board, the owner of the hotel in which I lodged, the entire school faculty, my fellow students—all of these and others, by their kindness, encouragement, and aid, contributed substantially to what I sought to achieve and to my happiness. Bless them all.

The best that Bess Evans gave me was given in frequent conferences in her office and her cottage and during the many hours we spent preparing for interschool debates. In working individually with me, her method was strictly tutorial and Socratic. What made it so effective was a student-teacher relationship that was close to the ideal: a wise, talented teacher and an eager, capable student working together in an atmosphere of mutual respect and affection. She gave me reading and writing assignments that were not required of the class, and she taught me the elements of research: how to use the library and how to take notes and arrange them topically in a logical sequence. When I had completed an assignment, we met and discussed what I had done.

During these happy sessions, in answer to her probing questions, I told her a great deal about myself, about my life in Casabianca, the trials and blessings of immigration to the new land, and the vague plans I had to further my education. Also, I sought from her an explanation of the strange phenomenon that had puzzled me after our arrival in McCleary—the absence of the clear-cut class distinctions we had known in the world of Casabianca, where the peasants and proletarians lived apart and never mingled with the upper classes, the citizens. In Elma, as in McCleary, the owners of the mill, the bosses, the merchants, and the common laborers all mingled freely and lived in pretty much the same way. One of the McCleary brothers had often been in our home drinking with father at the kitchen table, another operated one of the locomotives, a third was a friendly adviser to our family, and his two children had become my good friends. The phenomenon was pleasant. Now, six years removed from Casabianca, I was taking it in stride as another of the many blessings in the new land. But there must be a reason for it, and I was anxious to know what that might be. Could Bess Evans tell me where I might find an answer? Were there really no class distinctions in America? Was this what was meant by democracy? Was there more to this circumstance than explained by the political structure—a constitution, periodic elections, government by consent of the governed? Without then knowing it, I was groping for the ethical and philosophical basis of democracy. Bess Evans understood this, and she started me on a search that I would continue years later. What she learned of me from our frequent conferences and from her acute observation of my personality, she used as a basis for guiding me and furthering my education.

Bess Evans set me on the course that eventually led to my career as teacher, writer, and lecturer, and it was Bess Evans who added the word "ideal" to my vocabulary, and who first made me aware of idealism as a practical, imperative, and sensible way of life. It was she who introduced me to good and evil as philosophical concepts, matters that I would ponder years later in graduate seminars on the Platonic dialogues and, later still, in the classroom as a professor of English literature.

I have said that Bess Evans was a moral presence in the classroom. To me she was precisely that. Her neatness and propriety, her quiet smile and soft voice, the kindness in her eyes and her gentle behavior—all these attributes gave the impression that she was the embodiment of simple goodness. Priests and nuns, my "spiritual guides" during the early years in Casabianca, had made me fearful rather than reverent. In the classroom, Bess Evans inspired me with love and respect.

Elaborating what Laura had begun, Bess Evans made me aware of my ethnic heritage. I knew absolutely nothing about my native land, as a people or as a nation in the western world, neither did my parents and their fellow peasants. Italy was for us no more than the narrow, illiterate world of Casabianca, where we had come to terms with "the broad sameness of the human lot—hunger and labor, seed-time and harvest, love and death." That was the sum and substance of what we knew about the land we had left forever, and it was not readily conducive to a feeling of pride in our native land.

But there was, of course, more than ample reason for pride in my heritage, and it was ironic that my American teacher, in a brief conference in her cottage, should have made me aware of it. When she learned that I knew nothing about Florence, Pisa, or Siena, all famous cities within a few miles of Casabianca, she gave me a brief outline of Italian history, reciting names, dates, events, and eras that were fascinating and new to me. She equated Dante with Shakespeare, Galileo with Newton; and Da Vinci she proclaimed the universal genius without peer in any land. Historians would probably agree, she said, that western civilization owed more to Italy than to any other single nation.

Thus she inspired me to begin a course of reading in Italian history and letters that determined the course of my professional career. My doctoral thesis was about the influence of the Italian philosopher, Giordano Bruno, on the writers of the British renaissance. Later, when I began my career as a writer, I wrote mostly on the history of Italy and of the Italian immigrant in America. Had I yielded to the temptation to forget the Italian language, reject my origins, and melt into the melting pot—who knows what the consequences might have been! Not, I am sure, as happy for me as the ones I have experienced.

Henry Adams was right: A great teacher does affect eternity! While still in high school I was now able to pursue with intelligent purpose the course I had chosen in the summer of 1919. Having, thanks to Bess Evans, been made aware of the value of my Italian heritage, I could now progress to a serious consideration of its implications.

And thanks to her again for having taught me to read critically and having helped discover that I had an aptitude for literature and for writing. These subjects came easily to me; I enjoyed them. She praised my compositions and wisely urged me to write about my personal experience and my early life in Italy. She gave me books to read. One of these, toward the end of my second year in high school, was *Romola*. The class was then reading *Silas Marner*. Why did Bess Evans want me to read *Romola*? And why, after I had read *Romola*, did she have me read Wordsworth's narrative poem, *Michael*?

The setting for the novel is Florence; the time is from the death of Lorenzo the Magnificent, in 1492, to the end of the first decade of the next century. It is a quasi-historical novel, since some of the characters—Machiavelli, Savonarola, the Medici—are historical figures and much of the text is a paraphrase of historical records. It is a learned novel, philosophical and didactic.

Mary Ann Evans, who wrote under the pseudonym George Eliot, had a special affection for Italy and the Italians. She was especially fond of Florence, a jewel in the incomparable Tuscan landscape and the very center of the revival of learning known as the Renaissance. The writing of the novel *Romola* required extensive research in the history of fifteenth-century Florence. In writing it, Eliot very likely indulged in her love of the subject matter and the Italian language.

Did Bess Evans have me read the book because the subject matter was Italian and because, in the reading of it, I would learn something, as I certainly did, about my heritage? That must have been a reason for her choice, but I'm sure there was another, conceived not by Bess Evans the teacher but by Bess Evans the moralist. She wanted me to read the novel primarily for its message. Reading it carefully under her guidance, and discussing it with her during our conferences, I had no difficulty understanding the particular message she wanted me to see. Eliot spells it out clearly at the end of the novel, and Bess Evans carefully underscored it for me. What I failed to understand at the time was that Bess Evans intended the message as moral advice to me. This I surmised years later when I reread the novel as a student of English literature and remembered that Bess Evans had had me read Wordsworth's *Michael* when I had finished *Romola*.

The reader may remember the message of the novel emphasized at the end of the book. Romola, the disillusioned widow of Tito Melema, is speaking to Lillo, her husband's illegitimate son, sixteen years of age, who has just expressed a desire to become "a great man," something that would not hinder him from "having a good deal of pleasure." Whereupon Romola warns him: "There are so many things wrong and difficult in the world that no man can be great unless he gives up thinking much about pleasures and rewards."

Then, without naming him as such, she tells the boy about his father: "There was a man to whom I was very near, so that I could see a great deal of his life, who made almost everyone fond of him, for he was young and clever and beautiful, and his manners to all were gentle and kind. I believe, when I first knew him, he never thought of anything cruel or base. But because he tried to slip away from everything that was unpleasant, and cared for nothing else so much as his own safety, he came at last to commit some of the basest deeds— such as make men infamous. He denied his own father, and left him to misery; he betrayed every trust that was reposed in him, that he might keep himself safe and get rich and prosperous. Yet calamity overtook him. . . . " He was murdered by his father whom he had betrayed.

There is substantially the same message in the Wordsworth poem. In order to pay a claim on his few acres, the reward of a lifetime of labor, Michael sends his son, Luke, to the city to earn the necessary funds. But the son in pursuit of the pleasures he discovered in the metropolis, gives himself over

> To Evil courses; ignominy and shame
> Fell on him, so that he was driven at last
> To seek a hiding place beyond the sea. . . .

Self-indulgence in the pleasures of the flesh leads to ruin. Such was the lesson the moralist, Bess Evans, hoped I would derive from the reading she had assigned. She was interested in shaping character to the high requirements of her moral absolutism, and perhaps she knew me well enough to conclude that I might "slip away from everything that was unpleasant" and take the path to ruin. All I know is that I have never studiously avoided the pleasures of the flesh. On the contrary, I have danced, played (not at cards!), loved, and feasted in America's abundance, without growing fat, ruining my liver, betraying trusts, or avoiding the unavoidably unpleasant. Nay, more than that! In obedience to my nature, and following what I learned from the ancient Greeks for whom the supreme art was the art of living, I even made something of a career of urging others to discover the good that is in bread and wine.

The puritan in Bess Evans would probably have supported Malvolio and dismissed as irreverent nonsense Sir Toby's rebuke: "Dost thou think, because thou art holy, there shall be no more cakes and ale?" When we discussed *Romola,* had she called my attention to the fate of Savonarola and warned me that the search for truth might entail suffering, her advice would have been more realistic.

While her simple goodness was too narrow to include the goodness that is in cakes and ale, it was broad enough to include the goodness inherent in education and reason. This was most apparent to those of us who were privileged to work with Bess Evans in the debate program.

The organization of an extensive and meaningful debate program at the high school was her idea and pet project; in achieving it she proceeded with characteristic care. With the assistance of certain of her colleagues she canvassed the student body for likely candidates and had each one of us try out for a place on the debate squad. The tryout itself was a rigorous—and somewhat frightening—test designed to discover those candidates who had both serious intent and skill. Each of us was asked to prepare and extemporaneously present an oral argument on a given proposition. In order to assure complete fairness in the trial, Bess Evans asked two of her colleagues to join her in judging the candidates. In this way a squad of several students was chosen. Then we competed with each other for a place on the teams that represented the school in interschool debates. It was my good fortune to survive the tests; thus began my career as a debater both in high school and in the university.

Bess Evans had no interest in debate as a forensic game. Thus conceived, as it too frequently is, the emphasis is on winning an argument; as such, debate has little, if any, educational value. It encourages sophistry, the suppression and distortion of evidence, verbal bravura, and other such tricks of demagogues and charlatans. When rivalry between schools is intense, there is also the temptation, not always resisted, to stack the judges. The sort of extracurricular wrangling for the sake of trophies was not debate as conceived by Bess Evans.

For that most extraordinary teacher, debate was a means to the highest educational end: the cultivation of the student's reasoning faculties. This was basic and fundamental. There were also some more immediately practical objectives. In debate, as a student learned to reason and draw conclusions from a set of facts, he also learned how to construct an argument and present it orally. He received some instruction in methods of research. Also, since debate propositions were usually formal statements of current social problems, debaters received some practical experience in applying reason to their solution.

Bess Evans repeatedly emphasized the importance of what she called creative citizenship. By this she meant two things: an awareness of current social problems and a willingness to work rationally and cooperatively toward their solution. Thus, we debated such subjects of current interest as the sales tax, the League of Nations, and the compulsory arbitration of industrial disputes. Relying principally on the state library, we compiled bibliographies and read the available material. Then the squad met with the coach to discuss what we had read, define the issues, and construct broad, preliminary briefs for the affirmative and negative positions. Thereafter each participant was required to construct his own argument and submit it to the coach for criticism. And when the argument was put in final form, Bess Evans drilled us in the art of oral presentation.

Thus we worked together, young and eager students of both sexes, with a teacher whom we admired and respected, and came to grips for the first time in our young lives with issues that were the subjects of our collective inquiry. Given our immaturity and the complexity of the subjects we dealt with, we were naturally often over our heads. The best we could do was to paraphrase or quote the authorities, most of whom we understood imperfectly, and to try to do so in a manner that was clear and persuasive. Though we had feelings and leanings and were predisposed one way or the other on some of the issues, we had no real ideas of our own. This didn't matter. What mattered was that we were learning to reason well in all matters, and to search for rational solutions to complex social problems. This is what Bess Evans repeatedly emphasized. Not once did she urge on us the necessity of winning an interschool debate. An argument soundly constructed and effectively presented was in itself a victory.

Such was the debate program as planned and supervised by Bess Evans. I have no idea what others who were my good friends and capable associates remember about it, nor do I know how they would assess its value. I do know, however, what it meant to me. With the possible exception of the courses in English, my participation in that new and exciting labor of the mind did more to further my education than any other discipline school had offered up to that time. Hitherto in school I had read, remembered, and recited. In debate I was now required to read, to reflect, and to reason. I learned something about the process of inference, the elements of elementary logic, and the art of public speaking.

With the perceptive guidance of Bess Evans, I discovered that I had a degree of natural ability, an aptitude for debate and oratory that she and others of the faculty and community urged me to cultivate. Among these others was Judge Austin Griffiths, a visiting jurist in the Superior Court of Grays Harbor County. After he had judged one of our interschool debates he was kind enough to join us for cider and doughnuts and give us the benefit of his judicial criticism. During the little party he asked me questions about my background, complimented me for doing well, gave me good advice on how to manage a closing rebuttal, and urged me to go to the university. "Continue with debate," he said, "and plan to study law. You have the makings of a fine lawyer." Naturally I was pleased, though I seriously doubted that I had sufficient talent to become a university debater.

However, I did continue with debate at the university and with more ease and success than I had hoped for. Immediately after I graduated and began my legal studies, I was granted a fellowship in the English department to teach a course in argumentation. Since my degree was in history, the only academic credential I had for the job was my record as a college debater. Two years later, with the same credential supplemented by courses in law, when I was about to begin my graduate studies for the doctorate in English, I received my first full-time academic appointment: instructor in English in a small private college in the west. For the next fifteen years I was on the faculty of the speech department at the university; and in 1936, in collaboration with a colleague, I published a college textbook: *Argumentation and Public Discussion*, which the philosopher John Dewey graced with an introduction. In 1945, now with a doctorate in English, I left the speech department and joined the English faculty. Since I had no formal academic training in speech, I am indebted to debate, particularly as taught by Bess Evans, for the course of my career.

However, I have an even greater debt to debate: the research it involved was the beginning of my political education. We did not debate such esoteric issues as how many angels can dance on the head of a pin. We dealt with the subjects that were the immediate concern of enlightened citizens. In proposing or opposing any given political or economic policy (such as joining the League of Nations or buying on the installment plan), our endpoint was the promotion of the general welfare. In the course of our inquiries and discussions, we discovered that on every important social issue there were views variously labeled liberal or conservative, radical or reactionary. Having noted this, it was inevitable that we should also discover that the conservative view was usually espoused by industry and the rich, while the liberal view was that of labor and the poor. In the same way we became acquainted with the concept of human rights: the rights of labor, the rights of capital, the rights of women, the rights of the common man. Thus, without making the necessary historical connections, we were coming to grips with some fundamental realities of American political and economic history from colonial times to the present. We were getting the elements of a political education.

No subject we debated was so politically instructive as the proposition that all industrial disputes should be submitted to compulsory arbitration. There was a reason for the timeliness of the subject and the urgency of the issues it raised. We were living in a region where employers and employees were engaged in a bloody struggle over the issues of unionization. The lumber barons of the Pacific Northwest united to keep unions out of the industry and to destroy the ones that had gained a foothold in it. Their most effective and uncompromising opponents in the conflict were the IWW, the Industrial Workers of the World. Both parties did not hesitate to use club and gunfire to achieve their ends. The scenes of their two bloodiest battles in the Pacific Northwest were but a few miles from the school where we young students were debating the merits of compulsory arbitration of industrial disputes!

One battle had occurred three years before we began high school. On November 5, 1916, on the Everett waterfront, the agents of the mill owners and the IWW met in a gun battle of such savagery that it came to be known as the Everett Massacre. While we young debaters were reading the literature on that "infamous event," another occurred that came to be known as the Centralia Massacre. The date was November 11, 1919. The adversaries were the IWW and the American Legion, acting as the self-appointed exterminator of "radical agitators." The casualties were five—four downed by gunfire and one by lynching. Twelve members of the IWW were charged with first degree murder and brought to trial in Montesano, a few miles from Elma and the county seat of Grays Harbor County. The trial began in February 1920; our debate squad attended one of the sessions. Those who castrated and lynched a member of the IWW were never brought to trial.

These massacres were the culminations of continuing skirmishes between labor and industry over the issue of the unionization of labor, and we, as young debaters, were close to the grim realities of industrial conflict. We were observers of the politics and economics of the lumber industry, and, as such, we were getting the elements of a political education not available in the classroom.

The research I had done on the subject of compulsory arbitration had left a number of questions unanswered. In reading the literature on the Everett Massacre, I had come upon a phrase that puzzled me. Some writers referred to these conflicts as skirmishes in the class struggle. What did that mean? I had also noted that the parties to a dispute invariably based their claims on certain rights. David Clough, owner of mills and a formidable power behind the Everett Massacre, refused to confer with union representatives on the issue of wages and working conditions. The mills were his. He had a right to operate them as he pleased, to pay what wages he pleased, and to hire and fire as he pleased. That was the official stand of the lumber barons. The spokesmen for the workers insisted that they had a right to a living wage and a right to impose on the employer certain minimum standards of safety in the mill and logging camp. The IWW asserted their right to meet, speak freely, and organize. Obviously, if Clough was right, the workers were wrong. Who was right in claiming a right?

In answer to these questions, Bess Evans continued to educate my mind. Theoretically, she said, there are no classes in America—no ruling aristocracy, no hereditary landlords, no nobility. All men are created equal. However, there are the rich and the poor, the whites, blacks, yellows, and browns. And many Americans, rich and poor alike, insist that all nonwhites constitute an inferior class and treat them as such. But they are wrong. Our system of government is founded on the proposition that all men are created equal.

(As I learned years later, her answer was, in substance, precisely what Justice John M. Harlan of the U.S. Supreme Court had put in legal terms in *Plessy v. Ferguson,* a case decided in 1896. The issue was the constitutionality of a

Louisiana statute that required railway companies to provide "equal but separate accommodations for the white and colored races." The court decided that the statute was not unconstitutional, for the reason that the separation of the two races did not imply that the colored was inferior to the white. In a dissenting opinion, Justice Harlan argued that it did and was therefore unconstitutional. Then he stated the law: "In the view of the Constitution, in the eye of the law, there is in this country no superior, dominant, ruling class of citizens. There is no caste here. Our Constitution . . . neither knows nor tolerates classes among citizens.")

Our system of government is founded on the proposition that all men are created equal! That was reassuring. And Bess Evans quoted from Lincoln's Gettysburg Address. But, she warned: That is the ideal; and you may discover that the reality is something different. There are the rich and the poor, and the one tends to exploit the other. They really don't mingle and live in pretty much the same way. This may not be so obvious in McCleary and Elma, but it will be apparent in the city, as you will discover for yourself someday. The rich live on one side of the tracks, the poor on the other. It is not the law that separates them, for in the eyes of the law they are equal. Wealth is the great divider in America. Some day you will know what this means.

Her comments were at once provocative and disturbing. My observations in McCleary and Elma had been superficial. She clearly implied that I had much to learn, and, of course, she was right. But I was fascinated by Lincoln's words, "Four score and seven years ago our fathers brought forth on this continent, a new nation, conceived in Liberty, and dedicated to the proposition that all men are created equal." And Bess Evans reminded me that this was the ideal, and that all men should strive to make it the reality.

In answer to my question regarding rights she told me that American citizens have certain rights guaranteed in the Constitution, that the precise nature of some of them is not clear, and that, as I continued my education in the university, I would realize the extent to which certain rights are disputed. In the meantime, however, she asked me to remember that a given right must not be so exercised as to interfere with the rights of others. David Clough had a right to operate his mills as he pleased, but he did not have the right to interfere with the rights of the workers to be fairly paid for their labor. Whether he did or not was a question of fact for an impartial judge to decide. For this reason it was very important, for the welfare of the community, that all industrial disputes be submitted to arbitration and preferably to voluntary arbitration. Both parties should, of their own accord, nominate someone to examine the facts and draw reasonable conclusions from them as we do in debate. This seemed to me very sound reasoning.

As we talked generally about democracy, which she was trying to make me understand was something more than periodic elections and government by consent of the governed, she did a most unexpected thing: she directed me to the poet Walt Whitman, whom no other teacher had ever mentioned. I cannot possibly exaggerate the relevance to my political and general education of my discovery of Walt Whitman, coming as it did when I desperately needed an emotional as well as intellectual basis for my self-assertion and self-esteem as a citizen of the new land. What one is taught during the first ten years of life is not easily rooted out. Growing up as a peasant lad, at the bottom of the social scale, I was schooled in obedience and taught not so much to respect as to fear my superiors. The Virginia landowners who bought indentured servants in the latter part of the seventeenth century understood this. They selected the ones who were fifteen and sixteen years old because, having been accustomed to discipline and severe punishment, they were docile, obsequious, and not yet mature enough to rebel.

This was essentially my situation at sixteen years of age. I had led a "revolt" in school; I had asserted myself on the platform, the gridiron, and in the classroom. However, these had been premature gestures, sporadic thrusts in a direction I did not clearly see. I lacked the emotional and intellectual basis, the deep conviction of equality, for honest and effective self-assertion. I still lived in some fear of my "superiors."

The works of Walt Whitman greatly contributed to my intellectual maturity. While I did not understand everything of this poet who was not even understood by his fellow poets, I understood enough to be moved to deep reverence for the "inspired interpreter of the soul of America." In her quiet way, articulating every syllable with precision, Bess Evans read to me the following from Whitman: "Love the earth and the sun and the animals, despise riches, give alms to everyone who asks, stand up for the stupid and crazy, devote your income and labor to others, hate tyrants, argue not concerning God, have patience and indulgence toward the people, take off your hat to nothing known or unknown, or to any man or number of men, go freely with powerful uneducated persons, and with the young, and with mothers of families reexamine all you have been told in school or church or in any book, and dismiss whatever insults your own soul. . . ."

Thus spoke the bard to the lad from Casabianca, and something deep and dormant in me replied, "I shall!" Never again would I fear the frown of the great.

CHAPTER V

O Brave New World!

Never again! There was no longer any terror in Boss Johnson's frown when I began my university studies in the fall of 1922. Speaking to me through her great poet and prophet, America had asked me to reexamine all that I had been taught in church and school and to purge myself of all that I should find offensive. Most offensive of what I had been taught in Casabianca was the crude medievalism that required one to bend the knee and stand uncovered in the presence of one's "superiors." Never again! Henceforth the knee would bend in reverence and respect, never in fear.

I was now half way into my nineteenth year, free and independent, ready to stand frowning, brow to brow, with logger and timber baron, unafraid, spurred by ambition, and confident that I had the necessary talents to achieve whatever goal I should choose. I had worked four summer seasons and been paid a man's wages, completed my apprenticeship in the use of the crosscut saw and the double-bitted axe, and sweated along the rails as a section hand for the Northern Pacific railroad. I had milked cows, churned butter, and cooked breakfast for loggers and tradesmen in the Elma Cafe. In promoting father's domestic economy and the continuing excellence of the Pellegrini table, I had taken game from the hills and fish from the streams, slaughtered rabbits and chickens, and assisted at butchering hogs and calves. I had written essays and a narrative poem in imitation of Walt Whitman and had them published in the school paper. I had achieved a certain ease on the speaker's platform. Could anyone have been better prepared to take up the challenge in what was called the University of a Thousand Years?

It was, indeed, a university, and I entered it with more ease and less apprehension of the unknown than I had felt in proceeding from elementary to high school. This was once again thanks to Bess Evans' preparation. She had given me some idea of what to expect: the critical approach to knowledge, the quest for truth, the ethical content of higher learning as a continuing inquiry toward a definition of what Christian and pagan philosophers called, respectively, the summum bonum and the good. Beyond courses and textbooks, these were the matters to engage our young and eager minds.

Bess Evans was so pleased with my response to her instruction that she was certain I would easily make the university debate team. I dearly hoped she was right, but I was not convinced of my ability. To persuade me that I should attempt the university debate team, Bess Evans urged me to go to the city to attend university debates and see for myself that their excellence was not beyond my competence. I followed her advice, and Bess Evans went with me on my first visit.

It was during my senior year, at the height of spring, a few days after my nineteenth birthday. Although I have forgotten much of the content of that exciting experience, I remember certain things as vividly as if they had occurred only yesterday. We arrived early and took seats in the center section and near the front in a large auditorium that had both a balcony and a gallery. At the front of the hall, above the orchestra pit and against a gently stirring purple curtain was placed a finely built lectern with a chair immediately behind it. On either side of the lectern were a table and two chairs; on each table was a pitcher of water and two glasses. I had never seen such impressive preparations for a debate.

Nor had I expected that a debate, even a university debate in the big city, would be attended by so many people. They kept coming down the several aisles and occupying vacant seats until the entire first floor was filled to capacity. As the audience grew, I thought of the few dozens who had attended our high school debates; I felt that I was way beyond my depth, and that I could never muster the poise and the degree of self-control necessary to speak effectively before so large and, no doubt, so sophisticated an audience.

Then, the big moment—the debaters appeared simultaneously from opposite sides of the stage, carrying an imposing burden of books, and followed by the chairman. They then sat at their respective tables. What we had come to see and hear was about to begin. I leaned toward Bess Evans, tremulously seeking moral support, and she leaned toward me so that our heads touched. I slipped my right arm under her left and took her hand and our fingers intertwined in a tight clasp.

I have long forgotten the proposition debated, the name of the chairman, the names of the visiting debaters, and the identity of the university they represented; but I remember very well the young men who represented our university. They were an impressive team. Even before they had uttered a word I found myself wondering what chance I might have to equal them. When they spoke I listened with concentrated attention and observed each one with care. They were university calibre—urbane, polished, poised, flawless, and in perfect command. They spoke with the confidence and authority of grown men. Were they typical university debaters? If so, a peasant lad a few years away from Casabianca might very well admire, but he stood no chance to equal them.

When the debate was over I was discouraged. The confidence I had felt as a high school debater had been seriously undermined by the excellence of the university men. Bess Evans insisted that I was potentially the equal of these young men. Very well. She knew me better than I knew myself. So we agreed that my immediate goal in the university should be to make the debate team.

Among the university debaters who had impressed me most were Julian Matthews and Robert Macfarlane. Strikingly handsome, impeccably groomed, and of aristocratic bearing, they were second and third year law students respectively, and each in time became a distinguished attorney, the latter proceeding from general counsel to the presidency of the Northern Pacific. Those two became my idols. I would strive to equal them; and I too would study law. My goals thus set, I began my university studies in the fall of 1922.

This morning, when I went to the lavatory in the university library, I saw something that made me sad. On the front of the little metal box that dispenses toilet tissue, I read the following graffiti, recently written in blue ink: "U. of W. Diploma. Free. Take One." Who, I wondered, as he sat there relieving himself, had written such a cynical commentary on the worth of a college degree? Was it an indictment of this or of all universities? Was he a student or teacher? What had prompted so cryptic a statement of disillusionment? If I could identify the critic and persuade him to level with me, what would be his story? As these questions formed in my mind, I became more and more interested in trying to determine whether the cynic would prove to be a disgruntled failure seeking a scapegoat or a perceptive social critic whose judgment on the worth of a college degree was completely objective. Assuming that it would prove to be the latter, it then occurred to me to ask whether such a judgment could have been made in this university fifty years ago. Or, perhaps, I should ask whether I or any of my intimate friends would have made such a judgment or taken it seriously if made by anyone else. The remainder of this chapter will be in large measure an answer to this question.

When I was a student, and later a teacher, in the twenties, the university, compared to what it has become today, was to me and my intimate contemporaries well-nigh utopian. The campus itself was idyllic. Located about four miles from the city center on a gentle rise in the terrain, it was a six hundred acre tract of lawns, indigenous shrubbery, and forest. There were a dozen or so buildings, the newer ones, including the library, were Tudor-Gothic in style. Four of these constituted the liberal arts quadrangle: education, commerce, home economics, and philosophy. In 1925 there were about six thousand students and two hundred and seventy-five faculty. An aging army sergeant, unarmed, but with authority rendered impressive by a red motorcycle, was employed to keep intellectual discussion from becoming too violent.

Such was the campus—spacious, pastoral, arcadian, and one of the most serene and beautiful in the country. The physical plant was not obtrusive. The few buildings, tucked away among the trees on so large a tract, were no more than adequate to house the university community. The center of university studies was the liberal arts quadrangle, for at that time the university was primarily an undergraduate institution. The most distinguished of the university's faculty had tiny, unpretentious offices, and the president, one of America's leading educators, lived on the campus.

It was a community in a real sense and it was autonomous, organized, and interrelated. Each class had its governing body and a sequence of traditional yearly activities. Each of these activities was the responsibility of an appropriate committee. There were the Freshman Mixer and Frosh Frolic; the Sophshindig and Hello Day; the Junior Jinx and Junior Girls Vodvil; the Junior-Senior Roundup, the Prom, the Senior Soiree. Each class had—or planned to have—its distinctive garb. Freshmen wore green skullcaps; juniors and seniors wore cords, the latter adding thereto red vests with gold numerals. In order to distribute identity and honors to more than class officers and members of the various committees, the classes held hotly contested elections to choose the most handsome man and woman, the best politician, the best male and female dancer, the one with the biggest feet, the man with the most powerful physique, the girl with the best line, and the biggest fusser. There were also all-university functions: the Varsity Ball, the Cadet Ball, the All-University Mixer. And there was a Tolo Dance to which women invited male companions, an unconscious prelude to women's lib.

The several classes related to each other in a variety of interclass competitions in sports and academic pursuits, competitions that were taken seriously. There were also all-university activities, such as the school paper, the yearbook, the humor magazine, debate societies, honorary societies, and a wide variety of clubs. Participation in these was encouraged and eagerly sought, on the theory that such work as it entailed would add significantly to the student's preparation for life outside the gates of the university. Thus each student had an identity, or an opportunity to establish one. He was a person rather than a thing or a number in the hidden recesses of a computer.

The faculty were a close-knit group. The various departments, schools, and colleges were then rather small, some of them quartered in the same or adjoining buildings. The departments of history, philosophy, psychology, and political science were all in one building; by this very fact the physical distance that separated colleagues was negligible. The professors in the various disciplines were not yet engulfed and insulated in a proliferating bureaucracy or departmental bigness, and the department executives were primarily teachers whose burdens of office routine were borne by competent secretaries. Thus the colleagues lunched together, played cards in the faculty club, entertained each other, exchanged ideas, and discussed the promise of certain students; through these interdisciplinary associations they developed a sense of community, an awareness of being professors in the university rather than narrow specialists in a given discipline. They quoted each other in their lectures, and when one of them published a classic in letters and achieved a national reputation, he dedicated the work to a colleague in political science.

The professors also had ample time to confer with students, for they were not yet obliged to work long hours behind locked office doors doing research in order to meet the challenge to publish or perish. Students in the twenties did not generally complain, as they do now, that professors were not available for conferences. There was no occasion for such remonstrances, since any student was welcome to walk with a professor at the end of the class hour, and to be smoked at by the professor, as Stephen Leacock once said they do at Oxford, for as long as he could endure the smoke of Benson and Hedges. Faculty members served as advisers to students during registration and participated in student life in a variety of ways. Isn't it ironical that, when a scholar is being considered for a position in a department today, the first thing he wants to know is how much he will have to teach? How much of the working day will he have to devote to doing what he will be paid to do? Isn't that incredible! What he wants and usually gets, if he is a scholar with a reputation, is an appointment that will allow him plenty of time for research and publication so that he may add to his bibliography, increase his reputation as a productive scholar, and position himself for lucrative offers from other universities.

In the 1925 yearbook, the president of the university wrote as follows: "The University is the scion of Western Civilization, the inheritor and transmitter of the art, science, and philosophy of the ancient Universities of Paris, Bologna, and Oxford. It is also a child of young America, taking its stature, strength, and grace from the rich, favorable, free life of the Pacific Northwest."

Forty-five years later, the president of the associated students, writing in the yearbook for 1970, had this to say: "It's no good coming here to be educated if you can't learn anything because the things taught don't count in the real world and are taught by those who can't communicate them anyway."

In this brief profile of the university in which I began my studies in the fall of 1922, there is an implied comparison with what the university has become today. I am not passing a final judgment on what it was then nor on what it is now. I felt the need to give a summary description of the university community in which I continued the education of the mind in the middle twenties. In the remainder of this chapter I shall give an account of the ambience in which

I continued my studies, particularly as it relates to the central theme of this narrative—my interest in the rights of man. In the next chapter I shall explain how that interest took on the intensity of a passion.

Once again I acknowledge the extraordinary good luck that attended all my efforts; what I have accomplished was made possible more by good fortune than by exceptional personal resources. As Shakespeare's Bolingbroke achieved the throne by luck rather than by craft, so I progressed toward the achievement of my goals by taking hold of opportunities rather than by making them. I do have a peasant's instinct for survival, and, given America's opulence, I can keep bread on the table. But I have no genius for overcoming what appears to be hopeless adversity. A. E. Houseman, in his essay on *The Name and Nature of Poetry,* confesses that his verse is akin to a "morbid secretion," and that he has seldom written poetry unless he was "rather out of health." Not so with my own labors. I require health and a glimpse of the light at the end of the tunnel in order to be productive. For me it was pure luck that father settled in the opulent Pacific Northwest. Had he established our home in a ghetto of one of the large eastern cities, I doubt that I would have fared so well. Once again it was my good fortune that when I began my university studies, the university community was such as I have described, the time was the middle twenties, and my preparation to meet its challenge was such as Bess Evans and other teachers had provided.

What, then, were the mood, temper, and intellectual climate in the nation and in the university, when I left McCleary, ceased being a provincial lad, moved to the big city, and sought my place in the university community? The answer may be stated in two words: optimism unlimited. When I began reading Ely on economics in the fall of 1922, ably interpreted by a very persuasive professor who later became educational director of the American Banking Institute, the golden and roaring twenties were on the launching pad, and only the most perceptive critic could see that the crash landing was only a few short years away. During most of the time between the launching and the crash, the presidency was in the trust of Calvin Coolidge, who continued his predecessor's quest for normalcy but left the plotting of the course to the unfettered captains of industry and finance. If we may trust the indices for the period between 1922 and 1929, industry and finance did well. The national wealth increased from $306 to $353 billion, the value of man-ufactures jumped from $59 to $67 billion, and the national income increased at the rate of $30 billion a year.

Secretary of the Navy, Curtis Wilbur, in a speech before the Connecticut Chamber of Commerce, on May 7, 1925, justified everyone's confidence in the booming economy with these impressive statistics: "Americans have over twenty millions of tons of merchant shipping to carry the commerce of the world, worth three billions of dollars. We have loans and property abroad, exclusive of government loans, of over ten billions of dollars. If we add to this the volume of exports and imports for a single year—about ten billion dollars—we have an amount almost equal to the entire property of the United States in 1868; and if we add to this the eight billion dollars due us from foreign governments, we have a total of thirty-one billion dollars, being about equal to the total wealth of the nation in 1878." The course was indefinitely upward. Could anyone fail to believe that prosperity had come to stay?

The sense of material well-being and the certainty that the spiral upward was without visible end was strikingly reflected in the bourgeois sector of the Italian colony in the city. Since I was secretary of its Commercial Club, I had an opportunity to observe the phenomenon at close range. The active members of the club were shopkeepers, building contractors, artisans, insurance and fiscal agents, and salesmen of one sort or another. There were two doctors, an attorney, a pharmacist, the publisher of an Italian weekly, a printer, and several bootleggers. Most of them, except for the professional few, were of peasant and working class origin with little or no formal education; but they were shrewd, aggressive, and richly endowed with the acquisitive instinct. In less than two decades in America they had progressed from worrying about the daily bread in their native villages to making good money. Not fortunes, but, for them, good money. They drove automobiles, lived heartily and well, and faced the future with confidence. At the home of one of them— he was grossing two grand a week in the liquor traffic—after a feast in celebration of Columbus Day attended by politicians who "loved Italians," the host distributed cigars and lit them with a flaming dollar bill. (I had been invited with the understanding that I would make a little speech on the marvels of Italian civilization.)

In the community in those days it was heresy to doubt that the golden twenties would become anything but more golden. In any period in history those who prosper and are happy are secure in what an English social critic has called a "calm belief in the finality of the order of things." In the twenties such a belief was pervasive in the university community no less than in the world of affairs. There was no organized challenge to the status quo. Faculty and students shared a sense of well-being. Faculty dispensed and students acquired knowledge, confident that they were preparing themselves for a comfortable post in an order of things that was final in structure but infinite in opportunities. There were, of course, perceptive and unheeded critics, but they made no waves. Their cynicism was academic and therefore irrelevant. One of them, a professor of history, advised his students to vote for Coolidge, but the reason he gave was preposterous: "A vote for Coolidge is a vote for the revolution." A community that was essentially a carefree haven of happiness and well-being was only amused by such heresy.

When I registered in the university at the beginning of my freshman year, it was my good fortune to have as an adviser a distinguished professor of classics. This was important, for the professor was an amiable, friendly scholar who made me feel immediately at home in the university community. As Bess Evans had, he noted my Italian name, pronounced it correctly, and told me that the president of the university was of Italian descent. He was obviously interested in the fact that I was an Italian immigrant and fluent in my native language, for at that time I was possibly the only Italian student in the university who had come to America as an immigrant at ten years of age. He asked me questions about my family's immigration, the reasons for it, and our settlement in McCleary—a place he had never heard of. Thus I had an opportunity to establish my identity and to tell him about my plans. During our extended conference—he seemed in no hurry to terminate it—he told me that he had traveled in Italy, and that in Florence he had acquired a rare copy of the *Divina Commedia,* from which he read me the opening lines in perfect Italian and with obvious pleasure. Thus the fact that I was Italian caused the professor to regard me with special interest.

When he had registered me for the fall term and planned the complete course of my prelegal studies, he urged me to consider the possibility of an academic career in either classics or romance languages and literature. The fact that I was Italian and knew the language would give me a certain advantage in those disciplines. I was flattered by his interest in my future and assured him that I would seriously consider pursuing that course. I did take his excellent course in Greek and Roman civilization, and I still remember something rather striking that he said in one of his lectures on Lucretius: "He dropped his plummet down the broad, deep Universe and cried: No God!" But although I did give some thought to pursuing the professional course he had suggested, nothing ever came of it. I was too determined to study law and proceed according to the plans Bess Evans and I had agreed on.

And now that I was settled in the university and well into my courses, I was ready to petition for membership in one of the debate clubs. There were four—two for women and two for men. After attending a meeting of both clubs as spectator, I chose the one that had the most congenial companions. However, my choice was subject to the club's approval, for membership in either club was by invitation; one was invited to become a member only after passing a rigorous test in the presentation of an oral argument. A date was set for the trial and the name of the judge was announced. He was Lewis Baxter Schwellenbach, then the most distinguished alumnus of the club. He was state commander of the American Legion, president of the Alumni Law Association, prominent in Democratic state politics, and he was being groomed for the governorship. When he died, rather young, in 1948, he had been a member of the University Board of Regents, U.S. Senator, Federal Judge, and Secretary of Labor in President Truman's Cabinet. That gentleman, four years a varsity debater, already distinguished and so full of promise, would judge the performance of all students who aspired to membership in the debate club. How charitable would he be? How exacting?

In preparing my maiden speech at the university, on the success of which so much depended, I decided to do some research on the man who would judge my performance. Accordingly, I consulted the yearbooks, and, to my horror, I discovered that when Schwellenbach began his career as a varsity debater in 1913 the proposition for intercollegiate debate was: "Resolved: That immigration of all unskilled laborers of the Slavonic, Italic, and Hellenic races of Eastern and Southeastern Europe should be prohibited." How shocking! How blatantly discriminatory! At the very time when our family had survived the test of Ellis Island and gained admittance to the new land, the universities of the west were debating the merits of a proposed law that would have excluded us. Lewis Schwellenbach had debated that proposition and lost. But he had upheld the negative! That gave me an idea. I would make my maiden speech on that subject and present an argument against the proposed law, expressing all the bitterness and resentment I felt. For at that time, the American Dream was becoming a vivid reality to me; I was beginning to feel the profound religiosity of "we hold these truths to be self-evident, that all men are created equal, that they are endowed by their Creator with certain unalienable rights. . . . "

To construct such an argument as would impress an attorney who had himself argued against the proposed law as a varsity debater, I needed a great deal of data that I did not have. Where should I begin? Perhaps my adviser, who seemed to be rather fond of Italians, could help me plan the research. Unfortunately, after a brief conference with me, he confessed he knew absolutely nothing about the subject and was shocked to learn that anyone should want to keep those nice Italians out of the country. However, he directed me to the reference division of the library, and there I found willing and capable guides to help me find what I needed. It was my first of many happy and productive encounters with reference librarians, and I must say that they are a very special breed of men and—mostly—women. I have found them so helpful, so obliging, so persistent, that I now hesitate to seek their aid, for fear that once they undertake a search they may never abandon it.

So I began my research immediately with the aid of the reference librarians. While I was a schoolboy in McCleary, I had learned something about literacy tests and the agitation against further immigration from southern and eastern Europe as reported in the Italian newspaper, but it was while I was doing the research for my maiden speech at the university that I learned about the magnitude of that agitation. I learned also that many distinguished Americans had joined Presidents Cleveland, Taft, and Wilson in opposing the exclusion of immigrants from southern and eastern Europe and in rejecting any such test as literacy. President Wilson had stated their case perfectly when he had said that such tests were tests of opportunity rather than of character or fitness. I also made the convenient discovery that, at the very time that Mr. Schwellenbach was opposing the proposed law as a varsity debater, President Taft was vetoing the literacy bill just before he left office in 1913.

Of these data I fashioned an argument on the thesis that the proposed law made a mockery of the finest traditions of American democracy. Since our incomparable society was predicated on the divine principle that all men are created equal, then, I insisted, the Italic, Slavonic, and Hellenic races must not be judged inferior to the Nordics by an act of Congress. I concluded by stating my own personal bias against the proposal and expressing my own sense of gratitude for the fact that such a bill had not been enacted into law when my family sought admittance to the new land in 1913. The argument, I felt, was irrefutable, and I indulged in a bit of pride that, as a young immigrant from Italy only a few years away from the crude medievalism of Casabianca, I could align myself with distinguished presidents in defense of the finest traditions of American democracy. The question now was, would Mr. Schwellenbach be persuaded? And—there's the rub!—would I be able to present it effectively?

Here there was cause for anxiety. Since debate was a major university activity and the debate clubs were training camps for varsity debaters, competition for membership was very lively. Furthermore, practically all students who were intent on a degree in law were advised to seek membership in one or the other of the clubs. Thus the clubs were very selective in order to keep the membership down to a number that would give each one an opportunity to participate in the debate activity. Therefore, the trial for admission was not a mere formality; it was designed to be a serious test of competence, and also a means of deflating the ego of freshmen who thought too well of themselves. Very likely I was such a one. I did have confidence in my ability to pass the test. I had won every debate in high school and received the praise of a judge of the Superior Court. Nevertheless, I faced the challenge with much anxiety: this was the major league and I was a bush leaguer.

The trial was held in the evening, in the moot court of the Law School, on the fourth floor of the commerce hall. There were about a dozen trying out that evening. The order of appearance was determined by lot. I drew number seven. The speeches were to be no more than ten minutes. That meant that I would have to be on pins and needles for about an hour. When finally my name was called, I had just passed the most uncomfortable sixty minutes in my life. However, when I got to the platform and stood behind the lectern, I felt strangely at home. I arranged my notes on the lectern, firmed my stance, paused briefly, as Bess Evans had taught me, and then I addressed Mr. Schwellenbach. He smiled and bowed his head in acknowledgment of my address. Whereupon I began: In the spring of 1913, when I was ten years of age, and our family was making plans to immigrate to America from Italy,

the varsity debaters at the university were debating this proposition: Resolved, that immigration of all unskilled, and so on. This evening I propose to
present a brief argument against that proposal. At this point, Mr. Schwellenbach, obviously remembering the debate he and his colleague had lost, rear-
ranged himself on his chair and leaned slightly forward as if the better to hear
what I might have to say. He seemed very pleased and attentive, as I proceeded to indicate the line of argument I intended to pursue. And I, pleased
that he seemed so pleased, became so engrossed in savoring my initial success, that I lost my train of thought. My mind went blank!

Fortunately I had wit enough to remember Bess Evans' advice: "If at any
time you lose your train of thought, don't panic. Pretend that the silent in-
terval is a dramatic pause and refer to your notes. If they are in good order,
there is no occasion for anxiety. You will find your place and be able to continue." By good order, she meant that the notes were, as she had taught us, a
point by point outline of the argument, clearly arranged on large numbered
cards. My notes were in good order. When darkness descended on me I was
standing beside the lectern. I moved deliberately behind it, consulted my
notes and—thank heaven!—I was able to continue. A friendly nod by Mr.
Schwellenbach assured me that he was no less relieved than I. I felt that he
was with me, and with his moral support I concluded my maiden speech at
the university without any further difficulty. When I left the platform and
made way for contestant number eight, I was confident that, except for that
moment of horror, I had done my best. And Mr. Schwellenbach would decide whether my best was good enough.

I was not in the least surprised when I was notified on the following day that
I had been admitted to membership in the club. Pleased, yes. Immensely
pleased; but not surprised. And not because I had an overblown image of
myself as a debater. I knew that I was a rookie and had much to learn about
the art of oratory before I could compete with any hope of success for a place
on the varsity debate squad. Julian Matthews and Robert Macfarlane were
still my idols, and I had a long way to go before I would have their poise,
urbanity, and knowledge of politics and economics and before I could aspire
to be their peer.

The reason I was not surprised was something other. It had been another
bit of my continuing good fortune that, in presenting an argument in defence

of a view he had unsuccessfully defended as a varsity debater, I had identified myself ideologically with Mr. Schwellenbach. This, added to the fact that I had done rather well, had made him charitably disposed toward me. I wasn't certain of this but it was what I had felt as I observed his reaction to my presentation.

Later, after the trials, when we all met to refresh ourselves with the usual cider and doughnuts, that feeling had been strengthened. He chatted with me as a liberal democrat and told me that, in 1913, it was practically impossible for a negative team to win a debate on that proposition, so widespread was the opposition, among conservative Americans, against further immigration from southern and southeastern Europe. He did not tell me that I had passed the test—the winners would be notified the next day. But I felt that he was praising me by implication.

In any case, whether he had been charitable or judged me strictly on merit, I was now a member of the debate fraternity and on my way toward the goals I had set for myself. I stated at the beginning of this chapter that I entered the university with more ease and less apprehension of the unknown than I had felt in proceeding from elementary to high school. The factors that contributed to that ease of accommodation with the university community were my association with Bess Evans, my visits to the campus to hear university debates, and what I had learned during the preceding three years. I had had three years of debate experience, been introduced to great nineteenth-century writers, felt the frightening vulgarity of the Everett and Centralia Massacres—and I had become a man. To these were now added two other factors: the appointment of the professor of classics as my adviser and my membership in the debate club. During registration week I had the privilege of being received in his office by a senior professor who liked Italians, knew something of our language, and took a personal interest in my career. In less than a month I was admitted to membership as a novitiate in the debate fraternity. In so brief a time, and with such ease, I had begun to find my place in the university. Not many country lads had it so easy.

I had expected that membership in the club would be a prelude to membership on the varsity debate squad. And it was. I had not expected that it would be the open sesame to what I shall call the inner university. And here I must explain that in the liberal arts college, as I learned rather early in my undergraduate days, there were two universities: the outer and the inner. The one was the world of matter, the world of the many; the other was the world of spirit, the world of the few. The quality of the one is suggested by the phrase "in the good old college days." Note the connotations! It was the essentially untroubled world of sports, class activities, class attendance, Greeks and independents, social life, periodic examinations, going steady and being pinned, and the day-to-day advancement toward a degree in education, history, business, or whatever. The movement from matriculation to baccalaureate did not normally entail a spiritual or intellectual conversion. The graduate of the outer university shared, perhaps unconsciously, the business community's "calm belief in the finality of the order of things."

Not so with the majority of faculty and students in the inner university. Its quality was suggested by the phrase "the quest for certainty," which was used by the philosopher John Dewey as the title of a book much discussed at the end of the decade. It was the narrow world of intellectual companionship, of the quest for truth, of the perennial search for the meaning of life, the definition of the highest good. It was a world where the better student met the better faculty on substantially equal terms and worked together as associates in the quest, where one was expected to reason well in all matters, to reexamine all one had been taught in church and school, and to dismiss whatever offended one's soul. It was a world that employed criticism and doubt as means of arriving at truth, a world perhaps a little afflicted by Hamlet's "scruple of thinking too precisely." However, it was also a world of hope and optimism, as I shall presently show, and of creative citizenship, for what its scholar-citizens ultimately sought was the just society.

The outer university was ever present—palpable and plainly visible to all. It engulfed one immediately. The inner was hidden and had to be found. The search for it, the effort to find it and become a part of it, was the better part of one's education. Perhaps I might have sharpened my vision, searched for it, and found it without aid. However, the fact is that I was introduced to it rather early by certain members of the debate clubs. Certain upperclass members, students of philosophy, literature, and the social sciences, who had become my intellectual companions and were of the inner university led me into it before I was fully prepared for membership in it. Thereafter, it was up to me to become a part of it; the measure of my success in so doing was that I eventually became private wine maker to the professor of philosophy who was universally regarded as the presiding deity of the inner university. A latter day Ganymede to Jove.

Optimism unlimited! Such was the pervasive mood and temper of the little world in which I lived, worked, and played during the better part of my undergraduate years. We were optimistic about our own future and about the destiny of the human race. We wore no rose-colored glasses; we were skeptical, critical, and realistic, but the facts at that time, precisely sixty years ago, justified our vision of the future.

Consider a few of the facts that gave us a sense of complete security that each of us would assume his proper place in society. I have already described the golden state of the economy in the twenties. We were all then free to choose a profession or a business career with the certainty that we could embark on such a course without any hindrance whatever and find immediate employment when the course was completed. I shall give an example that is fairly typical. When I entered law school, applicants were not screened and subjected to interviews and tests nor were they required to produce recommendations and a specific scholastic record. One simply registered as a matter of course for the first-year courses in law. The total enrollment was about 150. The law school was growing and the dean was proud of the fact that it was growing. He welcomed anyone who had finished the prelaw course. And no one who entered the law school was in the least concerned about finding his place in the legal profession upon graduation. I myself had been promised employment by the prosecuting attorney even before I had completed my first year. In brief, our optimism about our own future was completely realistic. Furthermore, we were comfortably aware of being citizens in a most extraordinary land. Its resources were seemingly without limit. The enterprise and ingenuity of its people had been demonstrated in the phenomenal progress in industry and commerce during the six decades following the Civil War. Also, the guidelines for a healthy and happy society were written into the Declaration and the Constitution. All we needed to assure an indefinite amelioration of that society was an unwavering loyalty to the immutable and profoundly religious principles declared to all mankind in those documents.

When my companions and I turned our thoughts from contemplating our own happy, personal prospects to reflect on the destiny of the nation and of the human race, our optimism was no less securely based. There may have been, in the twenties, such seers and prophets as could see the beginnings of what plagues the current generation: the food and energy crisis, the imminent exhaustion of unrenewable natural resources, the pollution of the total environment, the very real possibility that in another century the planet Earth will be dead. If there were such seers and prophets, their cries of doom were not heard above the roar of the roaring twenties. The critics whom we heard and to whom we listened, warned of dangers of another kind: corruption of Teapot Dome magnitude in government; the perils implicit in unfettered laissez-faire, financial speculation, imprudent use of installment buying; "the Mitchel Palmer raids" as a serious infringement of the civil liberties guaranteed in the First, Fourth, and Fifth Amendments; and the increasingly imperialistic direction of American foreign policy. These were present, palpable evils, but they were remedial. They could be attacked at the ballot box by the removal from office of the servants of privilege and the election of representatives who believed in the American Dream and were loyal to it. Nevertheless, we listened with some alarm.

Thus we became political activists. We did not march or demonstrate, for there was no occasion to do either. But we read the social critics, kept current on issues, and discussed, analyzed, and made speeches for worthy candidates and causes. We engaged in what Bess Evans had urged on her students—creative citizenship. We did this with zeal and passion, for we believed in progress as the gradual amelioration of society and the human lot. We believed in the infinite perfectibility of man and of the human race, and we were convinced that human nature could be changed.

We believed all of this because we were idealists, young romantics, and because it was reasonable to hold such beliefs. We were reading Walter Lippman, Russell's *Proposed Roads to Freedom,* the Socratic *Dialogues.* In the trial and death of Socrates, a subject on which the presiding deity of the inner university delivered a celebrated yearly lecture, we saw the dramatization of man's dignity. We discussed with passion what Socrates meant by the supreme good as a goal attainable and to be striven for. We were caught up in the fervor of the romantic poets and believed that if winter came, spring could not be far behind. We had the will to believe before we had to read James on the subject. And while Tennyson's Victorian faith had been shaken by Darwin, *The Origin of Species* had strengthened our secular faith in the evolutionary process from primeval slime to the "... one far-off divine event; To which the whole creation moves." By definition, the event was, indeed, far off, but we had no doubt that it was a demonstrable reality.

During those years, I was particularly elated, for I tended to equate what we believed with what was happening to me. An event that had been far off was now at hand. The process of what sociologists call acculturation was well under way. In a dozen years since I had entered the first grade in Mc-Cleary, the goals I had set for myself were now within reach. I had become completely American without having lost my Italian identity, and my Italian descent was beginning to pay dividends. Most of my friends had part-time jobs: one was working for the Associated Press, one was working in the library, and another was selling butter to sororities and fraternities—living off the fat of the land! But I was earning my way as an interpreter for the superior court—in criminal cases that involved Italian immigrants and for one or both of the litigants in civil suits. Meanwhile I was in law school. I had been selected by the dean to nominate an astute senior for the presidency of the law association; after he had been elected, my fellows elected me yell leader of the law school!

However, my legal studies were about to be terminated. Once again I had come to a crossroads and had to make a crucial decision. I must choose between the law and literature, or, since these need not be mutually exclusive, I had to choose between an academic career and the practice of law. The choice was difficult and I wavered. I liked the law as a discipline, and I enjoyed reading and pondering the decisions of such cultivated jurists as Holmes and Cardozo. But I was not certain about spending my life in the hurly-burly, earning my bread in the service of litigious persons—which now included corporations. On the other hand, my interest in literature and philosophy, particularly ethics and epistemology, was deepening day by day. I enjoyed the life of the mind that I was living with my companions. I was strongly attracted by the peace and serenity promised by an academic life, as I saw it reflected in most of the professors who were now my close friends. Several of my companions who had come to the university intending to study law were now in graduate school in English. Furthermore, I hoped that some day I would write. Such considerations as these made the practice of law seem, perhaps unjustly, rather grubby. The spur that I needed to abandon law was supplied by the offer to teach English in a small private college. Thus I decided to work for a doctorate in English and earn my bread in academia.

The offer of a job teaching English, when my undergraduate degree was in history, was very flattering. Since I knew Italian—the dividends kept coming in!—the professor who taught the Chaucer seminar had told me that when I returned to the university I might take his course and investigate the possible influence of Boccaccio on the Troilus and Criseyde story. That, too, had been very flattering. I had already fancied myself a young professor, lecturing to my peers, drawing reflectively on Benson and Hedges (the cigarettes of the presiding deity), writing essays, and pondering the contours of the good society—a sort of happy cross between Milton's *l'Allegro* and *Il Penseroso*.

Thus, when I was graced by the prospect of so bright a future, the optimism that I have described above was intensified. I reread two books that had once strengthened my faith in the far-off divine event and given it eloquent expression. When I had entered the university and aspired to become a varsity debater, Julian Matthews and Robert Macfarlane had been my idols. By diligent labor and with the aid of great teachers, I had closed the gap between myself and them. Now that I was about to enter academia, I had other idols. Among them were the authors of these two books: One of them was G. Lowes Dickinson. His little classic, *A Modern Symposium*, I had used in my class on argumentation. Another book of his, *Justice and Liberty*, I had first read while taking a course in social ethics. It is a political dialogue. The speakers are a banker, an aristocrat, and a professor. I quote from the section of the book where the subject discussed is human nature, the nature of man and the ideal. The banker has just defended the essentially Hobbesian view that man is a brute—stupid, greedy, cowardly, and narrow-minded—and that life is nasty, brutish, and short. Whereupon the professor replies:

"This animal, Man, this poor thin wisp of sodden straw buffeted on the great ocean of fate, this ignorant, feeble, quarrelsome, greedy, cowardly victim and spawn of the unnatural parent we call Nature, this abortion, this clod, this indecent, unnamable thing, is also, as certainly, the child of a celestial father. Sown into the womb of Nature, he was sown a spiritual seed. And history, on one side the record of man's entanglement in matter, on the other is the epic of his self-deliverance. All the facts, the dreadful facts at which we have timidly hinted, and which no man could fairly face and live, all those facts are true; stop at them, if you will! But true also is the contest of which they are the symbol, real the flood no less than the deposit it has left; real, of all things reallest, the ideal! Do not conceive it as an idea in somebody's head. No! Ideas are traces it leaves, shadows, images, words: itself is the light, the fire, the tongue, of which these are creatures. Poetry, philosophy, art, religion, what you will, are but its expression; they are not It. Thought is a key to unlock its prison, words are a vessel to carry its seed. But It is Reality of Realities, fact of facts, force of forces. It refutes demonstration; it unsettles finality; it defies experience. While all men are crying *impossible,* it has sped and done. Even in those who deny it, it lies a latent spark; let them beware the conflagration when the wind of the spirit blows. . . .

"Looking at the thing as straight as I can, and in what philosophers call a calm moment, I find in men a real fact, the impulse to create the ideal, and this I represent to myself as a seed sown into the soil of Earth with her insufficiency and insecurity, of the flesh with its needs and desires. What there from grows up is the tree of human history, receiving its form from the seed, but its matter from the soil and air, warped and stunted, battered, mutilated, broken, but always straining upward to the light and the sky, and throwing out branches and bearing leaves by the law of its inner impulse. At any moment, then, we may, indeed we must, say, at once that man is a spirit, if we look at his ideal form, and that he is a brute, if we look at his stuff; at once that his Society is bad and that its shaping soul is good; at once that his history is a sordid chronicle of crime, and that it is a solemn school of righteousness. The one is not true and the other false; the truth is the Whole. . . . The ideal is not utopian, in the sense in which that word is commonly used. It has always reference to contemporary facts, is engendered by and against them, and is itself part of the process that is working out. Though it appear in heaven it is not an unapproachable star; it is the light struck from the friction of the contest."

That is irresistibly provocative! And as I read it now, six decades later, and notwithstanding the gloom generated during the last decade, I am deeply moved. Man's impulse to create, as we but think on what man has created since Dickinson wrote, is even more demonstrably a fact now, a fact of nature, a part of the whole truth, than it was then. And so is the life of reason, since the impulse to create is but reason made manifest. If only we could— and we can, we must—redefine the ends toward which that impulse is directed, away from destruction and toward construction, away from waste and toward conservation, away from greedy competition and toward generous cooperation. If, in planning our course for tomorrow, we have the good sense to remember before it is too late, the late Bertrand Russell's farewell: Remember the human family and forget the rest! then we may very well redirect ourselves toward the future prophesied by H. G. Wells in his little book, *The Discovery of the Future:*

"We are in the beginning of the greatest change that humanity has ever undergone. There is no shock, no epoch-making incident—but then there is no shock at a cloudy daybreak. At no point can we say 'Here it commences, now; last minute was night and this is morning.' But insensibly we are in the day. If we care to look, we can foresee growing knowledge, growing order, and presently a deliberate improvement of the blood and character of the race. And what we can see and imagine gives us a measure and gives us faith for what surpasses the imagination.

"It is possible to believe that all the past is but the beginning of a beginning, and that all that is and has been is but the twilight of the dawn. It is possible to believe that all the human mind has ever accomplished is but the dream before the awakening. We cannot see, there is no need for us to see, what this world will be like when the day has fully come. We are creatures of the twilight. But it is out of our race and lineage that minds will spring, that will reach back to us in our littleness to know us better than we know ourselves, and that will reach forward fearlessly to comprehend this future that defeats our eyes.

"All this world is heavy with the promise of greater things, and a day will come, one day in the unending succession of days, when beings, beings who are now latent in our thoughts and hidden in our loins, shall stand upon this earth as one stands upon a footstool, and shall laugh and reach out their hands amid the stars!"

By a happy coincidence, that book was published in 1913, the very year when I began the discovery of my own future. When I reread it, some dozen years later, I myself was laughing and reaching out my hands amid the stars. And had I known then about Prospero's Island, I would most certainly have exclaimed with Miranda:

> How beauteous mankind is! O brave new world
> That has such people in it!

CHAPTER VI

The End of the Dream?

I have forgotten who among us had been the first to read Wells' *Discovery*, but after we had all read it and felt the exaltation of its eloquence, my debate companions and I occasionally stood, symbolically, upon a footstool and rehearsed our speeches. A few blocks from the campus there was a wilderness that in the preceding century had been a part of the forest primeval. Scattered among the trees and indigenous shrubbery were the stumps of the giant conifers that had been felled fifty years before. In spring evenings when the dogwood was in bloom and the sap flowed and the stars were bright, we quickened the blood's flow with draughts of homemade and forbidden wine and laughed our way thither. Standing on the ample surface of one of the stumps, we took turns whipping ourselves into shape for the next debate. Often we recited poetry. And always one or the other of us, reaching out his hands amid the stars, recited the concluding sentence of the *Discovery*.

One of the companions was a Jew, and I mention the fact because he was the first Jew I had ever known. Nor had I known that Jews were a persecuted race. Therefore, I was puzzled when the fellow who told me he was a Jew seemed surprised that I hadn't noticed that he was a Jew. What the hell was there to notice? I had noticed what was perfectly obvious: that he was a dedicated student with a keen analytical mind and a devastating wit, that he was effective on the platform, grave, abstracted, and not given to levity. It was in part for his benefit that we warmed ourselves with wine—to loosen him up, make him smile, even apologetically, as if smiling were a sin and the unwrinkling of the brow a loss of time. And the strategy worked. After a draught or two from the bottle—the wine was young, potent, and a trifle sweet—the woes of the world fell from his slightly stooped shoulders, the young Disraeli smiled, elfishly, leaped upon the stump, and delivered our credo: "All this world is heavy with the promise of greater things. . . ."

In choosing the teams for the various interclub debates, it was the policy of the club to assign a freshman to work with an upperclassman. I was assigned to work with this man. Since he was in his first year in law school and a skilled debater, I considered myself very fortunate that he was to be my partner in my first interclub debate. With him as my tutor, given his skill and experience, I felt that he and I would be a team to be reckoned with in all interclub debates. Had I known him then, as I came to know him later, I would have had other reasons for being thankful that he had been chosen to be my tutor. Of all the skeptical companions, he was more completely skeptical. Their skepticism was largely intellectual; his was intellectual, emotional, and disturbing.

It has been said of the Italian poet, Luigi Pulci: *Non crede in niente dal tetto in su.* He believes in nothing from the roof upward. That could possibly have been said of him. However, he felt the need to believe, and what disturbed him was that he hadn't yet been able to define what he ought to believe. As we drew closer to each other and exchanged ideas and confided in each other, I learned that he was struggling to come to terms with Karl Marx and economic determinism! That, at the time, was all Greek to me.

He was a sweet and gentle person, but the woes of the world lay heavy on his shoulders and he died young, probably from sheer mental exhaustion. While I had the pleasure of working with him I learned from him more than mere debate strategy.

Since he was a complete student and self-supporting, he was very busy; the only time he and I could conveniently work together on the debate subject was in the evening while he worked for the Associated Press. I have forgotten what he did, but whatever it was, it left him some time for his studies. One evening when I joined him in his little cubbyhole of an office, there were several books on his tiny desk. As he put them aside to clear a space for me, he handed me one of them and asked me if I had read it. It was a volume of the works of Thomas Paine: *Common Sense, The Rights of Man, The Crisis*

Papers. When I told him that I had never heard of Thomas Paine, he proceeded to tell me something about the man and his work. What a revelation! That evening we did no work whatever on the debate subject; for he talked at great length and with considerable excitement about the "philosopher of the American Revolution" and urged me to read the book as soon as I could find the time. When we returned to the campus late that evening, he loaned me the volume. As soon as I got to my room I read the whole of *Common Sense*. Never had I read anything so exciting since Bess Evans had introduced me to Walt Whitman.

How strange that none of my teachers thus far, and some of them knowing that I was anxious to learn the elements of American history, had told me about Tom Paine! Hadn't they read *Common Sense*? When I looked at the first of *The Crisis Papers*, I remembered that the opening sentence had been used as an exercise in a typing class in high school: "These are the times that try men's souls." I had remembered it not so much for the sense as for the sheer beauty of the diction, and it had never occurred to me to ask whence it came. Nor had the teacher volunteered the information. Why had that particular sentence been chosen as an appropriate exercise in typing? Because it had become a celebrated line, such as Dante's *Nel mezzo del cammin di nostra vita*, and presumed to be known by every schoolchild? I never knew, nor did I ask. Looking at it now, I see that it contains half the letters of the alphabet, including all the vowels. By repeated typing of that short sentence, consisting of eight monosyllabic words, the student would learn to find the five vowels and eight of the twenty-one consonants on the keyboard. What an unintended service the philosopher of the American Revolution had rendered the teacher of commercial studies! And what an opportunity she had lost for doing some memorable and creative teaching!

"These are the times that try men's souls. The summer soldier and the sunshine patriot will, in this crisis, shrink from the service of their country; but he that stands it *Now*, deserves the love of man and woman. Tyranny, like hell, is not easily conquered. . . ." Now, class, let's forget the typewriter for a moment and note what we have here. Willy, what were "the times"? How did they "try men's souls"? Who is a "summer soldier," a "sunshine patriot"? What "tyranny" is alluded to there? Who wrote those memorable words?

Had the teacher proceeded in this manner, that class itself would have been a memorable experience, and I might have begun, while still in high school, a line of inquiry that would have shed some light on the root source of the Everett and Centralia Massacres and of the tyranny of Boss Johnson. But to the teacher of commercial subjects, that memorable line was no more than a useful exercise in typing. So I must express my gratitude to the first Jew I had ever known for having introduced me, at the very beginning of my college career, to Tom Paine and, through him, to the whole subject of political philosophy.

In a sense, my tutor and companion in debate, by placing in my hands that book, prepared me for instruction I should get later from certain of the great teachers in the liberal arts college. They and their young assistants, principally in philosophy, political science, and American literature, were democrats in the tradition of Jefferson. They were all so liberal, intellectually honest, and faithful to the quest, that they had not escaped the surveillance of the self-appointed guardians of morals and the status quo. They all knew Tom Paine well, and they would lecture with commanding authority on *Common Sense*, *The Rights of Man*, the nature of government, the origins of the American Revolution, and the development of the American commonwealth.

Common Sense is not a book; it is an extended essay, a monograph. But its pages are weighted with a boldly stated political philosophy, much of it original: the essentially economic origins of government; the doctrine of the continuous reaffirmation of the social compact—opposed to the view, defended by Burke and the old Whigs, that government derived from a perpetual civil contract that bound those who executed it and their "heirs and posterities forever"; the idea that sovereignty inheres in the majority; the celebrated dictum that "that which a nation chooses to do, it has the right to do." Much of this, of course, escaped me when I first read *Common Sense;* but what impressed me profoundly, and what I had no difficulty whatever understanding, was his merciless attack on monarchy and hereditary succession. On this subject he wrote with such Disraelian mockery that the Tories could only express their contempt of him in sputters of disgust: "Mankind being originally equals in the order of creation, the equality could only be destroyed by some subsequent circumstance: the distinctions of rich and poor may in a great measure be accounted for. . . . But there is another and great distinction for which no truly natural or religious reason can be assigned, and that is the distinction of men into Kings and Subjects. Male and female are the distinctions of nature, good and bad the distinctions of Heaven; but how a race of men came into the world so exalted above the rest, and distinguished like some new species, is worth inquiring into. . . . "

Having begun his inquiry by referring to scripture and finding that monarchy was "ranked as one of the sins of the Jews," he continues: "These portions of scripture are direct and positive. They admit of no equivocal construction. That the Almighty hath here entered his protest against monarchical government is true, or the scripture is false. And a man hath good reason to believe that there is as much of kingcraft as priestcraft in withholding the scripture from the public in popish countries. For monarchy in every instance is the popery of government.

"To the evil of monarchy we have added that of hereditary succession; and as the first is a degradation and lessening of ourselves, so the second, claimed as a matter of right, is an insult and imposition on posterity. For all men being originally equals, no one by birth could have a right to set up his own family in perpetual preference to all others forever, and tho' himself might deserve some decent degree of honours of his contemporaries, yet his descendants might be far too unworthy to inherit them. One of the strongest natural proofs of the folly of hereditary right in Kings, is that nature disapproves it, otherwise she would not so frequently turn it into ridicule, by giving mankind an *Ass for a Lion.* . . . England since the conquest hath known some few good monarchs, but groaned under a much larger number of bad ones; yet no man in his senses can say that their claim under William the Conqueror is a very honourable one. A French bastard landing with an armed Banditti and establishing himself King of England against the consent of the natives, is in plain terms a very paltry rascally original. It certainly hath no divinity in it. . . . "

As I record these lines now, some sixty years after I first read them, my pulse still quickens with excitement. Paine's immediate purpose was to convince the colonies that they should unite, draw up a charter, and declare their independence of England—of George III, whose folly and cruelty were the "best commentary upon the foolishness of hereditary monarchy." Having suggested how such a union might be democratically effected, he raised and answered the following question: "But where, say some, is the *King* of America? I'll tell you, friend, he reigns above, and doth not make havoc of mankind like the Royal Brute of Great Britain. Yet that we may not appear to be defective even in earthly honours, let a day be solemnly set apart for proclaiming the Charter; let it be brought forth placed on the Divine Law, the Word of God; let a crown be placed thereon, by which the world may know, that so far as we approve of monarchy, that *in America the law is King.* . . . "

And there you have it: a government of laws, not of men! *The Rights of Man,* a much longer treatise, was somewhat more difficult but equally exciting: "Every history of the creation, and every traditionary acount, whether from the lettered or unlettered world, however they may vary in their opinion or belief of certain particulars, all agree in establishing one point, *the unity of man;* by which I mean that all men are all of *one degree,* and consequently that all men are born equal, and with equal natural rights, in the same manner as if posterity had been continued by *creation* instead of *generation,* the latter being only the mode by which the former is carried forward; and consequently every child born into the world must be considered as deriving its existence from God. The world is as new to him as it was to the first man that existed, and his natural right in it is of the same kind.

"The Mosaic account of creation, whether taken as divine authority or merely historical, is fully up to this point, *the unity or equality of* man. The expressions admit of no controversy. 'And God said, Let us make man in our own image. In the image of God created he him; male and female created he them!' The distinction of sexes is pointed out, but no other distinction is even implied. . . .

"Hitherto we have spoken only (and that but in part) of the natural rights of man. We have now to consider the civil rights of man, and to show how the one originates from the other. Man did not enter into society to become *worse* than he was before, not to have fewer rights than he had before, but to have those rights better secured. His natural rights are the foundation of all his civil rights. But in order to pursue this distinction with more precision, it will be necessary to mark the different qualities of natural and civil rights.

"A few words will explain this. Natural rights are those which appertain to man in right of his existence. Of this kind are all the intellectual rights, or rights of the mind, and also all those rights of acting as an individual for his own comfort and happiness, which are not injurious to the natural rights of others. Civil rights are those which appertain to man in right of being a mem-

ber of society. Every civil right has for its foundation some natural right pre-
existing in the individual, but to the enjoyment of which his individual power
is not, in all cases, sufficiently competent. Of this kind are all those which relate to security and protection. . . . "

For this reason, then, were governments originally founded: to protect the
individual in the enjoyment of those rights which he, acting alone, could not
secure. Historically, governments have arisen from several sources: superstition, power, the common interests of society, and the common rights of man.
"The first was a government of Priestcraft, the second of Conquerors, and
the third of Reason. . . .

"It has been thought a considerable advance towards establishing the
principles of freedom to say that government is a compact between those
who govern and those who are governed; but this cannot be true, because it is
putting the effect before the cause; for as man must have existed before Government existed, there necessarily was a time when Governments did not exist, and consequently there could originally exist no governors to form such a
compact with. The fact therefore must be that the *individuals themselves,*
each in his own personal and sovereign right, *entered into a compact with
each other* to produce a Government: and this is the only mode in which
Governments have a right to arise, and the only principle on which they have
a right to exist. . . . "

Here, indeed, simply, clearly, and boldly stated, is the philosophical basis
of self-government, the sacred doctrinal core of democracy! Competing
political philosophers may very well ask some embarrassing questions about
the assumptions on which it is based, and historians may very well point out
that much of Thomas Paine derives from John Locke. But such challenges
are academic and for academics; they in no way affect reality. Tom Paine
reached the mind of the colonial yeomanry where more sophisticated philosophers had failed, and the natural rights, written into the Declaration as the
Creator's "unalienable" endowment to man, have been universally accepted
as such wherever men have aspired to self-government.

What I have quoted above should be fashioned into a catechism and
taught to every schoolchild in America. For is it not self-evident that every
member of a self-governing society ought to know the philosophical basis of
his rights and duties? Is it not common knowledge that the unalienable rights
must be daily secured against every generation's George III and Boss John-

son? Is it not axiomatic that he most effectively defends, who best understands the virtue of that which he is asked to defend? And is it not deplorable that even the majority of college graduates are not likely to know more of Tom Paine than the man's name? The times that tried men's souls were the years when the colonists were called upon to assert their rights against the tyranny of George III; and the summer soldier and the sunshine patriot were the timid who failed to rise to the opportunity.

When I read *The Crisis Papers* in 1923 and understood the issue that was to be settled on the battlefield, my reaction was akin to what I had felt six years before, on April 6, 1917, when America had declared war on Germany. The press of the day carried daily accounts of horrible atrocities committed by the Germans. "With impudent audacity"—the phrase was President Wilson's—the savage Huns were impaling Belgian babies on their bloody bayonets. Moved by such accounts to bitter loathing of the monster enemy, I wanted desperately to be among the Yanks who were going "over there," to put an end to atrocities and "make the world safe for democracy." But I was too young to bear arms, so I argued with the summer soldiers and the sunshine patriots in our home who sought ways to avoid doing their duty. Of course, I was a young boy, fascinated by the gun and the uniform, and I was deceived by the propaganda. For it is possible today to argue that it was a mistake for America to join one set of predators in Europe against another set, in a war that settled nothing of importance to mankind and set the stage for all the wretchedness that followed. But on the record, and two hundred years after the event, no American will argue that the Declaration and the War of Independence were tragic errors. Tyranny must be resisted wherever and whenever it seeks to deprive man of his unalienable rights. Fortunately, in 1917, I was too young to bear arms, but in 1923 I found myself regretting that I was one hundred and forty-seven years removed from the opportunity to stand with those who earned the love of man and woman.

I must now try to explain more fully what has been implicit in much that I have written thus far, the reason for my passionate affirmative response to Walt Whitman, Tom Paine, and all the liberal thinkers I would come to know thereafter in the related areas of political economy and jurisprudence. One of the pleasant ironies in my life was the rather early realization that, having left it, I was learning many things about my native land that I most certainly would never have known had I not emigrated. I have already stated that it was Bess Evans who first called my attention to Italy's exalted status among the nations of the West, and it was after I had come under her benign influence in high school that I got a glimpse of what I have called the crude medievalism into which I was born. When I read Whitman and was thrilled by his bold imperative to reexamine all you have been told in school or church and dismiss whatever insults your own soul, it was that crude medievalism I wanted to purge myself of.

But I could never quite define it or see it as clearly and exactly as a surgeon must see the pathology that he seeks to remove. In other words, at that time I did not know what medievalism was as a philosophy, a world view. I knew the symptoms, but not the disease. It was Tom Paine who provided the necessary diagnostic insight. After I had read *Common Sense* and *The Rights of Man,* supplemented by other reading, I knew enough to know what I had been early taught that was offensive to my soul. This I can best explain by commenting on a key declaration in *Common Sense:* "But there is another and great distinction for which no truly natural or religious reason can be assigned, and that is the distinction of men into Kings and Subjects."

That statement I accepted as an absolute truth. And still do! John Adams, in a letter to his wife, quoted General Lee to the effect that Tom Paine had "genius in his eyes." He must have had it in the very depth of his soul. However, I did not accept that statement as an absolute truth simply on the authority of the "philosopher of the American Revolution." Remembering Bess Evans' advice that one must learn to reason well in all matters, I could not see then, nor can I now, that such a distinction could be justified in reason. Since it had not been ordained by God and was repugnant to reason, the distinction must have been the work of the devil; all the evil consequences that were implicit in it were the crude medievalism of which I must purge myself. All the consequences save one: that crude medievalism was the ultimate cause of our immigration to the new land.

I now had at least a rough idea of the philosophy of medievalism. The distinction of men into kings and subjects implied a society divided into rigid classes; the hierarchical arrangement in Heaven—God, archangels, angels—repeated on earth—God, the king, the nobility, the pope, the cardinals, the archbishops, and so on. It implied, also, the patriarchal arrangement of society, the law of primogeniture, and the complete domination of the lower by the higher order of beings. "He for God only, she for God in him."

This was the world in which I was born. I knew now that, chronologically, the Middle Ages came to an end in the middle of the fourteenth century, and that at the beginning of the twentieth century Italy was a constitutional monarchy. That was all in the history books; and it was no more than an academic reality. Perhaps the world of the citizens—the world of Rome, of Florence, of Venice—was modern, a world where people had rights guaranteed by a constitution. Perhaps. I knew nothing about that world. (I do know now, however, that in 1945 the world of Rome got rid of the monarchy and hereditary succession and became a republic!) All I knew was the world of Casabianca and that it was essentially medieval, crudely medieval, in the sense in which I now understand the term. It was a miniature government of superstition and priestcraft, where hereditary succession meant that, among the landless peasantry, the eldest son inherited the father's misery, and where duties were clearly defined and rights nonexistent.

The twin imperatives in that world were to believe and to obey. (About a decade after I left it, Mussolini added a third and turned it into a bumper-sticker slogan for the entire nation: Believe, obey, and fight.) Without strict observance of those imperatives, ruthlessly enforced by the petty, local hierarchs, that world would have collapsed by the weight of its own injustice. Accordingly, in school and in church, I had been taught the gospel of strict, unquestioning obedience to superiors. As for the rest, the catechism had been a litany of frightening thou shalt nots. Where I had not been taught in so many words, I had been made to feel that rich and poor, privileged and deprived, master and servant, man and woman, constituted an order ordained by God. And, of course, I had believed and obeyed. There had been no alternative. Being a mere boy, I had not learned to covet what I did not have, and I had yet to learn the meaning of *pazienza* and *sperare*.

But now I was no longer a boy. I was a university man, a world away from Casabianca, and in the process of becoming acquainted with philosophy and political economy. I now knew that the order in which I had been taught to believe had neither the sanction of God nor of reason. Knowing this, and understanding to my complete satisfaction the rationale on which that order was based, I could now purge myself of it completely, clear my mind of the myths and lies with which it had been defiled. Now I could do it. For some reason, as a student I needed to know precisely what I was rejecting and why. Now I knew.

For this same reason I had been curious, perhaps precociously so, about the meaning of democracy. I had been groping for its philosophical and ethical basis before philosophy and ethics were words in my vocabulary. I had sought an explanation for that strange phenomenon, first observed in McCleary, in the school and in the village—that strange and yet reassuring phenomenon of mill owners and workers and their children mingling freely and living pretty much the same kind of life.

Bess Evans had suggested that that had been a superficial observation and she had warned me that as I became better acquainted with America I would see for myself that the rich and the poor did not mingle as they did in Mc-Cleary. Of course, she was right. However, there was an element of truth in what I had observed; and I had become increasingly interested in discovering what underlay it. For even in the university community, the rich were not segregated from the poor. There were sons and daughters of wealthy parents and sons and daughters of poor parents. The former did not work their way through college; the latter were almost completely self-supporting. No one avoided me because I was the son of a peasant immigrant who worked as a section hand. We mingled freely as equals. This, too, was a reality. There had been nothing like it in Casabianca, and there must be a reason for it.

With the aid of my teachers I had begun my search for a convincing explanation. Bess Evans had contributed most significantly to the inquiry with what she had told me about rights guaranteed in the Constitution and her references to the Gettysburg Address and to Walt Whitman. But how strange that she had not referred me to "the philosopher of the American Revolution"! Was it possible that she had not read Tom Paine? I preferred to believe that she had considered me too young and rebellious to read the arch rebel of the American Revolution. In any case, I had now found what I had sought, the philosophical and ethical principles on which American democracy was based. Tom Paine had spelled them out so clearly and so convincingly in the passages I have quoted from his works. About a year after he had written *Common Sense,* its distilled essence was stated in the second paragraph of the Declaration of Independence: "We hold these truths to be self-evident, that all men are created equal, that they are endowed by their Creator with certain unalienable rights, that among these are Life, Liberty, and the pursuit of Happiness. . . . "

A society organized in accordance with these self-evident truths would certainly have the sanction of both God and reason. Such a society, conceived in the Continental Congress that produced the Declaration in 1776, became a formal reality twelve years later when on June 21, 1788, New Hampshire became the ninth and last of the necessary number of states to ratify the Constitution of the United States of America. The preamble to that great and exemplary document, written in the spirit of a compact executed among equals and reminiscent of the Mayflower Compact, explained why the Constitution was ordained and established: "We the people of the United States, in order to form a more perfect Union, establish Justice, insure domestic Tranquillity, provide for the common defense, promote the general welfare, and secure the Blessings of Liberty to ourselves and our Posterity, do ordain and establish this Constitution for the United States of America."

Thus at the end of my first year in the university, in the spring of 1923, nine years after I had entered the first grade in McCleary, I found the explanation for what I had first observed in that bustling frontier village. The first principle on which the government of the new land was based, its enduring foundation, was the proposition that all men are created equal. In terms of that ethical, essentially religious concept, I could now explain that strange phenomenon that had surprised and amazed all of us who had come from the Old to the New World. That concept, that self-evident truth, was structured into the very being of my companions in school and their elders, precisely as its opposite had been structured into me and my young companions in Casabianca. For that selfsame reason, their mingling freely together as equals came naturally to them while it as naturally amazed and surprised me. Our dissimilar behavior was in accordance with our dissimilar "human nature." For neither of us could have explained to the other the philosophical basis of the respective societies into which we had been born. If I understood that basis now, it was because as an immigrant to the new land, intent on making an intelligent adjustment to its noble traditions, I had felt the necessity to undertake the inquiry I have described.

Such, in brief, is what I had learned about American democracy near the end of my first decade in the new land. It was a sound beginning; it served my

purpose; it was all I needed to know at the time. Thereafter I would continue
my inquiry and make a secular religion of my reverence for the rights of man.

As I continued my university studies into the middle twenties, I came, as did
my companions, under the influence of the university's finest and most liberal minds in philosophy, history, literature, and political science. As I have
already stated, their common goal was the establishment of a just society.
One of their current interests was a line of inquiry that tended to debunk the
Fourth-of-July-rhetoric view of American history. These scholars led us to
the historical sources of the Declaration and the Constitution and taught us
to examine them critically in the context of history. This we did, with all the
eagerness and enthusiasm of young idealists. I regret to say that what we discovered with the aid of their scholarship and analytical minds was disillu-
sioning. As I looked back to the end of my freshman year, I realized that in my
deeply felt reverence for what I had discovered in Tom Paine, I had accepted
too uncritically what my masters called the "glittering generalities" of the
Declaration and the preamble to the Constitution. I had discovered the philosophical and historical basis of America's fluid, "classless" society. True
enough. I knew now that only in America one could be below the tracks today and above them tomorrow. There was no hereditary aristocracy, and on
the frontier there were no affluent first families. In 1900 Henry McCleary
had been an ambitious, shrewd mill worker, and in 1915 he was a lumber
baron and a millionaire. In such circumstances and in a land where all men
were presumably created equal, he could easily mingle at church on Sundays
with his mill workers, some of whom, doubtless, aspired to and would eventually become mill owners themselves. All of this I had learned; and it stood
the test of critical inquiry. No one could deny the facts. I had learned also the
self-evident truths and the unalienable rights on which the American government was based. These, too, were clearly declared and undeniable.

Where I had gone astray, however, was in failing to distinguish between
what had come to be known as the American Dream and the reality. As I understood it then, as did my companions and my best teachers, the dream was
the hope among men and women of good will after the Civil War that
America would move forward in accordance with the goals stated in the
Declaration; that the purposes for which the Constitution was ordained
and established would be gradually realized; and that during the succeeding

generations the American way of life would become, by degrees, the exemplary embodiment of all those truths and purposes. It was also a part of the dream that in the conduct of her foreign policy, America would never be guilty of land grabbing after the fashion of the Old World monarchies. As such, the dream was national, and within its framework, each individual would formulate and pursue his own dream.

If such was the dream, what was the reality? Whence the disillusionment? And what was the nature of the disillusionment? After the middle twenties, when I had taken a degree in history and noted with alarm the development of American imperialism, I began to have serious doubts that the dream was being realized, and that laissez-faire, or rugged individualism, was functioning to establish justice and promote the common welfare. At the beginning of the next decade, in the depth of the Great Depression, my doubts and disillusionment were so aggravated that I wanted to get to their root source. My understanding of the new land must not be fragmentary. In order to avoid this, and following the lead of my teachers, I must learn what I could about the historical antecedents of the Declaration of Independence and have a close look at the Constitution.

A critical reading of the events that prompted the colonies to declare their independence revealed beyond any doubt that the conflict had not been between colonial democracy and the tyranny of George III. The colonies were not a democracy and George III was not a tyrant. The last of the English tyrants who had sought to rule by divine right were the Stuarts, and they had been eliminated in the revolutions of the seventeenth century. The "glorious revolution" of 1688 had got rid of the last of them and effectively subjected successors to the will of Parliament. As for democracy as the rule of the majority under a system of universal and unrestricted suffrage, there was nothing even remotely like it in England and the colonies at the time of the Revolution. The suffrage was so severely restricted by property qualifications that only about one fifth of the male population had the right to vote.

Since there was no democracy in the colonies and no absolute monarchy in England, in whom did the ultimate power reside? England during the eighteenth century was ruled by the union of two powerful classes: landlords and merchants. One reliable historian has estimated that ten thousand landlords and merchants ruled the England of George III. In the colonies there

were three ruling classes: the merchants of the northern colonies, the tradesmen and landowners of the middle colonies, and the plantation aristocracy
of the southern colonies. Thus, on both sides, it was a "government of gentlemen, by gentlemen, and for gentlemen," without the slightest interference by
the mass of workers, landless farmers, indentured servants, women, or
slaves. Therefore, the conflict that culminated in the Declaration was between the two ruling classes described above. In England, the merchants and
landlords acted through Parliament and the crown; in the colonies, the various colonial governments, some operating under royal charters, acted in behalf of their respective ruling classes.

And what was the issue? What had provoked the colonies to address petitions to king and Parliament and finally to declare their independence and
accept whatever consequences might issue from it? The causes of the conflict
were primarily economic. The British empire under George III and for decades before, was based on the principles of mercantilism, a theory which,
among other things, regarded colonial trade as the property of the rulers and
the ruling classes of England. Thus the "function of the colonies was to produce raw materials for the use of the mother country to consume its man-
ufactures and to foster its shipping." The result of the theory, and the various
laws enacted by Parliament to implement it, was that the colonies were reduced to a position of economic vassalage to England. The effect of this
humiliation was that the colonial landlords and merchants were deprived of
the right to govern themselves as they pleased and to make what money they
pleased. All petitions for the redress of such grievances having been refused,
the colonies declared their independence.

Historically considered, the various petitions that the colonies addressed
to the crown before the Declaration were in accordance with British political
traditions that dated back to Edward the Confessor, the last of the Anglo-
Saxon kings and immediate predecessor of William of Normandy. It had
been the scrupulously observed custom of English kings to grant accession charters to their immediate subjects, normally the secular nobility and
church dignitaries in the centuries before the supremacy of Parliament was
established. In effect, such charters were bills of rights granted by the king to
the nobility and, later, to Parliament. The most famous of these was the Magna Carta. It became the most famous because of the dramatic circumstances
that attended its birth, and for Article Thirty-Nine, which in time came to be

considered the cornerstone of the English common law, and for its many confirmations. Especially during the struggle between Parliament and the Stuarts it came to be regarded as something sacred which embodied the very ideal of English liberties.

However, the Magna Carta itself as written by the barons and presented to King John, was just an elaboration of the accession charter of Henry I, and it differed in degree but not in kind from the charters that had been granted by the Norman and early Plantagenet kings. It made the church free, but it granted nothing to four fifths of the male population, the serfs, whose emancipation was begun two centuries after the Magna Carta and completed under the Tudors. After the Magna Carta, the most important charters were the Petition of Rights granted by Charles I to Parliament in 1628 and the Bill of Rights granted by William III to Parliament in 1689.

None of these documents was in the least concerned with the general welfare. Each one of them became a milestone toward the belated triumph of democracy in the late nineteenth and early twentieth centuries. The reason for this unintended consequence was that those who framed the charters, in order to put a good face on their greed, claimed their privileges in the name of the nation. For that reason, the elder Pitt could say that the "Magna Carta, the Petition of Rights, and the Bill of Rights form that code, which I call the Bible of the English Constitution." Well enough! Collectively, however, those charters may be fairly described as being petitions by privilege addressed to a higher privilege for more privilege. The petitioners were not in the least concerned with the rights of the common man and the general welfare.

The Declaration of Independence, taken as a rejected petition addressed to the crown, was essentially a late eighteenth-century version of the Magna Carta. Whereas in the Magna Carta the petitioners had been the secular nobility and the church dignitaries, in the Declaration they were the merchants, the landlords, and their servants in the various professions—collectively, the class that had prevailed in the struggle for power over the aristocracy by the end of the seventeenth century. In both instances what was, or might have been, granted was for the benefit of the petitioners only, not for the masses, who had no rights. Whereas in the Magna Carta the rights had been asserted on behalf of all "freemen" (property owners), in the Declaration, five and a half centuries later, they were claimed as the Creator's endowment to all men. Article Thirty-Nine of the charter stated that "no freeman shall be arrested, or detained in prison, or deprived on his freehold, or outlawed, or banished . . . unless by the lawful judgment of his peers and by the law of the land." In the Declaration that principle was brought up to date and enlarged to include such self-evident truths as that all men are created equal and endowed with certain unalienable rights.

Thus, in form and substance the Declaration was in the tradition of the Magna Carta. Nor could it have been otherwise; for as a body, the fifty-six colonial gentlemen who signed it were, though Americans, typical eighteenth-century Englishmen. Their values, their religion, their educational system, their Anglo-Saxon sense of independence and the sacredness of property, their political philosophy—all these components of culture derived from the mother country. Hamilton, John Adams, Madison, and other firm Federalists were direct descendants of English Tories; just as Jefferson, Sam Adams, Tom Paine, and Patrick Henry were in the line of English dissenters and independents. All of them, in the mother country as in the colonies, whether Whig or Tory, were learned in the *Two Treaties of Government*, for John Locke had not only defended and philosophically justified the "glorious revolution" that had established the supremacy of Parliament but he had also sanctified property by making its ownership one of man's unalienable rights.

One may fairly conclude, then, that if George III had attempted to make the merchants and landlords of England his economic vassals, as his parliament attempted to make the merchants and planters of the colonies subservient to its economic will, the ruling classes of England would have reacted precisely as did the ruling classes of the colonies. And instead of the Declaration of Independence another Magna Carta would have found its place in the archives of English liberty. Indeed, the two ruling classes, the eighteenth-century gentlemen of England and the colonies, were so much alike that one senses a sort of pride of family in what Lord Chatham said to his colleagues about their colonial brethren: "When your lordships look at the papers transmitted to us from America; when you consider their decency, firmness and wisdom, you cannot but respect their cause and wish to make it your own. For myself, I must declare and avow, that in all my reading and observation—and it has been my favorite study—I have read Thucydides and have studied and admired the master statesmen of the world—that for solidity of reasoning, force of sagacity, and wisdom of conclusion, under such a complication of difficult circumstances, no nation or body of men can stand in preference to the general congress at Philadelphia."

An Anglo-Saxon admiring Anglo-Saxon virtues! How just the praise! What wisdom, what command of language went into the writing of those "papers" transmitted from America! What patrician eloquence had been tapped in the very soul of the colonies to give just utterance to those mighty principles! I must confess that even in these sober, twilight years, I cannot read the first two paragraphs of the Declaration without an elated response to its high imperatives and the perfection of its language. The rhetoric of the self-evident truths, for anyone who is clearly committed to the democratic ideal and has a passionate regard for the rights of man, can never become stale or a series of mere cliches. Never! *Conceived in liberty! Dedicated to the proposition that all men are created equal! The unalienable right to life, liberty, and the pursuit of happiness!* The freshness of these phrases, their profoundly religious authority never wanes.

And this is so because the very conception of self-evident truths is an instance of man thinking, what Dickinson called "man's impulse to create the ideal." I have lived on intimate terms with illiterate peasants and intellectuals, and I have seen the impulse as frequently in the one as in the other. Samuel Johnson was an obnoxious Tory with a bloated belly stuffed with prejudices, a sage whose wisdom was often put in doubt by his facile judgments, such as "I am willing to love all mankind except Americans—rascals, robbers, pirates." But he had spurts of inspired insight, and one such was his observation that there is something in nature that abhors tyranny. To that I would add its corollary: There is something in nature that is drawn to the ideal, spontaneously, instinctively, and without instruction. I have seen the brute and the angel in man. They are neighbors. I was as startled by the juxtaposition as Lear was when he realized that Cordelia and her tiger sisters were the fruit of the same womb.

I have seen the ideal operating in certain peasants. Illiterate, or nearly so, their instinctive—perhaps spontaneous—behavior reflected the wisdom of Locke, Jeremy Bentham, and the Sermon on the Mount. (One such, in Tolstoi's *Anna Karenina,* solved Levin's moral problem: Is life worth the struggle? It is, the peasant assured him, if one lives it "in God's way." In God's way! According to the ideal, the undefined ideal because it is all-inclusive. Or if an attempt at definition is made, as in the novel, the result is a sort of parable of two peasants: one who lived for his belly, the other, for his soul.) Men and women who frowned severely at the mere mention of injustice and who smiled reverently when they talked of justice and liberty; whose concern for the general welfare emerged in well-ordered homes, where constant labor fairly distributed was condition to survival, social compacts designed to promote life, liberty, and the pursuit of happiness; who had a tacit understanding with neighbors to work together for the common defense against such evils as they could not cope with singly; who lived pretty much in the state of nature; whose decency was exemplary; whose honesty was beyond question; and whose sense of justice was faultless. We hold these truths to be self-evident.

Yes, even now, after more than fifty years in academia, I cannot read the first two paragraphs of the Declaration without an elated response to its high imperatives. And yet, when I had finished my undergraduate studies in the late twenties and begun my academic career in the early thirties, I had lost some of my reverence for it. My masters aided this disillusionment by causing me to note the difference between theory and practice, the "glittering generalities" and effective policy, the ideal and the reality. How could the men who signed the Declaration subscribe to the proposition that all men are created equal and endowed by their Creator with certain unalienable rights, when there were a half million slaves in the colonies and thousands of indentured servants? When women and 80 percent of the male population had no political rights whatever?

The same "glittering generalities" were repeated in the preamble to the Constitution: "We the people of the United States, in order to form a more perfect union, establish justice, insure domestic tranquility, provide for the common defence, promote the general welfare, and secure the blessings of liberty to ourselves and our posterity, do ordain and establish this Constitution for the United States of America." It is *we* the people. No one is excluded. The only qualification necessary to be included is membership in the human race. The framers of the Magna Carta had been more honest: they claimed rights only for freemen—property owners. When one proceeds from the preamble to the document itself, reading it with care, and examines the proceedings of the Constitutional Convention that drafted it at Philadelphia in the summer of 1787, two conclusions are inescapable: the Constitution was a masterpiece of statecraft and no amount of cynical debunking can detract an iota from that judgment. But it was not a great charter of democracy. The preamble was pure democracy; the document itself was not. Nor was it intended to be. The delegates to that historical convention, the great majority who easily held sway over its deliberations and whose political philosophy triumphed, had no faith whatever in the wisdom or political capacity of the people. They were aristocrats, not democrats. Their philosopher—apologist is the better term—was Alexander Hamilton, whose contempt for the "beast" majority is known to every schoolchild. They would have been perfectly at home with eighteenth-century English Tories.

However, they were perfectly aware that during the decade that followed the shots fired at Lexington on April 19, 1775, democratic ideas, as interpreted and urged by Tom Paine, Sam Adams, Thomas Jefferson, and other democrats, had gained such wide acceptance by the masses, that no form of government that did not confer on the people at least the form of political power would have the necessary support. Their task, then, was to devise a system that gave the people the illusion of power but not the substance. They succeeded so well in this that the document they devised and signed on September 17, 1787, was hailed throughout the world as a masterpiece of statecraft. It did not reject democracy outright; it stemmed its progress and delayed its triumph by more than a century.

The evidence is both clear and convincing that this is precisely what the decisive majority of delegates to the Constitutional Convention set out to accomplish. Sam Adams, Thomas Jefferson, Tom Paine, Patrick Henry, the great democratic leaders, were not sent by their respective states as delegates to the convention. When the convention assembled in Philadelphia only eleven years after the Declaration, its members included only six of the fifty-six bold men who had voted for independence—significant omissions from the assembly of fifty-five delegates who were to create the government as announced in the Declaration and the preamble. Furthermore, the controlling delegates were men of inherited wealth and social position—lawyers, merchants, planters, and established politicians. Thirty-one had university training. Elbridge Gerry and Edmund Randolph reflected the prevailing political philosophy of the convention when they argued that democracy was the origin of all political evils in the country. They feared what Shakespeare called the "vulgar many," and therefore excluded from their deliberations any representative of the disfranchised majority.

Turning from the members of the convention to the document itself, we note two significant omissions: *We the people,* in order to accomplish the many wonderful things, are not guaranteed the right to vote by the Constitution; and *We the people,* are not given the bill of unalienable rights announced in the Declaration. The House of Representatives shall be chosen every second year by the people of the several states; and it was left up to each state to determine who would have the right to vote. Since every state, in accordance with the political traditions of the mother country, granted the suffrage only to those who met the strict property qualifications, the representatives were elected by the minority property owners. We were well into the nineteenth century before the several states granted universal *manhood* suffrage. Strange that the Constitution itself should not have fixed *immediately* that basic unalienable right.

Even more strange was the failure of the delegates to include a Bill of Rights in the Constitution. It was not an oversight; James Mason, the delegate from Virginia, refused to sign the Constitution because it did not include such a bill. Several of the states, among them Massachusetts, New Hampshire, and New York, insisted on a series of amendments designed to protect personal rights—what Paine had called natural rights of the mind, intellectual rights—and to put restraints on the authority of the federal government. James Madison was therefore obliged to submit to the First Congress a series of such amendments, the first ten of which were ratified in 1891 and came to be known as the Bill of Rights.

The right that the Constitution did protect as sacred above all others was the right of every man to be secure in his property. Adam Smith, in his *Wealth of Nations,* had observed that civil government, "so far as it is instituted for the security of property, is in reality instituted for the defence of the rich against the poor, or those who have some property against those who have none at all." Madison and Hamilton, in complete agreement with that observation, maintained that government ought to "protect the minority of the opulent against the majority." And in number ten of *The Federalist,* Madison reasoned that since, in the very nature of things men differ in their capacity to accumulate property, some men have much while others have little or none at all, then the result of this disparity is that those who have little or nothing—the vulgar many—constitute a danger to the opulent minority. These being the brute facts of nature, the function of government must be to protect those who have against those who have not.

This was in line with the reasoning of John Locke who had listed life, liberty, and property as the natural rights all governments are instituted to secure. Jefferson, in the Declaration, in listing the unalienable rights, had substituted "the pursuit of happiness" for the word property. Had he been a delegate to the Constitutional Convention, he would certainly have argued the case for the people and insisted on a more democratic document. But he was not there, neither were Patrick Henry, Tom Paine, or Sam Adams. So the view of the Federalists had prevailed, and the opulent minority produced a Constitution designed not only to protect their property but to secure them permanently in office. The minority who had the right to vote in each state would elect representatives to Congress. That was a concession to the people. Senators, however, would be elected by the state legislatures; and the president would be elected by special electors chosen by the legislatures. Thus "we the people" had the illusion but not the substance of power.

In order that we might continue in the illusion without the substance, the Constitution made provision for amendments, but it made the amending process so difficult that no effort to change the Constitution in any substantial way would be likely to succeed. Just to set the amending machinery in motion would require a two-thirds majority of House and Senate or two thirds of the state legislatures. In the Virginia ratification convention, Patrick Henry presented an angry but perfectly reasoned argument against the proposed method of amendment, and he concluded by pointing out that "one twentieth part of the American people" could prevent a needed change in the Constitution. "Is this an easy mode of securing the public liberty? It is, Sir, a most fearful situation, when the most contemptible minority can prevent the alteration of the most oppressive government; for it may, in many respects, prove to be such."

Whether the opulent minority was contemptible or not, it did succeed in entrenching itself in power in the ways I have described, by the further means of giving the president the veto power the English monarch had lost a century before, and by extending to an independent judiciary the implied pow-

er of judicial review. In these ways the government of the new United
States, for all the radical rhetoric of the Declaration, was less democratic
than the government of England, where judges have never had the power to
declare acts of Parliament unconstitutional. All in all, the framers of the Constitution created a government that was much more a government of gentlemen, by gentlemen, and for gentlemen, than one of the people, by the people,
and for the people.

Such, in summary form, is what I had learned about the political realities of
the American Dream at the end of my second decade in the new land. Had
my masters led me astray? Had I consulted the wrong authorities? Were my
conclusions erroneous and my disillusionment unjustified? In order to check
on masters who may have been biased, and to understand what they meant
by glittering generalities, I felt the need to search for the historical antecedents of the Declaration and the Constitution. I was now a scholar-teacher
urging my students to do what I had been taught: get the facts, go to the
source of issues, and then draw the appropriate conclusions. Equally important, in pursuit of my own dream, I must build on solid ground and omit
nothing that would aid in understanding the spiritual underpinnings of
Whitman's fecund America. My understanding of the land that had done so
much for me, and promised to do so much more, must not be fragmentary; it
must be as thorough as I could make it. Thus, what I learned in the inquiry
recorded above gave me a better insight into what the founding fathers had
wrought. I then perceived it as the logical progression of the Anglo-Saxon
libertarian tradition implicit in the Magna Carta. My veneration for that
document was such that I hoped some day to go on a pilgrimage to Run-
nymeade, where the barons compelled King John to affix his seal to it on June
15, 1215.

The disillusion to which that inquiry added, however, must not be confused with cynicism. The optimism of which I have given an account in the
preceding chapter, both regarding my own and the future of mankind, the
belief in the eventual realization of the Dream, and the far-off divine event
survived these disappointments. The premises on which this optimism was
based was then, and remains now, too firmly rooted.

CHAPTER VII

The Ultimate Power

With all the passionate certainty of youth, well fed, well housed, superbly instructed, and auspiciously positioned to assume our respective places in the community, we believed in certain fundamentals: the sacredness and universality of natural rights as self-evident truths; the perfectibility of man and of human nature; the essential wisdom and good sense of the people; the ultimate triumph of what is right and good; the effectiveness of the franchise as a means of transcending the obstacles that privilege had put in the way of democracy.

We were Jeffersonians and believed, as he believed, that "truth is great and will prevail if left to herself; that she is the proper and sufficient antagonist to error, and has nothing to fear from the conflict unless by human interposition disarmed of her natural weapons: free argument and debate; that man is a rational animal, endowed by nature with rights and with an innate sense of justice." We shared his conviction that men "habituated to think for themselves and to follow reason as their guide" could be more easily governed than others "debased by ignorance, indigence and oppression." While Hamilton was busy putting together the U.S. Bank, Jefferson was building the University of Virginia, to be self-governed and based on the "illimitable freedom of the human mind." And we applauded.

But we rejected with the hauteur of young savants the essentially Hobbesian view that man is greedy, selfish, and brutish. We rejected it as the view of privilege, ably led by Hamilton, Adams, and Marshall, who considered themselves the best of Calvin's elect and attributed brutishness and beastliness to the toiling masses. We scorned it because it was not so much a philosophy as a prejudice, engendered by fear that what privilege had unscrupulously appropriated of the new land's bounty would be taken from it by the masses whom the Declaration had made aware of their unalienable rights.

Such were the premises in which our optimism was firmly rooted, and the disillusionment I have described had in no way impugned their validity. Furthermore, the great resources of mind and matter in the new land, made manifest in the progress that had been made in the six decades after Appommatox, strengthened the belief that what Wells had asserted in *The Discovery of the Future* was prophetic wisdom. Technological progress was swiftly carrying the blessings of the new land from ocean to ocean. By the middle twenties the legions of democracy had scored substantial victories: Slavery had been abolished and the Negroes brought within the protection of the Bill of Rights by the Fourteenth Amendment; the Sixteenth Amendment, ratified in 1913, had given Congress power to impose and collect income taxes; the Seventeenth, ratified the same year, had provided for the popular election of senators; the Nineteenth, ratified in 1920, had extended the franchise to women; and many of the states had adopted the initiative and referendum.

Nor was that the end of it. The sovereign people, in a display of the folly attributed to them by the Hamiltonians and, one supposes, in order to demonstrate to the world that they could be foolish as well as wise, ratified the Eighteenth Amendment on January 16, 1919. On that unhappy day, Justice Oliver Wendell Holmes gravely shook his hoary head. For years he had defended the people's right to be foolish, but he hadn't dreamed that they would exercise it in a way that would make sipping claret with one's dinner a crime!

Thus, that masterpiece of statecraft that had been so ingeniously devised to check the progress of democracy had been made more democratic. It had taken more than a century to transcend the obstacles that the Federalists had placed in the way to total self-government. From the meeting of the first Congress in 1789, to the time the women were granted the right to vote, one hundred and thirty-one years had passed. Think of it! It had been a long wait and a tough struggle to achieve that and the other amendments, but the victories were substantial and prelude to more. So we thought, as the twenties were drawing to a close.

And we thought, also, that self-government could promote the general welfare to a much higher degree than it had done hitherto, that it could gradually close the gap between the dream and the reality. By what means? Creative citizenship was the answer. We, the people, as citizens, had both rights and duties. By the judicious exercise of the former and strict observance of the latter, we could function creatively as citizens and govern ourselves accordingly. We had no doubt that this could be done. That so much had been done by the middle twenties was further proof that what the framers of the Constitution had accomplished was, indeed, a masterpiece of statecraft. They had made the amendment process extremely difficult, but they had made it an organic part of the fundamental law. We the people, men and women, had made use of it to become sovereign; in the final analysis we governed ourselves through agents chosen by ourselves.

For these various reasons, our optimism remained secure and firmly rooted, and the disillusionment I described in the preceding chapter did not degenerate into cynicism. It was, however, aggravated—it certainly was not diminished!—by what we further learned about the political and economic realities of government of the people, by the people, and for the people. Were we, the people, in fact sovereign? We had the total suffrage, but, when the chips were down, did we have the ultimate power? What follows is an account of the inquiry that led to these questions.

Although this is a personal narrative, I have frequently used the first person plural. This has not been a dodge, or the use of the editorial "we." The reason for it is that in much of what follows, my story merges with that of the young men and women whom I met when I began my university studies and who became my intellectual companions. We pursued the quest together and together we learned from the great teachers to whom I have several times referred. We were a little society of seekers, brought together by chance, most of us engaged in debate, taught and inspired by distinguished professors who had in common a discerning knowledge of American history and very liberal social views. For these reasons, I am very much aware that in writing this phase of my story I am writing with their tacit approval of the theme of my narrative.

We were all agreed on fundamentals. In the rather unusual circumstances, I doubt that any group of college students anywhere in America was better informed than we on subjects and issues that related to intelligent citizenship. Formally and informally we debated a variety of propositions: the Venezuela affair of 1895, the Monroe Doctrine, the League of Nations, the world court, Philippine independence, the closed shop, installment buying, judicial review. We stimulated each other, learned from each other and from the research involved in the debates. Inspired by our professors and following their lead, we became political activists dedicated to the task of perfecting self-government and promoting the general welfare.

The general welfare! The amelioration of society for the good of all. That was our teachers' gospel. Not once did they suggest that our education was an investment in material self-promotion. They placed more emphasis on our duties than on our rights, and they did not do so in any pious way. The duties of citizenship were pragmatic; their intelligent performance was a privilege and a means of contributing to the general welfare.

We also followed these teachers as disciples in their enlightened concern over current issues as grave as any that had stirred the hearts and minds of American statesmen: Could man devise ways to outlaw wars? Was there, as William James had argued, a moral equivalent to war? Were such outrages as the Everett and Centralia Massacres inevitable? These and other issues were as pressing as the one that had prompted Patrick Henry to utter the epic alternative: "I know not what course others may take; but as for me, give me liberty or give me death."

Of all the propositions we debated, none was so exciting as the doctrine of judicial review, a principle that was "wholly and exclusively American." It was first exercised by Chief Justice Marshall in *Marbury* v. *Madison,* February 24, 1803. There were several reasons for its particular urgency. As "America's original contribution to the science of law," the question of its democratic validity was of paramount importance to all of us as students of American political history. Two of our professors, in political science and American literature, had written with commanding authority on the subject.

A distinguished historian's book on the Constitution and the Supreme Court was being widely read and discussed, and the definitive biography of Chief Justice John Marshall had been recently published. Thus, we debaters, many of us law students, approached the subject with a certain professional fervor.

The jurists and historians who had argued the proposition earlier in the century had been concerned with an issue that was now largely academic: Had the framers of the Constitution intended that the Supreme Court should pass upon the constitutionality of acts of Congress? Had they granted the power explicitly or implicitly? Had the Supreme Court usurped the power from the beginning under Justice Marshall? Whether granted or usurped, the exercise of the power by the Court had occasioned a renewal of what came to be known historically as an "assault on the judiciary." Generally, jurists and historians who argued that the power was usurped were really opposed to judicial review on other grounds. Their case was impressively stated by Chief Justice Walter Clark of North Carolina in 1906:

James Madison and James Wilson, two of the leading framers of the Constitution, "favored the new doctrine of the paramount judiciary, doubtless deeming it a safe check upon legislation, since it was to be operated only by lawyers. They attempted to get it into the federal Constitution in its least objectionable shape—the judicial veto *before* the final passage of an act, which would thus save time and besides would enable the legislature to avoid the objections raised. But even in this diluted form, and though four times presented by these two very able and influential members, this suggestion of a judicial veto at no time received the votes of more than one fourth of the states.

"The subsequent action of the Supreme Court in assuming the power to declare acts of Congress unconstitutional was without a line in the Constitution to authorize it, either expressly or by implication. The Constitution recited carefully and fully the matters over which the courts should have jurisdiction, and there is nothing, and after the above vote four times refusing jurisdiction, there could be nothing, indicating any power to declare an act unconstitutional and void. Had the convention given such power to the courts, it certainly would not have left its exercise final and unreviewable. . . . In this country alone the people, speaking through their Congress and with the approval of their Executive, cannot put in force a single measure of any nature whatever with the assurance that it shall meet with the approval of the courts; and its failure to receive such approval is fatal, for, unlike the veto of the Executive, the unanimous vote of Congress cannot prevail against it. Of what avail shall it be if Congress shall conform to the popular demand and enact a bill and the President shall approve it if five lawyers, holding office for life and not elected by the people, shall see fit to destroy it? Is such a government a reasonable one, and can it be longer tolerated after 120 years of experience have demonstrated the capacity of the people for self-government?"

The Justice was absolutely right in this assertion that the Constitution does not expressly grant the power to the judiciary; but he was wrong if he meant that the reason for this was that the majority of the framers were not in favor of judicial review. He was also possibly wrong in denying that the exercise of the power was implicitly authorized by the Constitution. His argument that judicial review by judges appointed for life is undemocratic is irrefutable—at least in theory.

The distinguished historian Charles Beard has proved beyond any doubt that the controlling minds among the thirty-nine framers who signed the Constitution were unequivocally in favor of judical review, and in number seventy-eight of *The Federalist*, Alexander Hamilton argued persuasively that the Constitution implicitly authorized the judiciary to declare acts of Congress null and void on constitutional grounds. The view of William Patterson, a member of the Constitutional Convention from New Jersey, was substantially that of his colleagues who were most influential in framing the Constitution: "The Constitution is the work or will of the people themselves, in their original, sovereign, and unlimited capacity. Law is the work or will of the legislature in their derivative and subordinate capacity. The one is the work of the Creator, and the other of the creature. The Constitution fixes the limits to the exercise of legislative authority and prescribes the orbit within which it must move. . . . Whatever may be the case in other countries, yet in this there can be no doubt, that every act of the legislature repugnant to the Constitution is absolutely void. . . . I take it to be a clear position that if a legislative act oppugns a constitutional principle the former must give way, and be rejected on the score of repugnance. I hold it to be a position equally clear and sound that, in such case, it will be the duty of the court to adhere to the Constitution, and to declare the act null and void."

There is no doubt that this conviction was shared by nearly all the capable men who made the Constitution. However, it was their brilliant and ingenious leader, Alexander Hamilton, who argued most cogently, though not necessarily conclusively, that the principle of judicial review was implicit in the Constitution. He based his argument on the premise that where the Constitution is written, and therefore limited, the judges, in the performance of their prescribed duties, would be obliged to decide, when the occasion required it, whether a given legislative act was unconstitutional. In number seventy-eight of *The Federalist* he wrote as follows: "The complete independence of the courts of justice is peculiarly essential in a limited constitution . . . one which contains certain specified exceptions to the legislative authority; such, for instance, as that it shall pass no bills of attainder, no ex post facto laws, and the like. Limitations of this kind can be preserved in practice no other way than through the medium of the courts of justice; whose duty it must be to declare all acts contrary to the manifest tenor of the Constitution void. Without this, all the reservations of particular rights or privileges would amount to nothing. . . . "

According to Hamilton, then, the Supreme Court did not usurp the power to declare acts of Congress unconstitutional; it was implicitly granted by the Constitution. However, that left a very disturbing question unanswered: In order to remove the doubt, why wasn't the Court's authority expressly granted in the Constitution? That would have made the charge of usurpation untenable. There must have been good reasons for leaving so important a matter in doubt; and what these may have been, I need not now inquire.

As serious students of history and young debaters, we found the exploration of such issues both necessary and very exciting in our study of "America's original contribution to the science of law"; but as I have already stated, the question whether the Supreme Court's power was authorized by the Constitution or usurped was largely academic. At the time that we were debating the proposition, the Court had exercised the power for well over a century, and judicial review, for good or ill, had become a part of the American system of government, an organic part of the fundamental law. The live issue now was whether it was defensible on democratic grounds. Were the theory and practice of judical review in harmony with the Declaration and the preamble? Designed to promote pure democracy and establish the complete sovereignty of the people? Where, under the doctrine, did the ultimate power reside?

This course of inquiry was particularly exciting to me as I continued my search for what lay between the American Dream and American reality. Now a citizen and a student of law, having no property rights to protect, I was passionately aware of my vested interest in the rights of man. I had now learned from the great monk who had nailed his ninety-five theses to a church door in Wittenberg, another of the self-evident truths: the priesthood of the individual. What a heady discovery for a young man raised in a faith that required unquestioning obedience to the clerical hierarchy, and in which I had been vaguely uncomfortable even as a young boy! The discovery that I was now my own confessor made me feel as if I had been released from a sort of bondage, and I tended to assert my new freedom with all the unrestrained bravado of a young blood.

I had also felt the power of Milton's heretical imperative: "If every action which is good or evil in a man of ripe years were to be under pittance and prescription and compulsion, what were virtue but a name? I cannot praise a fugitive and cloistered virtue, unexercised and unbreathed, that never sallies out and sees her adversary, but slinks out of the race where that immortal garland is to be run for, not without dust and heat." In the excitement of trial and error, man must seek his identity and establish his own worth. Every man his own priest! No more priestcraft between me and the "Spirit that dost prefer before all temples the upright heart and pure." No more cowled intermediaries between the legislative enactment of the people's will and its execution as law. No one has the right, hereditary or otherwise, to impose his will on the people; but the people have the right to make their own mistakes.

In this mood, given a certain validity by my recently acquired citizenship, I began my research on the doctrine of judicial review. The mood described above predisposed me to a prima facie bias against it, but my interest in the subject so increased in intensity, that I continued my study of it beyond what was necessary for participation in the debate. I found the *Marbury* case, studied in its historical context, both exciting and instructive: it dramatized political shrewdness and the politics of power. My interest in the subject was sustained. (In the late thirties when President Roosevelt made the politically fatal attempt to control the Court by "packing" it, I occasionally lectured the doctrine of judicial review. I regretted the move he made because it was politically unwise, but I supported what he intended to achieve because the "nine old men" had traditionally served the rights of privilege more than the general welfare.)

My research on the subject led to a number of conclusions: Judicial review was plainly at odds with the spirit of American democracy; its defense by Hamilton and others was based on unwarranted premises; Marshall's exercise of the power for the first time, in the historic *Marbury* case, was politically—not judicially—motivated; once established, the power of the Court to strike down acts of Congress was used repeatedly to assert the supremacy of property over human rights when the two were in conflict.

This last was the harsh reality to which we young idealists could never become reconciled, for we could not conceive the ownership of property as a natural, a sacred right. On this issue we parted company with Locke and joined Jefferson, for this was the fundamental difference between them. Locke had argued that men possess rights to life, liberty, and property, and to establish governments to secure these. By substituting the pursuit of happiness for the property, Jefferson had introduced a revolutionary change in that justly famous declaration. We young idealists applauded the change. It was self-evident that man was endowed by his Creator with the rights to life, liberty, and the pursuit of happiness; it was not self-evident that He had similarly endowed him with the right to property. That right was derivative, a civil right, and it was not unalienable. Francis of Assisi had eschewed property and attained sainthood. On that matter we felt secure on both philosophical and esthetic grounds. For life, liberty, and the pursuit of happiness were things of beauty and joys forever. A mine, a mill, or corporate wealth were not. Of the two—property and human rights—we unhesitatingly exalted the latter above the former. The "illimitable freedom of the human mind," the dignity and inviolability of the individual! Nothing must ever prevail against them. Such was our credo.

Judicial review, which in effect placed the ultimate power in the judiciary, was a key link in the overall strategy of the statesmen who framed a government of gentlemen, by gentlemen, and for gentlemen. They framed a Constitution designed to check the will of the majority: property qualifications imposed on the electors in the several states would exclude many from the franchise; the legislators sent to Congress by property owners were to be checked by the Senate; both Congress and Senate were to be checked by the executive veto; and now, after the *Marbury* case, the Supreme Court, composed of judges appointed for life, would check both the Congress and the executive. The effect of these various checks and balances, as a distinguished historian had noted, was the reestablishment of the "old British system of politics, economics, and judicial control—this time grounded in American authority created by an American constitution." Measured against the promise of the Declaration and "We the people," the reality appeared to us dedicated students and young idealists a vulgar entrenchment of privilege, more Hobbesian than Lockean. "We the people" didn't figure in the equation at all.

As the sole arbiter of the meaning of the Constitution, the Supreme Court now held the ultimate power. Granted that, in accordance with the logic of the Constitution, it should rest there. Granted that, in the science of the law, judical review was a great and historic innovation. Granted even that its wisdom had been vindicated during better than a century of trial. Nevertheless, it was not in the spirit of the New World democracy. The judiciary, not the people, were sovereign. Furthermore, no other constitutional government in the western world was seduced to incorporate into its system "America's original contribution to the science of law." In the mother country, where first amendment rights have fared much better than here, an act of Parliament is not subject to judicial review.

This great and historic innovation, the brain child primarily of Hamilton, was judicial only in form; for, in substance, it was an economic device to secure the triumph of property over all other rights. Anyone who has read number seventy-eight of the *Federalist* and Marshall's opinion in the *Marbury* case, will know that one can make an impressively logical argument in defense of judical review. Reduced to its bare elements, it proceeds thus: The written and limited Constitution provides for three main divisions of government: the legislative, executive, and judicial. Each is assigned its specific function. The Constitution lists certain specific exceptions to legislative authority, such as the injunction against ex post facto laws. Therefore, any act of Congress the substance of which is forbidden by the Constitution, must be declared null and void. Granted. But by whom so declared? Since the function is judicial, by the judiciary. So runs the argument.

However, where it fails is in the several assumptions on which it rests. It is assumed that the Supreme Court is more capable of interpreting the Constitution than any other agency of government, such, for example, as a joint committee of the House and the Senate in cooperation with the executive. Such an assumption is wholly unwarranted, for both the executive and legislative branches of the government are normally dominated by lawyers. What reason, then, is there to justify the conclusion that lawyers, whom chance has elevated to the Supreme Court, will be more capable of interpreting the Constitution and more zealous in promoting its spirit and integrity than lawyers in the other two branches of the government? None whatever. The one group is not likely to be more infallible than the other, nor less prejudiced.

It is further assumed that Supreme Court judges will be uniformly judicial in their determination of constitutional issues, and that their judgments on constitutionality will be invariably objective rather than personal. These assumptions particularly raise doubt as to the democratic validity of judicial review, for judges who have absolute power and are secure in the exercise of it tend to legislate rather than to determine judicially. Justice Oliver Wendell Holmes, one of the few great dissenters, had this danger in mind when he noted in the course of one of his opinions: "Although research has shown and practice had established the futility of the charge that it was usurpation when this Court undertook to declare an Act of Congress unconstitutional, I suppose that we all agree that to do so is the *gravest and most delicate duty* that this Court is called on to perform. Upon this among other considerations the rule is settled that as between two possible interpretations of a statute, by one of which it would be unconstitutional and by the other valid, our plain duty is to adopt that which will save the act."

In another case, he alluded to the same danger when he wrote: "While the Courts must exercise a judgment of their own, it by no means is true that every law is void which may seem to the judges who pass upon it excessive, unsuited to its ostensible end, or based upon conceptions of morality with which they disagree. Considerable latitude must be allowed for differences of view as well as for possible peculiar conditions which this Court can know but imperfectly, if at all. Otherwise a constitution, instead of embodying only relatively fundamental rules of right, as generally understood by all English-speaking communities, would become the partisan of a particular set of ethical or economic opinions, which by no means are held *semper ubique et ab omnibus*." And on another occasion: "This case is decided upon an economic theory which a large part of the country does not entertain . . . the Fourteenth Amendment does not enact Mr. Herbert Spencer's *Social Statics*. . . . Some of these laws embody convictions or prejudices which judges are likely to share. Some may not. But a constitution is not intended to embody a particular economic theory, whether of paternalism and the organic relation of the citizen to the state or of laissez-faire. It is made for people of fundamentally differing views, and the accident of our finding certain opinions natural and familiar or novel and even shocking ought not to conclude our judgment upon the question whether statutes embodying them conflict with the Constitution of the United States."

Every one of the above strictures is proof on highest authority that too many judges tend to pass on the merits of an act of Congress rather than on its constitutionality. Justice Holmes, of course, was one of the few Supreme Court Justices who proved himself worthy of that high office and capable of performing that "gravest and most delicate duty." He was more a philosopher and a legal scholar than a lawyer. Flanked as he was by so many mediocre colleagues, he felt the need, as manifest in the quotations above, to scold them gently and to remind them that they should be judicial rather than censorious. One senses even a note of regret in Justice Holmes, especially in the first of the above quotations, that there ever came to be such an institution as judicial review. Had the doctrine been called socio-political and moral review, the name would have been more fairly descriptive of the substance of many of the Court's crucial decisions.

I need not deal further with what I learned in my study of the *Marbury* case and its consequences. I was opposed to the doctrine for two reasons: given my background and early training, I was suspicious of authority; and, remembering Shakespeare—"The abuse of greatness is when it disjoins remorse from power," an observation which a British statesman turned into a generalization, "Power always corrupts and absolute power corrupts absolutely"—my suspicion became total distrust. On this subject I shall have more to say later. For good or ill, the doctrine became a part of our judicial system. A brief review of how that power was used and what precedents were established by Marshall will be instructive.

CHAPTER VIII

The Abuse of Power

Justice Oliver Wendell Holmes must have had serious reservations regarding the wisdom of judicial review, for on one occasion he said, "I do not think the United States would come to an end if we lost our power to declare an Act of Congress void." One who has read *The Dissenting Opinions of Mr. Justice Holmes* is not in the least surprised that he should have been so skeptical about the ultimate validity of what Marshall's "judicial statesmanship" had made a part of the American system of government. For Holmes had no illusion about the Court. He was not seduced by the ceremony, the secrecy, the robed eminence of the justices, or their conventional isolation from the petty world of petty men. He saw it for what it was: an agency of government staffed by men, too often quite ordinary men. Given his clarity of vision and philosophic mind, it is not surprising that he should have regarded judicial review with such refreshing skepticism. Furthermore, since he achieved a reputation as the great dissenter, most of his dissenting opinions on constitutional issues were judgments on the Court's failure to use its power and authority judicially—judgments that questioned, indirectly, the wisdom and practicality of judicial review.

When I was much younger, I had no doubt whatever that judicial review was a vestigial remnant of the absolutism that America had heroically repudiated in 1776. Now that I am much older and have reviewed the Court's record as interpreter of the Constitution and sole arbiter of the constitutionality of acts of Congress and the legislature, I am less inclined to pass final judgment on its wisdom and propriety in a democracy such as ours. However, I am in complete agreement with Justice Holmes that, if the ultimate power were taken from the Court and given to Congress, the United States would not come to an end; in the protection of the rights of man, as against the rights of property, the zeal of the judiciary has been no more noteworthy than that of Congress.

Having examined the origin of judicial review, the political slant and motives of the justice who read it into the Constitution, and its theoretical justification, I shall now examine some of the cases in the adjudication of which that power was used. I shall proceed, as I have throughout this inquiry, from the point of view of one whose guidelines are the first principles of American democracy as set forth in the Declaration and the preamble to the Constitution. There would seem to be no other basis for such an inquiry: the authority of the Court was used either to secure the unalienable rights of everyone impartially and to promote the general welfare, or it was not. Those first principles, as self-evident truths so often quoted with pride and reconsecrated at Gettysburg, constitute our Magna Carta. We cannot, in honor or decency, pay them lip service and repudiate them in action.

John Marshall's tenure as Chief Justice extended over thirty-four years. During that time, by the charm of his personality and his adroitness as a lawyer, he completely dominated the Court and established certain precedents that are still respected today. Firm in his conviction that the sovereign power should be lodged in gentlemen of property, his monumental achievement, after his coup d'etat in the historic *Marbury* case, may be thus summarized: He established the supremacy of the federal government over the several states, the sanctity of private property, and the irrevocability of contractual obligations with little or no regard for the way they were incurred. He also laid the foundation for the broad construction school of interpreters of the Constitution. Whenever he found it necessary to achieve a certain end, normally political or economic, he simply read into the Constitution (as Justice Holmes later repeatedly refused to do) what was not expressly there.

Thus far historians of the Court and Marshall's biographers are in agreement. No one denies that such was his achievement and that it was monumental. They do not agree that, though great, he was necessarily wise. "Of social and humanitarian interests he was utterly devoid. One might as well look for the sap of idealism in a last year's stump as in John Marshall." Such was the judgment of Vernon L. Parrington, one of his severe critics, and there is ample justification for it. In 1827, the Court ruled four to three, with Marshall in the minority, that a New York bankruptcy law did not violate the obligation of contracts. It was a decision that angered the Chief Justice, for it favored poor debtors rather than rich creditors. The Court's opinion, tinged with Jeffersonian humanitarianism, was read by Justice William Johnson, the first great dissenter appointed by Jefferson and whose tenure was coextensive with Marshall's. He said, in part: "It is among the duties of society to enforce the rights of humanity, and both the debtor and the society have their interests in the administration of justice and in the general good, interests which must not be swallowed up and lost sight of while yielding attention to the claim of the creditor. The debtor may plead the visitations of Providence, and the society has an interest in preserving every member of the community from despondency—in relieving him from a hopeless state of frustration in which he would be useless to himself, his family, and the community. When that state of things has arrived, in which the community has fairly and fully discharged its duties to the creditor, and in which, pursuing the debtor any longer would destroy the one without benefiting the other, there must always be a question to be determined by the common guardian of the rights of both; and in this originates the power exercised by government in favor of insolvents."

Marshall could not understand a view so humane and just, and he dissented. After *Marbury*, he never again struck down an act of Congress. He had established the precedent and withstood the harsh criticism it had occasioned. Let the matter rest there and hope that his successors would honor and sustain the precedent. Accordingly, when, soon after the *Marbury* case, the Court, in *Stuart* v. *Laird*, had an opportunity to declare unconstitutional the Republican repeal of the Judiciary Act of 1801, Marshall avoided the issue and disposed of the case on other grounds. He had won what he dearly sought in the *Marbury* case. Why place that victory in jeopardy by a second coup d'etat?

He did not hesitate, however, to strike down acts of state legislatures in such celebrated cases as *McCulloch* v. *Maryland, Gibbons* v. *Ogden,* the

Dartmouth College case, and *Fletcher* v. *Peck*. In each of these the act of a state legislature was declared unconstitutional. I need not review the issues involved and the reasoning by which Marshall arrived at his conclusions, since those elements of the cases are not particularly relevant to my theme. What is relevant, and what disturbed the young idealist, were the precedents he established and the political and economic interests he served from the bench. In the *Dartmouth College* case, for example, a Federalist decided in favor of fellow Federalist trustees of the College. Dartmouth, under a royal charter granted in 1769, was run by a self-perpetuating board of trustees, gentlemen of wealth and Federalist allegiance. In 1816 the Republican-dominated New Hampshire legislature altered the charter and vested the administration of the college in a board of trustees appointed by the state. It was a democratic move in education and it was blocked by Marshall's anti-democratic Court. Ruling that a charter was the same as a contract—"a brand-new legal doctrine"—and therefore protected under the contract clause of the Constitution against impairment by state legislatures, Marshall declared the New Hampshire case invalid.

In the *McCulloch* case, as in the *Gibbons* case a few years later, Marshall expanded the powers of the federal government and curtailed those of states by reading into the Constitution whatever he needed to serve his political and economic ends. There were two issues in that case: Was the U.S. Bank, created by Congress, constitutional? Did Maryland have the power to regulate and tax its branches? Since the precise list of the powers of Congress does not include the establishment of banks, does it have that power by implication? Yes, said Marshall, and in order to justify his conclusion he expounded the Hamiltonian doctrine of implied powers, precisely as he had done in the *Marbury* case. Since the Constitution gives Congress certain specific powers, such as the control of the U.S. currency and the regulation of interstate commerce, it must also grant Congress by implication such other powers as are necessary for the performance of those functions. Hence, the power to establish the U.S. Bank was clearly implied in the power of Congress to regulate the currency; the Bank was therefore constitutional. Since "the power to tax involves the power to destroy," no state legislature has the power to tax branches of the U.S. Bank.

In these two cases Marshall elaborated the doctrine of what is variously called the "loose" or the "broad construction" of the Constitution. He stated it thus: "Let the end be legitimate, let it be within the scope of the constitution, and all means which are appropriate, which are plainly adapted to that end, which are not prohibited, but consist with the letter and spirit of the constitution, are constitutional." In plain English this means that a judge, when he finds it expedient to do so, on the authority of the Chief Justice, may read into the Constitution what is not there. In the *McCulloch* case that was done in order to check a people's legislature and advance the interests of bankers. Roger Taney, who succeeded Marshall as Chief Justice, might have concluded differently.

But what disturbed my young idealistic sensibilities was the failure of Marshall and his associates, in these and similar cases, to adjudicate judicially and in the spirit of the Constitution, particularly as professed in the preamble. In a sense, that single opening sentence was the most important part of the Constitution, for it spelled out clearly the worthy ends that were to be achieved by a strict adherence to the fundamental law. That great document, it must be remembered, was "ordained" and "established," in the name of the people, in order, among other things, to "promote the general welfare." If that be granted, as it ought to be, then in all cases where the public welfare is involved, the issue should be raised and most scrupulously considered. Yet, in deciding cases such as these examined here, it never occurred to Marshall and his associates to ask such questions as: In what ways is the general welfare promoted by denying a state the right to appoint the trustees of a college? In what ways is the general welfare promoted by denying a state the authority to regulate and tax a branch of the U.S. Bank?

The reason why such issues were not raised was that, according to Marshall, "the leading doctrine of constitutional law during the first generation of our National history was the doctrine of vested rights." He was also firm in his conviction that "the whole duty of government is to prevent crime and preserve contracts." Granted the validity of those premises, Marshall's decisions followed logically from them. But their validity was challenged by Roger Taney, Marshall's successor as Chief Justice. He reasoned from the premise that "the object and end of all government is to promote the happiness and prosperity of the community by which it is established." Thus, as one Chief Justice followed another, the pronouncements of the Court, in the adjudication of precisely the same issues, reflected, in Taney's words, "a change of emphasis from vested, individual property rights to the personal rights and welfare of the general community."

That change in emphasis was the determining factor in the case of *Charles*

River Bridge v. *Warren Bridge,* decided in 1837. The issue in that case was substantially the same as in the *Dartmouth College* case, decided by the Marshall Court nearly two decades before: "Whether the obligation of contract contained in a charter to a corporation authorizing the construction of a toll bridge was impaired by a charter, subsequently granted to another corporation, authorizing the construction of a free bridge paralleling the toll bridge." Taney decided that it did not. Therefore, the state statute that authorized the free bridge was constitutional. Whereas Marshall in the *Dartmouth* case had ruled that a charter, as a contract, granted exclusive rights by implication, Taney established the opposed doctrine that "in the absence of *express* words granting exclusive privileges in corporate charters, no such grants can be *inferred* as against the granting state." He did not deny that a charter was a contract. In direct opposition to Marshall he affirmed that such a charter must be *strictly* construed, and where exclusive rights are not *expressly* written into it, they must not be read into it by *implication*.

Which was the correct view? Since Marshall was intent on protecting vested property rights and Taney in promoting the general welfare, I felt that the view of the latter was more in harmony with the spirit of the Constitution and therefore correct. But I was not altogether happy with my endorsement of his view. In the *Dartmouth* and the *Bridge* cases, two opposed doctrines of constitutional interpretation were in conflict—the loose and the strict construction. In all honesty, I had to admit that I favored the latter because in the case at bar it led to the desired conclusion. Would I have supported the loose construction had that been necessary to reach the desired conclusion? The question disturbed me, for the choice of the mode of interpretation seemed based on expediency. In any given case one chose the mode that best served one's interests. Perhaps that essentially utilitarian view was politically sound, but there was something about it that was ethically repugnant. I again had occasion to wonder whether my passion for the rights of man was rooted in the fact that, having no property, my only vested interest was in human rights. There was scant consolation in this thought, but it was the sort of self-appraisal that must be taken into account. What determined whether one was a Hamiltonian conservative or a Jeffersonian liberal? Was it environment, family background, the extent of one's material possessions? Was my young Jewish companion right—that Marx had the answer? Later I would investigate that.

This sort of self-criticism should have tempered my reaction to Marshall's 1810 ruling in *Fletcher* v. *Peck* but it did not. The disposition of that single case represented everything in Marshall with which I differed: his rigid legalism, his indifference to the general welfare, his veneration of property rights and contractual obligations regardless of how they were incurred. At stake in that case was the title to millions of acres of valuable public land. One of the issues was whether a public contract was as sacred, binding, and irrevocable as a private contract. Another issue, hitherto undecided, was whether the Supreme Court had the authority to strike down a state statute on constitutional grounds. These issues were strictly judicial, and they could be adjudicated one way or the other in accordance with the law of contracts and the relevant provisions of the Constitution. There was another issue—social and ethical—that had no definitive judicial precedent and that would require the promulgation of a new legal principle. The initial transaction on which the claims in *Fletcher* v. *Peck* were based was admittedly conceived in fraud. Did that fact render those claims invalid? We shall see how Marshall disposed of this issue.

The case of *Fletcher* v. *Peck* had its origin in the greedy scramble for the thousands of square miles of virgin land that were the unparalleled bounty of the new land. It began during the new nation's first decade, gained momentum after the Civil War, and culminated at the close of the century in the extension of sovereignty beyond national boundaries. When there were no more domestic acres to acquire, by fair means or foul, those who had the power to direct the nation's foreign policy began to look elsewhere for spoils. It was then that, under the rationale of manifest destiny, the United States of America joined the land-grabbing imperialists of the old world, and astute judicial statesmen, such as Marshall, supplied the justifying legalisms and rhetoric.

Even before the union of the states was established under the Constitution, it was obvious that land was the prize to be attained in the new world. The towering forests, the plains, the subterranean treasures enriched anyone's private vision of the future. Those who were shrewd and sensed the direction in which the new nation would move knew that expansion would be westward. In 1803, the Louisiana Purchase added 828 thousand square miles to the nation's territory, thus doubling the area of the United States. When the expedition of Lewis and Clark returned to St. Louis, Missouri, on

September 23, 1806, the Pacific ocean was virtually established as the nation's western boundary.

Many men "had fixed their eyes, hopes, and purposes" on the western lands. Tillers of the soil, with no ambition other than to possess such land as necessary for a life of dignity and labor, were joined in pursuit by adventurers, speculators, and reputable men with money to invest. The resulting traffic in land was on such a large scale that it was "the most notable economic fact in the early years of the American nation." Unfortunately, it was dominated by unprincipled adventurers, whose wild speculations in western lands contributed significantly to the panic of 1819.

There was considerable precedent for the fraud that attended the land sale that was the subject in *Fletcher* v. *Peck*. In late seventeenth-century Virginia, "speculation in land was universal; exploitation was open and shameless; the highest officials took advantage of their positions to loot the public domain, resorting to divers sharp practices from tax dodging to outright theft. One gentleman added a cipher to a grant for two hundred acres, and although the fraud was commonly known, so great was his influence that no one disputed his title to two thousand acres. While governor, Alexander Spotswood issued patents for sixty thousand acres to dummy holders, who deeded the land to him after he had retired from office."

In 1789, six years before the transaction from which *Fletcher* v. *Peck* originated, the state of Georgia had disposed of twenty-five and one-half million acres to several land companies controlled by unscrupulous adventurers; when these tried to pay with worthless money, the state properly refused to accept it. The land companies who, in 1795, acquired the land that was the subject in *Fletcher* v. *Peck,* were "for the most part composed of men of excellent reputation." However, their agents in the transaction were guilty of fraud and thus placed the title of the buyers in jeopardy. The facts in the case were as follows:

The state of Georgia, through its legislature, sold to certain land companies more than thirty-five million acres of land at less than one and one-half cents an acre. The area was substantially the entire territory that later became the states of Mississippi and Alabama. The land was fertile, well watered, heavily wooded; its value had been tremendously increased by Eli Whitney's invention of the cotton gin in 1793. The competition for it was fierce, and the means employed by the victors in the scramble were scandalous.

"A saturnalia of corruption was in progress in the little village of Augusta where the legislature of Georgia was in session. The leading men of that and neighboring states, and a battery of lobbyists directed by General James Gunn, U.S. Senator from Georgia, were on hand to urge the enactment of the law necessary to effect the sale." The Senator himself "strode about the village arrayed in broadcloth, top boots, and beaver hat, commending those who favored the bill, abusing those who opposed it. In his hand he carried a loaded whip, and with this the burly Senator actually menaced members who objected to the scheme." It was bribery, however, that proved to be the persuasive means. In less than a week the act was passed and on January 7, 1795, became a law. "The greatest real estate deal in history was thus consummated" and "every member of the Legislature who had voted for the measure, except one, had shares of stock in the purchasing companies."

But they paid dearly for their betrayal, for when "the tidings of corruption attending the sale" became generally known, a wave of indignation swept across the state. "Men who lived near Augusta assembled and marched on the Capitol determined to lynch their legislative betrayers." Meetings were held in every hamlet, the land steal was angrily denounced, and Senator Gunn was burned in effigy. James Jackson, the other Senator from Georgia, left the Senate and was elected to the state legislature. With him as their angry and indignant leader, the people of Georgia elected a new legislature pledged to undo the dirty work of its predecessor. Jackson himself framed the rescinding statute. "It denounced the land sale act as a violation of both state and national constitutions, as the creation of a monopoly, as the dismemberment of Georgia, as the betrayal of the rights of man." And since its enactment had been secured by "atrocious speculation, corruption, and collusion," the sovereign state of Georgia had the authority to declare the land sale act, and all claims that arose from the sale, directly or indirectly, null and void.

The sovereign state of Georgia had acted quickly, but the land companies had acted even more quickly in disposing of the land to numerous investors in the middle states and in New England. Some were aware of the fraud; some were not. The average price paid was fourteen cents an acre. As soon as it became known that Georgia had annulled the land sale act and declared void all claims based on it, a number of rich and influential investors sought the advice of Alexander Hamilton. He told them, in substance, that they were secure. The sale of the land, as authorized by the Georgia legislature, was a contract. Therefore, the rescinding act was invalid because it violated the contract clause of the Constitution. The courts, he assured them, would be "likely to pronounce it so."

But there were others, as well versed in the Constitution and as eager to abide by it as Hamilton, who concluded differently. Among them were Senators Jackson of Georgia, Abraham Bishop of Connecticut, and John Randolph of Virginia. They defended the view that, when legislators betray their trust for their own corrupt advantage, the people have an unalienable right to abrogate any act in which the betrayal is attempted. Legislatures have the constitutional authority to pass and repeal laws. Accordingly, the rescinding act of the Georgia legislature, which "nipt in the bud a number of aspiring swindlers," was completely valid, and the courts would be obliged to deny all claims based on the abrogated act. Granted that the sale it authorized was a contract; but since the transaction was admittedly conceived in fraud, the courts would not be likely to validate it by resorting to the sacredness-of-contracts doctrine.

In consequence of these diametrically opposed views on the validity of claims based on an abrogated act, many land speculators appealed to the courts for adjudication. One of these was Robert Fletcher. He had bought fifteen thousand acres from John Peck, a Boston dealer in Georgia lands. When Fletcher learned that his title was in doubt, he sued Peck for the recovery of his purchase money. A circuit court judge decided in favor of Peck, and Fletcher appealed to the Supreme Court on a writ of error. Thus, the angrily debated issue was presented to Chief Justice Marshall for final adjudication. He delivered his opinion on March 16, 1810.

Had Marshall been less dedicated to the sacredness of contracts and less concerned about his own business interests, he might have disqualified himself from sitting in the Fletcher appeal. He was "profoundly interested in the stability of contractual obligations. The repudiation of these by the legislature of Virginia had powerfully and permanently influenced his views upon the subject. Also, Marshall's own title to part of the Fairfax estate had more than once been in jeopardy. At that very moment a suit affecting the title of his brother to certain Fairfax lands was pending in Virginia courts." Under such circumstances, judicial honor traditionally requires a judge to disqualify himself. But there was too much at stake in the case, issues that he wanted resolved in his own way; so judicial honor had to give way to judicial statesmanship.

Marshall proceeded to pass judgment and made *Fletcher* v. *Peck* one of the most celebrated cases of his long tenure as Chief Justice. There was no question about the authority of a state to make land grants on whatever terms it pleased. Nor was it seriously disputed that such grants were virtual contracts. Therefore, the sale act of 1795 was valid. Further, there was no question that a legislature of a sovereign state may rescind an act of its predecessor. However, the sovereign state of Georgia was a member of the sovereign union; and "that union has a Constitution which imposes limits to the legislatures of the several states." They may not, for example, pass ex post facto laws, nor laws that impair the obligations of contracts. The issue in *Fletcher* v. *Peck* was whether the Georgia legislature, in abrogating the sale act of 1795, had done what the Constitution enjoins. Under the doctrine of implied power, this was an issue that the Supreme Court must adjudicate. Accordingly, Marshall decided that the rescinding act was unconstitutional for the reason that it impaired the contractual obligations incurred by the sale act of 1795. Thus Marshall settled a matter that he wanted settled—as in the *Marbury* case—in his own way. Thenceforth, the Supreme Court would have the power to strike down acts of state legislatures on constitutional grounds.

Then he proceeded to dispose of the crucial issue raised in *Fletcher* v. *Peck,* the issue that had occasioned the violent debates throughout the nation. Did the admitted fraud in procuring the sale act of 1795 save the rescinding act from the constitutional injunction? It did not, for "the grant, when issued, conveyed an estate in fee—simple to the grantee, clothed with all the solemnities which law can bestow. This estate was transferable; and those who purchased parts of it were not stained by that guilt which infected the original transaction." It was regrettable that the legislators who passed the act were bribed, but a court of law could not examine the motives that operated in legislative assemblies and declare that "a law is a nullity in consequence of the impure motives that influenced certain members of the legislature which passed the law." Legislators are the elected agents of the people, and if the people choose unwisely, they must suffer the consequences of their choice.

Thus *Fletcher* v. *Peck* gave Marshall the opportunity he needed to settle another matter that he wanted settled his own way: to announce the new legal principle stated above. The precedent was now established for the maxim that a contract is absolutely inviolable no matter how corruptly derived.

However, "to the vast majority of the inhabitants of the United States," Marshall's opinion was furiously condemned in the Congress and legislatures of the various states by all except the most conservative Federalists. George M. Troup of Georgia called upon the national government to resist, by force of arms if necessary, the judgment of the Supreme Court: "It is proclaimed by the Judges, and is now to be sanctioned by the legislature, that the representatives of the people may corruptly betray the people, may corruptly barter their rights and those of their posterity, and the people are wholly without any kind of remedy whatsoever. It is this monstrous and abhorent doctrine which must startle every man in the nation, that you ought promptly to discountenance and condemn. If the arch-fiend had, in his hatred to mankind, resolved the destruction of republican government on earth, he would have issued a decree like that of the judges."

The language is harsh, but the decision that provoked it was shocking. Randolph and others condemned it with no less fury. Two decades later, Andrew Jackson appeared to have had the last word and have Marshall cornered, when he shrugged off the Chief Justice with: "John Marshall has made his decision, now let him enforce it." The words were clever and bold, but they did not affect reality. Marshall had made his decision and no amount of indignation would prevail against it. In stating his opinion, Marshall had said, referring to what the corrupt legislature had done, "The past cannot be recalled by the most absolute power." Unwittingly, he was speaking prophetically of what he had accomplished during the first ten years of his long tenure as Chief Justice. He had written himself into the fundamental law, and his successors on the Court would honor his precedents for decades to come.

In *Fletcher* v. *Peck* he had strengthened the law of contracts, put commercial intercourse in the young and growing nation on an even keel, brought acts of state legislatures under the scrutiny of the Supreme Court, and served notice on states such as Georgia and Virginia that their legislatures could not repudiate contractual obligations. Well and good. But he had also sanctioned other land speculations in which fraud was an element, and, in establishing the maxim that judges are not obliged to examine the motives that induce legislatures to enact a law, he encouraged the repetition of the fraudulent Georgia land sale act of 1795. For decades thereafter, unprincipled speculators (later robber barons) seeking state lands, grants, and franchises would not hesitate to use fraudulent means to achieve their ends; it was now official that, if their transactions should be challenged in court, the judges would not look beyond the contract.

This was regrettable, for a wise Chief Justice could have come to the opposite conclusion. In disposing of *Fletcher* v. *Peck,* he could have put all enterprisers, especially those doing business with the government, on notice that the Court would never sanction a transaction that smelled even faintly of fraud. He could have reasoned just as persuasively as he did in defending the sanctity of a government grant as a sacred contract. He could have appealed, as did the authors of the Declaration, to the Creator, or to natural law, or to the moral order of the universe, as sources of man's unalienable rights which the Court is duty bound to respect. Thus, he could have drawn a distinction between contractual obligations and the obligations of official stewardship. The former is merely legally binding; the latter is sacred and inviolable. Therefore, in accordance with the higher law, a contract based on desecration of that which is sacred and inviolable is null and void.

Alternatively, he could have based his decision on the doctrine of the general welfare, a concept that derives ultimately from the idea of natural law. Even though there was a contract, since it was conceived in fraud, the general welfare would be best served by declaring the contract invalid. In ruling thus he could have anticipated a famous declaration by Justice Holmes in *Olmstead* v. *United States*: "We have to choose, and for my part I think it a less evil that some criminals should escape than that the government should play an ignoble part." According to that wise ruling, it would have been a less evil that a contract conceived in fraud should be invalidated, than that the nation's highest tribunal should encourage unscrupulous enterprisers to bribe legislators and other government agents. Such a ruling, based on the general welfare doctrine and strictly honored by the Court thereafter, would have made speculators who sought public lands, grants, and franchises less likely to resort to fraud to achieve their ends. It would have discouraged the betrayal of official stewardship, which especially in a democracy must remain sacred and inviolable.

Or Marshall could have upheld the rescinding act of the Georgia legislature on the authority of John Locke, whose bias in favor of private property was no less intense than his own. Knowing that legislators may abuse their power as well as kings and magistrates, he had declared, in his *Second Trea-*

tise, that "the community perpetually retains a supreme power of saving themselves from the *attempts* and *designs* of anybody, even their *legislators,* whenever they shall be so *foolish* or so *wicked* as to lay and carry on designs against the liberties of the subject."

On these and other grounds, a wise Chief Justice could have asserted the interest of the community over business and sustained the rescinding act. He had the legal dexterity to pick his direction, but he was blind to all directions except that of the sovereignty of the federal state and the sanctity of private property. In the promotion and defense of these, Justice Marshall was resourceful, indefatigable, and invincible, but he was not wise.

Such was my judgment and that of my companions when, as law students, debaters, and young idealists, we had read the celebrated case of *Fletcher* v. *Peck.* We understood that, on strictly legal grounds, Marshall's decision was defensible. Our professor had made that clear—a contract is a contract, and that is the end. But we were shocked that the highest court in the nation, the self-proclaimed guardian of the Constitution, had condoned fraud. Unpardonable abuse of ultimate power! Fraud, bribery, political chicanery, intimidation, betrayal of public trust, the virtual stealth of millions of acres that properly belonged to the people—all that nastiness, evil, and greed crammed into one transaction, and the Supreme Court had sanctioned the dirty deal by sanctifying public grants as sacred contracts!

Even as Marshall had refused to look beyond the legalisms, so we refused to consider anything beyond the fact of fraud. Since the bare legalisms had been sufficient grounds for him to rule that the contract executed by the corrupt legislature could not be annulled by the act of its successor, so was the fact of fraud sufficient grounds for us to damn ab initio the entire transaction. For him the crucial issue was legal, for us it was ethical, what was at stake for him was vested rights in property, for us it was the interests of the community. We lacked legal dexterity and had no vested rights in property, but we had plenty of indignation and plenty of idealism. Thus armed, no one could have persuaded us that he was right and we were wrong. Even now, nearly sixty years later, I have no doubt whatever that it was right and proper for us to refuse to look beyond the fact of fraud and to believe as we did. When one is young and preparing to take a place in the community, it is better to have too much than too little idealism—better to be dedicated to the realization of a more just society than to the accumulation of a fortune.

When we were twenty-one, we lacked the knowledge and experience necessary to understand that there was some justification for what Marshall had done. The nation was young; its vast resources were in the first stages of development; the belligerence of certain states in asserting their sovereignty, anticipating the nullification movement in South Carolina led by John C. Calhoun in 1832, was threatening the union. Under these circumstances, it was necessary that the rights of business should be clarified, that enterprisers should be given some freedom in the management of their enterprises, and that the union should be strengthened at the expense of the more unreasonable pretensions of the states. We were too young and too inexperienced in the ways of the world to understand these expediencies except in a rather vague, theoretical way, and so we damned Marshall for having failed to consider fraud in *Fletcher* v. *Peck* and applauded ourselves for having refused to look beyond it.

To that extent our conclusions may have been vulnerable but our instincts were sound. We were partisans of the higher law even before we understood that the fundamental principles of democratic government had their source in that self-evident truth; even before we were old and wise enough to understand that honor, decency, honesty, and the inviolable dignity of man have their ultimate sanction in some higher law. On what other basis does one justify the reality of the rights of man? Of natural rights? Of the sacredness of that which is sacred? We supported honesty in government and all policies that we believed promoted the general welfare, so we rebelled against a Supreme Court decision that seemed to make a mockery of both.

The case came to be known, appropriately, as the Yazoo Land Fraud, because the land was largely in the Yazoo River country. In the history of constitutional law it was a landmark case, along with certain other cases decided by the Marshall Court. I found Marshall's decision in this case particularly offensive, as I have already noted. For this reason I have dealt with the case at some length, and I must now try to explain why the decision was particularly offensive to me—a reaction that was more emotional than intellectual.

The key to my reaction, as I understand it now, is in my attitude toward land, fraud, and any type of criminal behavior. How did my attitude toward land differ from that of my companions, and how can I account for it? Unlike my companions, I was born and lived the first ten years of my life in a land of scarcity, at the very bottom of the economic scale, and in a class where the concern and the challenge of each day was earning the daily bread. In that milieu the words "opportunity" and "investment" were unknown because the possibility of getting ahead and making money as an end in itself or as a means to power were unknown. I was born a peasant, as my companions were not, in a world of peasants, where everyone was a tiller of the soil—not a farmer, with acres and barns and livestock and plows, but just a tiller of the soil. My college companions, in their early childhood, began weighing the career options available to them. After a boy's childish desire to become an engineer and drive a choo-choo train had passed, they began to think of the trades, crafts, and professions. In the world in which I was born, I had no options whatever. In order to live I must take my place in the fields, learn to till the soil, and take from it my daily bread. Literally! For we prepared the soil, sowed the grain, ground the ripe kernels, and made bread with the flour.

All of this, of course, was changed when I arrived in America, but my origins determined my attitude toward the land and the course I would follow in developing my domestic economy. Land for me was never something to be bought and sold for a profit. There was no speculation in land and, therefore, no land speculators. There were only tillers of the soil of varying degrees of expertise. If one had the means, one bought land, but the goal was more and better bread for the table, not profit. In keeping with that hand-to-mouth sense of economy we acquired in the New World the land we had needed but could not afford to buy in Casabianca. We could have had a deed to it for practically nothing, but there was no need for legal ownership since the use of the land was given to us gratis. Had we been schooled in land speculation we might have bought hundreds of acres and sold it later for a tidy profit, but we were not. We were tillers of the soil, not speculators in land. So we took of the land only so much as we needed to improve the quantity and quality of our bread.

Thus, land as soil, in that typical peasant world of Casabianca, was actually our alter ego, something alive that required careful husbandry, the source of our bread that would yield generously or meagerly, according to how well or ill it was used. Since what land we had was severely limited and the possibility of adding to it nonexistent, we concentrated on mastering the arts of tillage and horticulture. The exercise of these arts was carried on in a spirit of friendly competition and cooperation. Given a tract of land, who in the community had perfected its total management—spading and harrowing, hoeing and fertilization, crop rotation and successive sowings—that the yield was the highest possible, season after season? How did Antonio manage to grow such excellent corn year after year? What magic spells did he cast over the land? There were, of course, no secrets, there were only the more and the less capable tillers. What Antonio had learned by diligent and intelligent labor (although he might encourage the belief that there was some magic in his methods), he readily passed on to the community. For competition among the Casabianca peasantry was not for the ownership of land or for its profitable exploitation but rather for the honor of being the acclaimed superior in the exercise of the common arts. It was only the indecently perverse who found any comfort in the fact that a neighbor's harvest was worse than their own.

The peasantry, cut off from the flow of history and civilization, knowing nothing of industry and finance, and entirely dependent on the land, developed a deep attachment to it and respected it as their alter ego: We live by the land and the land lives by us. The peasant's attitude toward it and management of it reflected not only sound empirical knowledge and common sense but also a veneration and a sense of the sacred tinged with superstition. In the fall after the harvest, scattered bonfires burned the land's parasites; in the spring the land was blessed by the village priest. Here and there, ensconced in some nook of the field, were iconic images, and lunar influences were observed in the sowing and the harvest. Also, there was the use of the word *governare*, which means to govern, but in Italian also means to minister to the needs of animals: *governare gli animali*. Thus, when the peasants applied fertilizer to the growing corn, they referred to the process as *governare*, an act of ministering to the needs of the soil and its growth.

They were also well aware, these simple folk who lived on intimate terms with the soil, that, in the mysterious scheme of life, the nine months process of human procreation was repeated in the soil's production of the twin staffs of life: bread and wine. The grain seed, lodged in the womb of earth in November, cropped nine months later in July. The vine, trimmed in February, produced the ripe grapes nine months later in October. These empirical data tended to humanize and, in a sense, sanctify the growth of the soil and to invest with a certain propriety the use of bread and wine in the celebration of the Eucharist. Bread was in itself sacred; if it were accidentally dropped, it was retrieved and blessed with a kiss. In a culture so elemental and wise, it was not considered sacrilegious for a pious peasant to stand at the head of the

Sunday dinner table and bless the occasion with the family's own bread and wine, the growth of the soil, the blessed fruit of their labor.

These attitudes, these customs, and the way of life they reflected were not left behind when we immigrated to the New World. In the land of plenty, except for the considerable improvement in material well-being, we continued to live pretty much as we had lived in the land of scarcity. By the time I was ten years of age, I had been permanently influenced by what I have related above. So much so that even now, six decades later, certain facets of my character—my idea of what is necessary to live happily, and, above all, my attitude toward the land—have their source in what I learned during the first ten years of my life. My memory of what I have here recorded is more vivid now than it was when I first read *Fletcher* v. *Peck*, but the essence of that memory was deeply embedded in my nature. In the six decades following my first, I have had time to reflect on the ethical and practical validity of what I learned as a young boy and to live in accordance with it.

I have never sought opportunities to make money by using money to make more money. I have known that that is the way money is made, but I have found the practice of the marketplace uncongenial to my nature. Thus, I have studiously avoided all species of investment. The world in which I have lived has always given me work to do, some of it hard work, but, on the whole, work that I have enjoyed. What money I have made has been more or less fair compensation for that labor, and it has been enough, more than enough, to raise a family and to live modestly, happily, and well. I record this as a fact and not necessarily as a virtue, for I cannot say that, having lived thus, I am a better man than my neighbor who has made money by using money to make more money.

Years ago I learned from a poet that a man should marry, beget a child, and plant a tree. The poet himself had married, begotten two children, and planted two thousand trees. In the normal course of events, given the milieu of my early years, I would have done precisely that without anyone's advice. Nonetheless, it was good to have a poet's blessings for pursuing my nature's bent. Accordingly, when I had sown my wild oats, and earned by labor the necessary means, I married, bought a house, begot three children, and planted the symbolic tree. The land on which the house was built was 6500 square feet—a tiny kingdom—and the castle itself no larger than necessary to house a royal family of five.

I was now a landowner, sole sovereign and lord of 6500 square feet of American land that hadn't been subsumed by the Yazoo speculators and their land-grabbing descendants. For the first time in my life, I had a vested interest in property, the contract for it duly executed with all the solemnities that law can bestow and rendered irrevocable and sacred by the precedents established generations ago by Chief Justice Marshall. That sacred document, as sacred as the Host in the celebration of the Eucharist, was wrapped in white linen and tenderly deposited in the vaults of the University National Bank. How ineffable the feeling of having a vested interest in property thus secured! I was beginning to understand and appreciate the sensibilities of the Chief Justice.

As a matter of fact, I was tempted to join the Federalist elite, but that temptation was annulled by the realization that I lacked the full credentials. For the transaction that had made me a landowner was conceived not in fraud, speculation, or political chicanery but in the sweat of my brow, in the thrift, industry, and attachment to the soil as a living thing—in the imperatives of my being structured into my nature when I was a young boy. So I remained with the Jeffersonian populace where I properly belonged and began a new life as a gentleman farmer. I divided my kingdom into quarter sections: one for the castle and its abutments, another for trees and shrubbery, a third for lawns and flower beds, and a fourth, approximately 1500 square feet, for the growth of edibles. In that most sacred of the four sections, I would do what in another book I described as "The Things My Fathers Used to Do." I would practice the arts of the peasant, with the talent I had inherited from my ancestry and the elements of which I learned as a young boy. By tilling the soil with the tools of the peasant, I would enrich the bounty of our royal table and also achieve a certain balance in the essentially sedentary life of the schoolteacher. I quote from the book I wrote forty years ago, ten years after I had acquired a vested interest in property:

"My labors in the family's bit of earth in Italy taught me very early in life the elements of agriculture: when to plant each vegetable; how to assist it to maturity; and when to harvest it for the table. . . . As I look back upon these experiences and contemplate them in terms of personality they helped me to mold. . . I can trace to them now, among other things, the realization, intimately personal, that there is real dignity in human toil; that labor with the hands has real worth in terms of man's physical and spiritual well-being. . . .

"Among the values by which I seek to live, and the source of which I can trace to my early years in Italy, is a *reverent attitude toward the soil and its growth*. The produce of the earth to me is sacred . . . I am thrilled and easily excited by any luxuriant growth on the face of the earth, for I know that the seed beneath the clod of earth today will sustain the body or inspire a poem tomorrow. . . .

"I do not mean, certainly, that one should worship carrots and make a ritual of bread and wine, although, I suppose, there are people who do both and yet somehow miss the point. Everything that man needs for the nourishment of his body and the elevation of his soul is as sacred as himself and should be so regarded. The wheat fields and the forests, the orchards and the vineyards, directly or indirectly—these put food in our stomachs and clothes on our backs. The man who has known the need of both, he who has competed with the animals for possession of tender shoots in the spring, will have no difficulty understanding what I mean when I say that we should look upon them as sacred gifts, to be used with discretion and bequeathed unimpaired to the children of tomorrow. If one does not realize how sinful man's behavior has been toward Nature's bounty, let him visit what were once the proud forests of the West. . . . "

I have quoted these fragments in order to show that even forty years ago, I could trace to my early years in Italy my sense of the sacredness of the land. It was not ownership, vested interest, the contract of acquisition—call it what you will—that was sacred and inviolable, it was the land itself and its produce. Sentimental? Romantic? Naive? Perhaps. In any case, it was this attitude that made the decision in *Fletcher* v. *Peck* particularly offensive to me, for the Supreme Court had sanctioned what was essentially an act of desecration—the criminal acquisition of land in order to make money. It was an evil precedent, and the Chief Justice had actually shrugged off the criminal element as unimportant.

My reaction to this phase of the case was colored by what a peasant boy had learned from a peasant father about strict obedience to the law. In a self-governing society people respect laws because they are made by themselves through their agents. These laws are their government—municipal, state, national—responsible, renewable at stated intervals, close at hand, and observable. The laws are an expression of the collective will. Not so in the peasant world of Casabianca where I was born and lived as a young boy.

There the society was essentially medieval—a master and servant society. The root evil was the complete exclusion of the peasantry from the governing process. This, to them, made the government—*lo stato*—remote, mysterious, and unalterable. Its power was arbitrary and absolute. Its laws were feared rather than respected. Long experience had taught us that any involvement with the state was invariably costly and unpleasant. Therefore, the best policy was strict obedience to the law.

At any rate, this was the policy my father pursued to the letter. Had he been more shrewd and crafty—and there were such among his peasant contemporaries—he might have considered possible ways of profitable transgression. But he was not; he was prudent to a fault—prudent to the point where the danger of getting in trouble with the law became an obsession with him. The obedience that he himself observed, he imposed on us children with frightening authority. Years later, as a student in the new land, I came to understand that the source of his gospel of obedience was fear of the law rather than respect for it. Given his temperament and the society in which he lived, his attitude was understandable. When I was a young boy, I felt the weight of his authority and was incapable of making that distinction. So I grew up with the notion that one was required to respect and obey the law as one was required to respect and obey the Church. The authority of each was absolute and beyond scrutiny. This idea was so rooted in my nature that, even after I had read Thoreau and intellectually approved what I read, deep down in me I felt that civil disobedience was as much a heresy as the transgression of the Lord's Ten Commandments.

It is true that when I first read *Fletcher* v. *Peck* I had acquired a certain degree of superficial sophistication, but in my attitude toward the law, I was still very much my father's son. For this reason I was baffled, amazed, and appalled by the fact that the Chief Justice of the Supreme Court had shrugged off as irrelevant the criminal element in the *Fletcher* case. My Jewish friend and partner in debate, who knew more history than I, had condemned Marshall's decision, but of the fraud he had said, cynically, "Oh hell! That sort of thing goes on all the time. Look at the Teapot Dome scandal." I did.

In trying to convince the Moor, Othello, that his Venetian wife, Desdemona, was unfaithful to him, Iago argued that Venetian women were crafty minxes unrestrained by moral scruples, and that "Their best conscience is not to leave it undone, but to keep it unknown." My Jewish classmate and partner in debate—a keen, analytical mind, well-read in history, and searching for the sources of evil in society—had already come to the cynical conclusion that what the establishment tends to regret is not so much the transgression as the failure of the cover-up. "What the hell! That sort of thing goes on all the time."

If that were so, what was the reason for it? What shaped the conscience of a Chief Justice who honored a contract conceived in fraud? Why did a government of gentlemen tend to place property rights above human rights? How could one account for land grabbers, robber barons, the unscrupulous, insatiable bloodsuckers of the new land's bounty? Was man, as Hobbes insisted, greedy and brutish by nature, litigious and belligerent? Or was he made so by heredity and environment, by the rules of the game?

In the late twenties, such questions as these were esoteric. The nation was enjoying prosperity and tranquillity on the installment plan. After the abnormal years of World War I, Harding had led the nation back to normalcy. His successor, Coolidge, announced that "the business of the United States is business." And since business was running the nation so well, there was nothing for him to do as president and titular head of his party. Therefore, and wisely, he chose not to run in the election of 1928. In such halcyon years, who cared about such questions as I raised?

My companions and I did because we were serious and well-informed students, and we knew, as the majority of the electors who put Harding in office did not, what I have recorded in the last three chapters. We were taught to keep our eyes fixed on the ideal; we believed that the best conscience is to live by that conscience's high requirements and that property rights should always yield to human rights. We believed what we were taught. So we continued our search for answers to such questions as I raised above.

I myself, as an immigrant from Italy, found ample reason in the halcyon twenties for becoming more and more concerned about the rights of man.

CHAPTER IX

. . . And the Chief
of These Is Property

At the turn of the century when America joined the land-grabbing imperialists of Europe, William James was convinced that we had come to the end of the American Dream. If his and the judgment of other anti-imperialists was premature, had the dream vanished into thin air by the end of the twenties? I cannot state with authority that at either date the dream had yielded to reality, but I do not hesitate to state that by the end of the third decade, my own faith in the dream was shaken. For as I continued my inquiry into the Supreme Court's use of its sovereign power, at times sustaining and at others opposing the executive and legislative authority, I became more and more convinced that the rights of man and the common welfare, so solemnly proclaimed as the cornerstone of the fundamental law, were being sacrificed to vested interests in property. As I read about the crudely bold beginnings of American imperialism that had disillusioned William James, how could I avoid being dismayed by what was happening to that other principle, likewise solemnly declared by the colonies, that all legitimate government is based on the consent of the governed? Did the historical data, beyond what I have already reviewed in the last three chapters, justify these grave doubts? Was my faith in the American Dream so severely shaken that it could not be regenerated? As I grew older, more amenable to compromise, and tempered my idealism with a more sober sense of what is possible, did I manage to recapture something of the faith I had in the early twenties? These are the questions I shall attempt to answer in what remains of my narrative.

The title of this chapter is taken from the opinion of Judge Van Orsdel of the United States Court of Appeals for the District of Columbia, in the case of *Adkins* v. *Children's Hospital*. To promote the moral and physical welfare of women in the District of Columbia, an act of Congress in 1918 provided for a minimum wage board to fix standards. The act was challenged on constitutional grounds in the district court and declared null and void by Judge Van Orsdel. In the course of his opinion he stated the premise on which the judgment was based: "The tendency of the times to socialize property rights under the subterfuge of police regulation is dangerous, and if continued will prove destructive of our free institutions. It should be remembered that of the three fundamental principles which underlie government, and for which governments exist, the protection of life, liberty, and property, *the chief of these is property*." On appeal by the board to the Supreme Court in 1922, Judge Van Orsdel's decree was affirmed in a five to four decision, with Justice Holmes delivering a bold dissent.

There is no need for me to review the course of reasoning that led to the majority and minority views. The remote precedents for Judge Van Ordsel's decision were the property views of Justice Marshall, and the English common law as interpreted by Sir William Blackstone a hundred and thirty years before: "So great is the regard of the law for private property, that it will not authorize the least violation of it; no, not even for the general good of the whole community." The substance of that view was affirmed by the Supreme Court as late as 1922.

In declaring the ends for which governments exist, had Judge Van Orsdel forgotten to include the pursuit of happiness, the protection of man's unalienable rights, and the promotion of the general welfare? So far as I am aware, no other judge had ever stated so boldly the priority of property over all other rights. In an earlier case, to which I shall presently refer, the Court had based its decision on the same principle, but it had done so in language that was less objectionable. I have quoted from Judge Van Orsdel's decision in the *Adkins* case because that principle, stated so blatantly, has been honored by the Court with a consistency that Justice Marshall would have applauded.

In a wide range of cases, adjudicated during the decades after the Civil War and culminating in three landmark cases in 1895, the Court used its sovereign power to protect vested interests in property at the expense of the general welfare, and, in one notorious case, at the expense of the rights of man granted in the Fifth Amendment. In one case, however, the Court honored the civil liberties guaranteed in the First Amendment. In 1867 it declared unconstitutional a state law that required clergymen to declare, under oath, that they had not given aid to the Confederacy, and also declared unconstitutional an act of Congress that required a similar oath from lawyers. However, the nullified law was directed against confederates, not subversives, but even so, the decision was by a bare majority of five to four. According to one historian of the Court, Fred Rodell, in his *Nine Men*, that decision is remarkable because it is one of only "three instances in the Court's entire history where the ultimate power of judicial review, in the veto of a Congressional law, has been clearly and significantly used in behalf of civil liberties."

After the long and distinguished tenure of Justice Marshall and Justice Taney, the Court was led by such undistinguished chiefs as Salmon P. Chase, Morrison R. Waite, and Melville W. Fuller. Indeed, it is a regrettable fact that, in the long history of the Court, from 1790 to 1930, less than a dozen chief justices had the range of learning, philosophic detachment, and judicial temperament that the nation has the right to expect of men who interpret the Constitution and wield the ultimate power. When the Court's decisions tended to favor property rights at the expense of human rights and general welfare, these few justices, because of their very competence, were invariably in the minority. Thus the most celebrated among them, Justice Holmes, achieved a sort of immortality as the great dissenter. In the exercise of judicial review, "America's original contribution to the science of law," it was inevitable that he and his accomplished associates should be remembered as the Court's scolding dissenters, for it is well known that, in the hurly-burly of politics, where power and spoils rather than the common welfare are the ends striven for, presidents tend to elevate to the supreme tribunal not legal scholars and philosophic minds but practical men who may be trusted to support their political views.

During the last four decades of the last century, when railroad barons and other tycoons of the gilded age exercised the decisive influence on government, the majority of men appointed to the Supreme Court had achieved reputations as attorneys for railroads and corporate enterprise. Both Fuller and Waite, as well as most of their associates, had been successful railroad lawyers. The influence that they exerted on the Court's decisions was revealed in *Santa Clara County* v. *Southern Pacific Railroad* decided in 1886. At issue was the constitutionality of a California law that imposed a higher rate of taxation on corporations than on individuals. Declaring that a corporation was also a person, the Court ruled that, as such, it came within the protection of the due process clause of the Fourteenth Amendment— "nor shall any state deprive any person of life, liberty, or property without due process of law." The California law was therefore unconstitutional. Samuel Miller, one of the distinguished justices alluded to above, who did not agree that property rights are prior to human rights, was so out of patience with his railroad lawyer brethren that he declared, with more integrity than tact, "It is vain to contend with judges who have been, at the bar, the advocates of railroad companies, and all the forms of associated capital, when they are called upon to decide cases where such interests are in contest. All their training, all their feelings are from the start in favor of those who need no such influence."

It was unfortunate that Justice Miller's learned and dissenting voice was no longer in the Fuller Court in 1895; in that one year the Court's decisions in three notorious cases established the complete triumph of the view that of the three fundamental principles for which governments exist—the protection of life, liberty, and property— "the chief of these is property." In one of these, *Pollock* v. *Farmer's Loan and Trust Company,* the Court declared unconstitutional the income tax law of 1894 that imposed a flat two percent tax on all incomes above four thousand dollars. In his argument against the law, counsel warned that, "If you approve this law, with its iniquitous exemption of four thousand dollars, and this communistic march goes on and five years hence a statute comes to you with an exemption of twenty thousand dollars and a tax of twenty percent upon all having incomes in excess of that amount, how can you meet it in view of the decision which my opponents ask you to render?" Then, in language that Judge Van Orsdel was to repeat more brazenly later in the *Adkins* case, he continued: "One of the fundamental objects of all civilized governments—we are informed—was the preservation of the rights of private property. I have thought that it was the very keystone of the arch upon which all civilized government rests, and that this once abandoned, everything was at stake and in danger." Well, it was not abandoned; in order to bring the most equitable of all tax laws within the intents of the Constitution, an amendment was required—the Sixteenth, ratified in 1913.

In the second of the three cases decided that year, *United States* v. *E. C. Knight Company,* the Court emasculated the recently passed Sherman Anti-Trust Law, "an act to protect trade and commerce against unlawful restraints and monopolies." The defendant, in the first real test of the Anti-Trust Law, was a sugar refining company. Chief Justice Fuller, speaking for the majority, conceded that the company, by buying up the stock of four other companies, had "acquired nearly complete control of the manufacture of refined sugar within the United States." However, drawing a surprising distinction between commerce and manufacture, he ruled that Congress, under the Constitution, could regulate the one but not the other, and that, therefore, the company's monopoly of sugar refining did not come within the prohibition of the Anti-Trust Law. Thus, once again, in a decision that encouraged manufacturing monopolies for another decade, vested interest in property prevailed at the expense of the general welfare.

In *re Debs,* the third of three cases decided in 1895, vested interests in property triumphed at the expense of civil rights guaranteed in the Fifth and Fourteenth Amendments: No person shall be "deprived of life, liberty, or property, without due process of law." In the Pullman railway strike in 1894, a federal judge in Chicago issued an injunction against Eugene V. Debs, leader of the railway union, ordering him to "desist and refrain from obstructing or stopping" the business of the railroads by any means whatever (including persuasion) or go to jail. Debs applied to the Supreme Court for a writ of habeas corpus. The writ was denied and Debs went to jail. The federal court had not granted him a jury trial as required by the Constitution and had acted without congressional authority. Nevertheless, Justice Brewer, speaking for the majority, "claimed for the federal judiciary the right to send men to jail, however, arbitrarily" in order to protect interstate commerce. Six decades later, Justice William O. Douglas, commenting on the *Debs* case, noted that the claim to judicial supremacy in that case "was made on behalf of vested interests that were callous to human rights."

Justice William O. Douglas, as a fearless defender of human rights particularly during the last twenty years of his tenure, followed the tradition of

Holmes and Brandeis, his immediate predecessors on the Court, and Hugo Black and Frank Murphy, his then associates. Had five such men dominated the Court from the beginning, there is no doubt whatever that the American judiciary would have established an exemplary record in the defense of civil liberties. Of the five, Douglas was the most blunt and the most unorthodox—appropriately so, as a man of the rugged mountains of the Pacific Northwest where he was more at home than in the salons of the East. Had he been born a decade later, I might now claim the privilege of having been his debate coach, for he achieved distinction as a debater in the college in which I began my academic career a few years after he had graduated. Had he been on the Court in the late twenties, he might very well have found a way to save Bartolomeo Vanzetti and Nicola Sacco from the electric chair. To their celebrated case I now turn my attention.

I turn to it for the reason that my study of the judicial process in that case, a proceeding that dragged on for seven years and three months, was a part of my political education. Furthermore, the defeat of human rights in that case added significantly to my disillusionment. After I had carefully examined the record of the trial and subsequent proceedings, I was convinced that Sacco and Vanzetti were the victims of a miscarriage of justice unparalleled in the annals of criminal law in America, and that, as Justice Douglas said of the *Debs* case, their execution was the ultimate triumph of political prejudice and "vested interests that were callous to human rights."

The two men were charged with murder on May 5, 1920, and they were executed on August 22, 1927. I followed the course of their trial and subsequent proceedings. Since the case was tried in Massachusetts, and not thoroughly reported in the press of the Pacific Northwest as in that of the East, I did not have access to the entire record until near the end of the twenties. In March, 1927, Felix Frankfurter published a detailed analysis of the case in the *Atlantic Monthly,* an essay that was soon thereafter expanded into a book titled *The Sacco-Vanzetti Case.* In 1928, Marion Denman Frankfurter and Gardner Jackson published *The Letters of Sacco and Vanzetti,* and in 1928 to 1929, Henry Holt and Company published the complete record of the case in six volumes. Other distinguished writers, such as John Dos Passos and Howard Fast, also published books on the case, but I read only *The Letters* and Frankfurter's carefully documented essay. On the basis of my study I reached the conclusion stated above. I became both intellectually and emotionally involved in the case that had, by that time, become an international cause célèbre. Furthermore, I became aware of the urgency and steadfast determination with which the conscience of America had raised its voice, unhappily in vain, in behalf of Sacco and Vanzetti. Anyone who reads the record with a mind free of all prejudice and bias, cannot escape the conclusion that the charge of murder for which Sacco and Vanzetti were tried was a mere pretext for sending them to the electric chair because they were outspoken radicals, agitators, and twice damned because they were marked by the Justice Department as alien agitators.

As to the facts and the single issue agreed on at the trial: On April 15, 1920, a paymaster and a guard of the Slater and Morril shoe factory in South Braintree, Massachusetts, were killed and robbed. The money taken by the murderers was approximately $16 thousand. On May 5, Sacco and Vanzetti were arrested; they were indicted on September 14, and put on trial May 21, 1921, at Dedham, Norfolk County, Massachusetts, with Judge Webster Thayer presiding. The killing of the paymaster and the guard was undisputed. The only issue was the identity of the murderers. Were Sacco and Vanzetti two of the several men who committed the crime? On this issue a mass of conflicting evidence was presented to the jury. The trial lasted about seven weeks, and on July 14, 1921, the jury returned a verdict of guilty of murder in the first degree. On April 9, 1927, a sentence of death was pronounced on the men by Judge Thayer; four months later, on August 22, Sacco and Vanzetti were executed.

Immediately after the verdict, an application was made for a new trial, based on exceptions properly taken to various rulings made by Judge Thayer during the trial. The request was denied. Subsequently a mass of new evidence was found by the defense and urged in support of further motions for a new trial. At this juncture in the proceedings there was a change in defense counsel. The attorneys who had conducted the defense and argued the first motions were dismissed, and William G. Thompson, a lawyer of great ability and a highly respected member of the Boston Bar, entered the case. It was he who argued the later motions in October and November 1923. Once again Judge Thayer denied the request.

In September, 1926, the judge was again asked to grant the defendants a new trial. The basis of this request was a confession by Celestino Madeiro that he had committed the crime as a confederate of a gang of professional criminals, a confession substantially supported by evidence gathered by the defense. Alleged also in the motion for a new trial was Judge Thayer's prejudice against the defendants. All motions denied, an appeal was made to the supreme court of Massachusetts. On April 5, 1927, that tribunal ruled that it found no ground, as a matter of law, for reversing Judge Thayer. Because of the limited scope of judicial review in Massachusetts, that court could not inquire, as the New York Court of Appeals and the English court of criminal appeal could have, whether the facts as set forth in the printed record justified the verdict. Thus, with the verdict not subject to review, the end had apparently been reached for resort to the courts, and a sentence of death by electrocution was accordingly pronounced.

An appeal was now made for executive clemency. Governor Alvan T. Fuller made a private investigation. On June 1, 1927, he appointed the president of Harvard, the president of the Massachusetts Institute of Technology, and Judge Robert Grant, as an advisory committee. On August 3, the governor, and on August 7, the committee announced their adverse decisions.

During the remaining three weeks before the execution, a number of influential citizens submitted to the governor evidence of Judge Thayer's prejudice against Sacco and Vanzetti because of their anarchistic views. Arthur D. Hill of the Boston Bar also submitted proof of Thayer's prejudice to both state and federal courts. By direction of Chief Justice Hall of the superior court, the issue of Judge Thayer's prejudice was brought before Judge Thayer himself, and Judge Thayer ruled that he had been without prejudice. As a last resort, proof of prejudice was made the basis for an appeal to Justice Holmes and Justice Stone of the United States Supreme Court, and to Judges Anderson and Morton of the lower federal courts. For one technical reason or another, none of which would have bothered Justice Douglas, the eminent jurists refused to intervene, and Sacco and Vanzetti were executed shortly after midnight on August 22, 1927.

That was the end of the ordeal of two immigrants who had come to the new land, not in search of bread, of which, according to the record, their families in Italy had an abundance, but for the enjoyment of the rights of man which the colonies had declared to all mankind in 1776. It was not, however, the end of the worldwide protest against that incredible miscarriage of justice in the proud commonwealth of Massachusetts. Should anyone doubt the quality and quantity of that unsparing criticism, let him examine what was published, not by fanatic partisans, but by respectable Americans, whose devotion to the fundamental law no one dared challenge, during the last stages of the trial and in the years thereafter. Even the recent historian of the Supreme Court Fred Rodell, writing more than a quarter of a century after the execution, makes this passing reference to the case and its most scholarly critic: Felix Frankfurter's "courageous and compendious defense of the murder-convicted anarchists, Sacco and Vanzetti, as victims of gross judicial injustice, made him a liberal hero, but did not prevent his being offered, a few years later, a seat on the stodgy Supreme Court of Massachusetts—which he declined."

In order to understand, or at least to have some sense of, the character of the defendants, one must read: (1) their letters, many written the day before their execution, and all of these brief but dignified expressions of gratitude addressed to men and women who had exhausted all available means to procure for them a fair trial; (2) their address to the court immediately preceding Judge Thayer's pronouncement of the death sentence; (3) Vanzetti's letter to Governor Fuller, and the *Statement* he dictated to the attorney, William Thompson, a few hours before the execution. All of these were happily included by Jackson and Frankfurter in their book, *The Letters of Sacco and Vanzetti*. The *Statement* was also published in *The Atlantic Monthly* for February 1928 and reprinted in *The New Republic*.

In my summary of the case I have given only the procedural facts; for it was primarily on the procedural impropriety that the various requests for a new trial were based. But even on the basis of so brief an account as I have given, with no attempt to edit or color the facts or question the validity of the grossly conflicting testimony of the identifying witnesses, and of other evidence introduced by the commonwealth in its attempt to pin the crime on the defendants, one cannot seriously doubt that Sacco and Vanzetti were denied the opportunity to establish their innocence. Indeed, it seems incredible that both federal and state supreme courts and Governor Fuller and his advisory committee, so urgently requested by a number of influential citizens, would not permit so reputable a member of the Boston Bar as William G. Thompson, to submit to a jury the new and convincing evidence of his clients' innocence. Incredible, but true. When these final appeals were made, Frankfurter's analysis had been published. Why did the conclusions of so eminent a legal scholar fail to persuade the governor and his advisory committee that, as a matter of elementary justice, Sacco and Vanzetti should be granted a new trial? I raise but make no attempt to answer this question.

On the issue of their guilt or innocence, I offer the following excerpts from Frankfurter's analysis: "Hitherto the methods pursued by the prosecution, which explain the convictions, rested on inferences, however compelling. But recently facts have been disclosed, and not denied by the prosecution, to indicate that the case against these Italians for murder was part of a collusive effort between the district attorney and the agents of the Department of Justice to rid the country of Sacco and Vanzetti because of their Red activities. . . . Hitherto the defense has maintained that the circumstances of the case all pointed away from Sacco and Vanzetti. But the deaths of Parmenter and Berardelli (the paymaster and the guard) remain unexplained. Now the defense has adduced new proof, not only that Sacco and Vanzetti did *not* commit the murders, but also, *positively,* that a well-known gang of professional criminals *did* commit them. Now a new trial has been demanded because an impressive body of evidence tends to establish the guilt of others." Of the attorney William G. Thompson, who entered the case in October 1923, he has this to say: "The espousal of the Sacco-Vanzetti cause by a man of Mr. Thompson's professional prestige at once gave it a new complexion and has been its mainstay ever since. For he has brought to the case, not only his great ability as a lawyer, but the strength of his conviction that these two men are innocent and that their trial was not characterized by those high standards which are the pride of Massachusetts justice."

The frequently repeated declaration of their innocence was stated thus by Vanzetti: "I am not only innocent of these two crimes, but in all my life I have never stolen and I have never killed and I have never spilled blood." And their attorney, William Thompson, at the conclusion of the *Statement* he had taken from Vanzetti a few hours before the execution, has this to say: "I was impressed by the strength of Vanzetti's mind, and by the extent of his reading and knowledge. He did not talk like a fanatic. Although intensely convinced of the truth of his own views, he was still able to listen with calmness and with understanding to the expression of views with which he did not agree. In this closing scene the impression of him which had been gaining ground in my mind for three years was deepened and confirmed—that he was a man of powerful mind, and unselfish disposition, of seasoned character, and of devotion to high ideals. There was no sign of breaking down or of terror at approaching death. At parting he gave me a firm clasp of the hand and a steady glance, which revealed unmistakably the depth of his feeling and the firmness of his self-control . . . I then turned to Sacco . . . He rose from his cot, referred feelingly though in a general way to some points of disagreement between us in the past, said he hoped that our differences of opinion had not affected our personal relations, thanked me for what I had done for him, showed no sign of fear, shook hands with me firmly, and bade me goodbye. His manner was also one of absolute sincerity. It was magnanimous in him not to refer more specifically to our previous differences of opinion, because at the root of it all lay his conviction, often expressed to me, that all efforts on his behalf, either in court or with public authorities, would be useless, because no capitalistic society could afford to accord him justice. I had taken the contrary view; but at this last meeting he did not suggest that the result seemed to justify his view and not mine."

Whether it seemed to justify or actually did justify Sacco's conclusion may be debatable. What is not debatable is the fact that, in that particular instance, a sovereign state in a capitalistic society had not accorded him justice. There is some reason to doubt that, given the temper of the times, any other state would have accorded total justice to Sacco and Vanzetti in the early twenties. The World War had not made "the world safe for democracy," as President Wilson had promised. The behavior of the victors at the peace conference, bickering over the division of the spoils, tended to generate widespread disillusionment, and the success of the Russian Revolution encouraged an intensification of activities by all species of radicals. The threat which these posed to the status quo, real or imaginary, was met in the several nations by a variety of repressive measures against all radical agitators. Particularly in America, the intolerance of heretical views reached a peak of hysterical intensity during the three years following the war. With the approval of President Wilson, the more surprising since he was a liberal, Postmaster General Burleson continued his wartime surveillance of the press and the mails. The state of New York expelled socialists from its legislature. Many of the states enacted a variety of antiradical laws. Beginning in the fall of 1919, the date of the Centralia Massacre, Attorney General Mitchel Palmer launched his war on the Reds. Proceeding as if the Bill of Rights were not a part of the fundamental law, he "arrested suspected persons wholesale, permitting the use of provocative agents to stir up 'seditious meetings,' insisting on the deportation of aliens rounded up by detectives from the Department of Justice, and tolerating, if not authorizing, constant resort to the third degree," as C. Beard has written. In a single day, January 2, 1920, he carried out raids in thirty-three cities and took 2700 persons into custody. In the spring of that year, in the state of Massachusetts, his agents, in collaboration with the local police, simply added two others to his long list of Reds brought to trial for their outspoken heresy.

Indeed, when Sacco and Vanzetti were arrested, May 5, 1920, "they were not confronted with the charge of murder; they were not accused of banditry; they were not given the remotest intimation that the murders of Parmenter and Berardelli were laid at their door. They were told that they were arrested as suspicious characters" and questioned about their radical views. Vanzetti was scheduled to speak at a public meeting a few days hence. Two of their friends had been recently deported. A third was held incommunicado by the Department of Justice. On the day of their arrest, fearing that they themselves and other associates were about to be apprehended, they had been engaged in gathering and hiding subversive literature. Thus, since they knew themselves innocent of other crimes, they assumed that they were being arrested for their radical activities. Had they been charged with publicly professing their anarchistic views, of which they were clearly guilty, they might have had their day in court and been deported and soon forgotten. The grave error made by the prosecution was in charging them with murder; there were too many people who knew them well and who were convinced, from the very beginning, that they were innocent of that crime. These organized the defense committee. As the trial dragged on and doubt of their guilt began to approach a conviction of their innocence, men of the integrity of William G. Thompson joined the defense, and the conservative *Boston Herald,* initially opposed to the defendants, made a frank reversal of its position. Furthermore, influential people throughout the world offered their moral and material support. Thus, because of that mistaken prosecutorial strategy, the case of Sacco and Vanzetti became "one of those rare causes célèbres which are of international concern."

My own involvement in the case, once I had studied the record, was little else than that of an indignant censor of the gross judicial injustice that had denied the two men an opportunity to prove their innocence. However, what had affected me profoundly was the fact that the conscience of America had been outraged and come to the aid of two humble immigrants, one a fish peddler and the other a cobbler. That fact in itself was as much a part of the reality as the gross injustice that had sent two men to the electric chair. What is the conscience of America? Is it not now, and has it not always been, that innate sense of decency, essentially religious, that requires of men and women an unwavering fidelity to the American Dream? And what of the dream itself, to which I have so often referred in this narrative? It is not a rhetorical abstraction, a fanciful vision conjured by dreamers in their ivory tower. It is something concrete, unequivocal, the concept of the unalienable rights of man, derived from a higher law, agreed upon in council, and proclaimed as the cornerstone of the fundamental law. In the conscience of America, it is the ever-present awareness of this as the end and goal of all legitimate governments, of our government, our Republic. As such, it has always had its uncompromising advocates, from those among the founding fathers who declared it to all mankind in 1776, to their heirs in the successive administrations and generations down to the present day.

Those advocates were there, convincingly present, in Norfolk County, Massachusetts, doing their utmost to keep the dream alive. They were the conscience of America, symbolically present in William G. Thompson, a man worthy to be its symbol. Having exhausted all avenues to judicial remedy he withdrew his counsel from the case but did not abandon Sacco and Vanzetti. He sought other means to prevent their execution and remained with them up to the time that they were strapped to the electric chair. His presence in their cell, with death at the door, when he could do no more than record their last words and give them his hand in friendship was an agonizing experience he could have easily avoided. But he did not. He was there, in the fullness of his integrity, symbolically there as the conscience of America, resolute, uncompromising—even though in vain! As so many times in the past, the petty men who were in power and callous to human rights, prevailed over those who kept faith with the dream. Being young, idealistic, and a student who had always revered his great teachers, it seemed to me incredible that the petty Thayers could prevail over such exemplary Americans as Frankfurter and Thompson. But the harsh reality was that they did; and that something in the system made their victory possible. That fact and others added to my disillusionment.

One of these was the landing of U.S. marines in Nicaragua in support of the conservative Adolfo Diaz against the liberal insurrection of Augustino Sandino. Another was the moral and material support of the fascist dictatorship in Italy by the U.S. government and the business community. As debate coach in the college where I began my academic career, I set my young debaters to work on propositions designed to explore the issues raised by such policies. Were they in harmony with the principles of American democracy? Since we had declared to all mankind that all legitimate governments rest on the consent of the governed, were we ever justified in intervening in the internal affairs of another country? Could we, in honor and decency, give aid to the dictatorship of Benito Mussolini who had silenced all opposition, put an end to constitutional government in Italy, and boasted that he had buried "the more or less decomposed body of the Goddess of Liberty?" One may well imagine our answer to these questions.

In our study of the historical background of the intervention in Nicaragua, we had occasion to review the course of American imperialism that had so disillusioned William James and other anti-imperialists. It began on July 20, 1895. England and Venezuela were engaged in a controversy over the boundary between British Guiana and Venezuela. Secretary of State Richard Olney addressed a belligerent note to the British government, stating that British pressure on Venezuela would be regarded by the United States as a violation of the Monroe Doctrine. With blunt arrogance he warned: "Today the U.S. is practically sovereign on this continent, and its fiat is law . . . because, in addition to all other grounds, its infinite resources combined with its isolated position render it master of the situation and practically invulnerable as against any or all other powers."

This was the language of a bully and not of such diplomacy as might have been expected of the heirs of the founding fathers. The implied dependence on power became the established policy of imperial America for the next decade. There is no need to give here a detailed account of what is common knowledge—the war with Spain, the conquest of Cuba and the Philippines, the annexation of Hawaii. What is relevant is that once again the rights of property prevailed over the rights of man and the conscience of America. The leaders of the imperialists were Theodore Roosevelt, Senators Albert Beveridge and Henry Cabot Lodge, and Alfred Thayer Mahan, the persuasive advocate and historian of naval power. These men and their many followers, in and out of government, supplied the rhetoric, the pretexts, and the myth of manifest destiny necessary to establish the nation on an imperialist course and to convince it that the United States must remain "practically sovereign on this continent."

It was by sea power—the building of a navy equal to that of England—that it remained so. "Gridley, you may fire when you are ready." "The American flag is up and it must stay," exclaimed Senator Lodge. "We are a conquering race," boasted Senator Beveridge. It was ironic that the imperialists should be led by Senator Beveridge from Massachusetts, since the principle that governments derive their just powers from the consent of the governed, as set forth in the Declaration, was written for the first time in the constitution of that state and properly recorded in the preamble: "We, the people of Massachusetts, do ordain and establish. . . . " Thus, the principle that governments derive their just powers from the consent of the governed was written into Massachusetts' fundamental law. Seven years later, the framers of the federal Constitution, in writing the preamble, followed the example of Massachusetts: "We the people of the United States . . . do ordain and establish. . . . "

If Henry Cabot Lodge had forgotten or willfully repudiated that principle, other Bostonians had not. Allied against the imperialists were the anti-imperialists, led by such distinguished Americans as Charles William Eliot and Charles Eliot Norton of Harvard, and Speaker Thomas E. Reed in Congress. Among them was also President Cleveland, who had unwittingly set the imperialist course by his Secretary of State's arrogant note to Great Britain. These and their many followers organized the Anti-Imperialist League. They were the keepers of the dream who took the Declaration of Independence seriously and kept faith with the proposition, reaffirmed in the Gettysburg Address, that governments derive their just powers from the consent of the governed. When the "conquering race" had conquered by virtue of its sea power, the anti-imperialists opposed the ratification of the Treaty of Paris unless it specifically excluded the annexation of the Philippines and Puerto Rico. A petition to that effect, signed by ex-President Cleveland, President Eliot of Harvard, and other distinguished Americans, was addressed to the Senate. The plea was in behalf of the dream. Once again, the conscience of America, invariably the defender of human rights, had to yield to vested interests callous to those rights.

For, on their own testimony, what had moved the imperialists to conquest, under the banner of manifest destiny, in the Pacific and the Caribbean, was not the liberation of oppressed people, but land hunger and greed for raw materials and new markets for American manufacturers. If such a blatant departure from American ideals and principles of government had disillusioned such men as William James, Thomas Reed, and Charles Eliot and Charles Norton of Harvard, how could I and my intellectual companions resist disillusionment? We were young and idealistic. We had been taught to keep faith with the dream. We, too, had taken the Declaration seriously. When we reviewed the course of events from the days of Marshall to the present and learned that property rights normally prevailed over the rights of man, how could we avoid wondering whether there might not be something amiss with the system itself that accounted for the triumph of the one over the other? How could we explain the Teapot Dome scandal or the fact that while the judiciary was denying Sacco and Vanzetti the right to prove their innocence in a new trial, the executive branch was giving away chunks of the public domain to vested interests? Our belief in the immutable principles declared to all mankind by the founding fathers was so firmly rooted, however, that we did not despair of finding answers to these questions.

We were now in the first year of the Great Depression. There was hunger in the land of plenty. I had returned to the university to continue my graduate studies and earn my bread as a teaching fellow. As a citizen schooled in the finest traditions of American democracy, a disillusioned but dedicated disciple of the great teachers who had taught me the duties of creative citizenship, what should I do? Should I assume the cynicism of Henry Adams who in the late nineties threw up his hands in despair, declaring that "society today is more rotten than at any other time . . . one vast structure of debt and fraud"? It was not in my nature to be thus cynical, for there was a great deal in that society that was young and vital and sensibly idealistic. What was needed was a strategy that would secure the gradual ascendency of the conscience of America. My Jewish colleague in debate was convinced that there was something in the system itself that accounted for the too-frequent triumph of vested interests over human rights. A book on *The State* by the Marxist Harold Laski had led me to believe that my Jewish friend was probably right. Why not continue my inquiry and attempt to find out for myself? Man must act in accordance with the imperative of conscience and conviction. The founding fathers had acted on such an imperative, and so would I. I thus pursued a course that led to the crisis mentioned earlier in this narrative, and it is to that sad story I now turn my attention.

CHAPTER X

The Great Image of Authority

On April 11, 1912, the "unsinkable" *Titanic* left Southampton on her first transatlantic voyage. Having taken on passengers at Cherbourg and Queenstown, she sailed for New York at 2:00 P.M. on April 11, with 1316 passengers and a crew of 891.

Eleven stories high and four city blocks long, capable of developing a thrust of fifty-five thousand horsepower, built with a double bottom and sixteen watertight compartments, she was the queen of the White Star Line's fleet of transatlantic liners. Built in the Belfast shipyards of Harland and Wolff under the direction of Thomas Andrews, who incorporated into his design the phenomenal technological progress of a century, no one disputed the claim that she was the greatest engineering achievement of all time. Since she could float with any two of her sixteen watertight compartments flooded, she was deemed unsinkable. One of the deck hands, when asked by a lady passenger in whom there remained a trace of doubt, whether the *Titanic* were really unsinkable, replied, "God himself could not sink this ship."

The faith of the lowly in the invulnerability of the ship matched that of the mighty, for there were more passengers in third class than in first and second class combined. Among the latter, some of whom had paid $4500 for the maiden voyage, were such titans of the business world as Guggenheim,

Astor, Ryerson, Strauss, and Rothschild. The builder of the ship and the president of the White Star Line were also aboard. Collectively the human cargo was worth $250 million.

At 9:00 A.M. of April 14, near the end of the third day at sea, the *Caronia* warned of icebergs in the sea lanes ahead. During the next twelve hours, the same warning was repeated by four other ships. None of these was taken seriously by the command of the *Titanic*. By 10:30 P.M., the temperature of the sea had dropped to thirty-one degrees. At 11:00 A.M., the *Californian*, only a few miles away, once again sent a warning message, but the wireless operator of the *Titanic* answered that he was busy and cut her off before she had given the location of the icebergs. Forty minutes later, the razor edge of a mountain of ice cut a fatal three hundred foot gash on her starboard side. Within an hour, five of her watertight compartments were flooded, and, at 2:20 A.M. on April 15, the icy water of the North Atlantic closed over the "unsinkable" *Titanic*.

She carried lifeboats for only one third of her capacity, and these were lowered only partly loaded. Notwithstanding the several warnings relayed to the command, her speed among the floating bergs was a confident twenty-two knots. There had been no boat drills and the launching had been late and confused. Since "God himself could not sink this ship," why prepare for a danger that did not exist? However, of the 2207 men, women, and children aboard, 1502 perished, and the vast majority of the victims were immigrants in steerage bound for the land of promise.

It was in the gloomy early thirties that I read with my students Hanson Baldwin's celebrated essay "R.M.S. Titanic," and as we discussed the dramatic documentation of the narrative, it occurred to me that there were interesting and suggestive parallels between the great disaster at sea in 1912 and the Great Depression of 1929. They were both needless and preventable human tragedies. The root source of each was man's pride in his achievement; this often creates the illusion of infallibility and militates against the prudence that would require adequate planning to avoid possible failure. But icebergs make no allowance whatever for man's pride, and economic policies, once translated into action, have economic consequences. Thus, in the tragedy at sea an indestructible technological structure was destroyed, and in the Great Depression an absolutely sound economic structure collapsed.

The prosperity of America on the eve of the crash was unprecedented in the history of western civilization. Mass production of consumer goods, and the perfection of technological skills had produced a golden age. The value of manufactured products was $1 billion in 1850, $11 billion in 1900, $61 billion in 1923, and $67 billion in 1929. The total national wealth in 1922 was $306 billion and in 1929 it was $353 billion. In 1925 there were 25 million families in America and more than 20 million automobiles, 15 million telephones, and 3 million radio sets—conveniences and luxuries scarcely known to the common man elsewhere. The movie houses had a daily attendance of about 25 million. The silent sage in the White House assured the prosperous citizenry that "the business of America is business." So it was, with two chickens in every pot and a car in every garage. In September 1929 stocks soared to fairyland heights, with the lowly as well as the mighty engaged in the "money-making orgy." With these data as proof, the architects of the golden age were as convinced of its permanence as the builders of the *Titanic* were certain of its unsinkability. Their political agent and prophet was Herbert Hoover. When he accepted the nomination for the presidency in 1928, he declared that, "We in America today are nearer to the final triumph over poverty than ever before in the history of any land. Given a chance to go forward with the policies of the last eight years, we shall soon with the help of God be in sight of the day when poverty will be banished from this nation. . . . No one can deny the fundamental correctness of our economic system."

Faith in this judgment by those who wielded the ultimate power was such that they failed to heed the warnings of economic danger ahead. Economists of the stature of Thorstein Veblen and John Maynard Keynes, who had prophesied the ruinous economic consequences of the Versailles Treaty, warned that the "unprecedented prosperity" rested on insecure foundations. Business profits from 1919 to 1928 had increased by 20 percent, from $55 to $65 billion, and profits on speculation in stocks had increased 300 percent. But the wages of the masses, the major buyers of consumer goods who purchased largely on credit, had increased by only 12 percent. During that decade of prosperity, there were always from three to four million unemployed. The price of wheat had fallen from $2.16 a bushel in 1919 to $1.00 in 1928; farm bankruptcies had increased from 997 in 1920 to 5,679 in 1928. By 1929, construction, manufacture of automobiles, and the purchase of durable consumer goods had begun to decline sharply, while the continuing boom was fed by reckless speculation in securities that had no relation to real wealth.

These warnings of danger were unheeded by the high command as were others even more ominous. When the *Titanic* struck the iceberg that destroyed her, the immediate reaction was that the incident was merely an inconvenience. The word from the ship's command, as it came to the passengers, was: "There is talk of an iceberg. The ship might have to return to Belfast to repair whatever damage may have been done." When on October 24 and 29, 1929, 13 and 16 million shares respectively changed hands in the stock market, the captains of industry dismissed the activity of frightened investors as a temporary panic that would blow over. It did blow, but it was a ruinous hurricane. On November 13, $30 billion in the market value of listed stocks were wiped out. By June 1932, such losses had increased to $75 billion. And yet, President Hoover, speaking for such giants of the business community as J. P. Morgan, Thomas Lamont, John D. Rockefeller, Sr., and Andrew Mellon, refused to budge from his conviction that "the fundamental business of the country, that is, production and distribution, is on a sound and prosperous basis."

When five of her watertight compartments were flooded, the command was obliged to acknowledge that God himself could not now save the "unsinkable" *Titanic*; when in March 1933, nearly four years after the crash, banks were closed by executive order, industrial output was cut in half, one-third of the nation's railroad mileage was thrown into bankruptcy, farm mortgage foreclosures were the order of the day, and fifteen million Americans were unemployed—then all but the most stubborn and self-deluding men of state and business had to admit that what had seemed to be a "temporary panic" was in fact a Great Depression. As in the great disaster at sea, the vast majority of the victims were the poor. Millions were living in "Hoovervilles," and others in what was delicately called "genteel unprosperity." There had been other depressed periods in the nation's economy—in 1873, 1893, 1907, 1921, for example—but none had been a collapse of the magnitude of the Great Depression.

Now the wealthiest nation in the world, the most advanced in the techniques of production, had to ponder seriously the incredible paradox of poverty and starvation in the midst of plenty. It was admitted on all sides that widespread misery was not caused by scarcity and overpopulation. The nation's larders were either full or potentially full. There was talk of overproduction, a sophisticated way of saying that the ten to fifteen million unemployed lacked the means to buy what the nation could produce. In these circumstances, how could one avoid the conclusion that widespread misery was the consequence of a defect in the system itself? Variously called laissez-faire capitalism, production for profit, or rugged individualism, its political and economic votaries were alike bankrupt of diagnosis and remedy when the crash came in 1929. They understood the system so imperfectly that they had failed to see the ominous signs mentioned above. Its most sophisticated and persuasive critics were the advocates of a planned economy—the socialists and the Communists. If they had the answer, why not listen to what they had to say? For this reason I joined the Communist party in the early thirties. I have forgotten the exact date. I chose the Communists rather than the socialists for personal and not ideological reasons.

It was not an act of folly, an ill-considered move prompted by the impatience of youth and an unrealistic idealism. Nor was it prompted by narrow, selfish motives. I was employed throughout the depression and living well enough. And as for keeping bread on the table: What I had learned about the craft of survival as a boy in a land of scarcity stood me in good stead in a land of abundance. I was able to take the Great Depression in stride, with rabbits in the backyard, a kitchen garden, and the resources of the forest.

Nor was my joining the party a commitment to an ideology imperfectly understood and accepted with the fervor of a fanatic. Certain of my companions and I who made that decision sought knowledge and not a pat ideology. As I have tried to explain during the course of this narrative, we had been taught to reason well in all matters, to have respect for the facts, to disabuse our minds of all facile prejudices, and to search for the truth—to seek for the solution of social problems in accordance with the inductive method and to accept whatever hypothesis came nearest to accounting for all the facts. As novitiates in the academy, we taught our students the sound methodology we had been taught; we were interested, informed, and critical participants in the political life of the community as we had been taught to be. Furthermore, we were the heirs and disciples of such noted liberals of the late nineteenth and early twentieth centuries as John Dewey, J. Allen Smith,

Charles A. Beard, Charles Norton and Charles Eliot of Harvard, and Vernon Louis Parrington, one of our great teachers. We had accepted their liberalism, not so much in the spirit of obedience to revered masters, but because their criticism of the course of American political and economic history had stood the test of reason. Above all else, we had kept faith with the American Dream as we understood it.

Thus, we were, in a very important sense, true conservatives rather than radicals, for we sought to conserve the finest American political traditions as declared to all mankind by the founding fathers. In order to make these traditions living realities as the ethical basis of American life, we were willing to compromise, to experiment, to regard the fundamental law as a means of implementing the rights it declared—to reject legal precedents that militated against the general welfare and to surrender, if necessary, the "dogma that property is to be the master of political power." In our support of the unionization of labor, our opposition to the use of the injunction in labor disputes, and our conviction that "freedom of contract begins only where equality of bargaining power begins also," we were in accord with the conservatism of Justice Holmes rather than with the regressive views of Justice Marshall. In brief, our conservatism was such that, in order to preserve the best that was implicit in the American Dream, it required the extension of the democratic processes to the economic sphere. For a genuine conservatism in politics, as the conservative Edmund Burke had warned, is as well "an ability to improve as a disposition to preserve."

However, the men who wielded the ultimate power were unwilling to make these accommodations to the urgencies in the decades immediately following World War I. Either they did not know, or failed to take seriously, the profoundly humane but thoroughly practical principles of government written into the Declaration and the Constitution. One could not help but wonder how much of the unique and creative early history of this extraordinary land such men as John D. Rockefeller and James J. Hill actually knew. In any case, whether they either did not know the principles or failed to take them seriously, it was unfortunate that such men should have been at the center of power during the four decades preceding the Great Depression. They had no constructive philosophy of government, a fact well established by the collapse that was the consequence of their political and economic policies. They and their associates in government operated on the unwarranted assumption that their prosperity and the welfare of the nation were identical. Thus, they pressed their enormous advantage, by whatever means proved effective, to prevent labor from unionizing and matching their power at the bargaining table. They exploited child labor and opposed a child labor amendment. They secured high protective tariffs and opposed a tax on income. At the time of the Great Depression they had successfully resisted the enactment of such social services as are now provided for in the Social Security Act, and which are now a part of the American system.

In the three decades following the Civil War, these views and policies, which were essentially petty rationalizations for greed, may have had some relevance to the hurly-burly of what Mark Twain called the gilded age, but in the twenties and thirties they were definitely regressive. We deplored the fact that they should have prevailed. In the decade of the twenties, the nation was in its Indian summer, a period of much needed reassessment and renovation. After the immense harvest of the preceding half century, attended by shameful waste that was aggravated by the World War, America needed a political and economic philosophy rooted in the assumption that the two necessities of the new era were conservation and a more even distribution of purchasing power. It was known then, though unfortunately not as widely and conclusively as it is known now, that the stock of irreplaceable natural resources was running low. Meanwhile, business prosperity had not sufficiently increased the purchasing power of the many. After the decades of wasteful exploitation of natural resources, with wealth concentrated in the hands of the few exploiters, the era of prudent management of the nation's entire economy had inevitably arrived. What was urgently needed was a sound and ethically oriented statesmanship in the economy and in government. Unfortunately, we embarked on the decade on the Harding-Coolidge-Mellon assumption that "the business of America is business." Toward the end of the decade, the best that their successor in the White House could offer was a continuation "of the policies of the last eight years." Soon thereafter the result of those policies brought the nation's economy to the brink of ruin.

Yet, in fact, what ruin was threatened? Was it not a fact that all we had to fear was fear itself? As I have already noted, I, personally, did not despair of keeping bread on the table. Living in the spacious and prodigal northwest, with the resources at hand mentioned above, skilled by heredity in stretching a dime to its ultimate limits, I could never take the Great Depression, viewed as a crisis that threatened my bread, quite as seriously as my bourgeois contemporaries. What alarmed them initially was the fact that it was "a sudden stop to the gluttony of the boom" twenties. But I had known penury and real scarcity; for that reason even the severely curtailed menu of the depression years seemed an abundance. What alarmed me primarily was the fact that the system had produced a spurious gluttony and promised more than it could deliver. As for bread on the table, I have never forgotten having seen a man on relief buying a dozen oranges with his food stamps. Oranges were luxuries, not necessities. When I was a child in Italy I considered myself lucky if I got an orange once a year, at Christmas.

For these reasons I was able to see from the very beginning that the abundance we had before the crash was absolutely unimpaired after the crash. The newspapers announced the "loss" of fifteen, thirty, seventy-five billion dollars. Not really. What was lost was the "market value of listed stocks," for the most part fictitious paper value. What money was "lost" had not been lost at all; it had merely changed hands. The nation's capital goods, its raw materials, vast resources of land, its technological skills, its looms and forges and network of railways—these were all precisely as they had been before the crash. Nothing was really lost. The nation's larders were full. Sooner or later we would get to them. This fact came home to me with such force that I accepted as an absolute truth the statement that all we had to fear was fear itself.

I was encouraged in this view by the fact that the various recovery plans proposed by the experts were all based on the assumption that our land was still the land of plenty, that we were plagued not by scarcity but abundance. The Townsend Plan, the Swope Plan, the various types of planned economy and collectivism, Production for Use, the New Deal itself—all of these were proposed ways of getting the people to the nation's larders. In other words, as a distinguished economist put it, "a more even distribution of purchasing power is essential to the maintenance of prosperity and the preservation of economic stability." A planned economy. Production for use rather than for profits. These were the realistic imperatives, the rational, effective ways of achieving a "more even distribution of purchasing power." The intelligence that had produced the greatest productive machine of all time must now be used to create the most equitable system of distribution of all time. We had the intelligence and we had the resources. So what, in real fact, was lost?

These proposals were not new. They were included in the unheeded utopias of the past. More recently, in 1892, the Socialist Labor Party had gone to the electorate with the proposition that, "Man cannot exercise his right of life, liberty, and the pursuit of happiness without the ownership of land and tools with which he works." The proposal was bold and it may have been sound and realistic, but it was premature. While we were then well into the panic of 1892, no one listened to the visionary socialists. Now, however, the Great Depression charged these radical proposals with a new persuasiveness. And there was talk of "the coming revolution." Not among the "proletarians," the masses who were the principal victims of the Great Depression. There was, in fact, no proletariat in America, no union of wage earners more or less aware of the class struggle and of itself as the exploited class. The word itself was an abstraction imported from class-conscious Europe, where Marx was something more than a "dull German philosopher with a beard."

There was, however, in the America of the thirties, a reality of which the term was descriptive—the mass of wage earners, unemployed or threatened with unemployment, who were the principal victims of the crash. But there was no talk among them of "the coming revolution." Indeed, a most amazing phenomenon of the Great Depression was the stolid patience with which the people who suffered most by the collapse endured the common misery. They had known depressions and panics before, and the system had always somehow corrected itself. The current depression seemed to make them inert with unbelief that anything of such unaccustomed gravity could happen so unexpectedly. There were no demonstrations in the early thirties, no marches against the citadel of power, no mass movement of wage earners united on a platform of radical change. These were to come later. By tradition and habit, steeped in the myth of rags to riches, the masses were basically loyal to the acquisitive society. A visual document of the Great Depression, widely circulated, tells the whole story: A man and a woman, in the bitter cold of winter and bundled in overcoats that had seen better days, are selling apples on the street at a nickel apiece. With winter at hand, could spring be far behind? In other countries, such as Italy and India, the man and woman would be begging; here, victims of the collapse of capitalism, were selling for profit. Just as the Republican administration, the masses "were waiting for nothing more drastic than the return of prosperity." It was by no means certain that Hoover would not be reelected in 1932.

If the masses were biding their time and waiting for the return of prosperity, where was the talk of the coming revolution? It was precisely where it had always been historically when societies were ready for a radical change of an epochal nature—among the intellectuals. John Ball had prepared and led the peasants in the revolt of 1381; Tom Paine, Sam Adams, Thomas Jefferson, and other intellectuals had planned and led the revolution of 1776; and, more recently, without Lenin and his select associates there would have been no Russian revolution. Thus, early in the critical thirties, the center of revolutionary ferment was among the intellectuals in the nation's academies, publishing houses, salons of Park Avenue, and studios of Hollywood. For it was to them—the critical observers of the current scene, the men and women who knew history, who were not easily deceived by appearances, who perceived that we were in a crisis of unprecedented gravity—that the Great Depression appeared the last twitch and spasm of moribund capitalism from which we could only be saved by unprecedented radical measures.

The intellectuals perceived also that the crisis was worldwide. The World War, the greed-inspired Treaty of Versailles, and our heavy investments in Europe had completely eroded the last vestiges of isolationism. A fundamental economic derangement anywhere in the western world had repercussions everywhere. The economy of every major country was tottering. In Italy and Germany a dictatorship of the right had saved capitalism and destroyed democracy. Mussolini and Hitler were intervening in Spain on behalf of their brand of dictatorship under Francisco Franco. In Russia the revolution seemed to be progressing toward its promised goal. Bernard Shaw had visited Moscow and returned full of praise for what the Russians had achieved and for what they planned for the future. Sidney and Beatrice Webb had come out of retirement in their seventies and gone to the USSR to crown their great achievement as social scientists with a definitive study of—*A New Civilization?* The brutal Moscow trials had not yet been staged (that *is* the proper word) and Stalin had not yet revealed the fullness of his evil nature.

In these circumstances, the imperative in America was to proceed from a collapsed capitalism to a planned society, an economy of production for use rather than for profits. To achieve that worthy goal, revolutionary changes of a socialist nature were required in the nation's economy. The alternative and the danger was fascism, for in the early thirties there was substantial basis for faith in the Russian experiment. Such, in brief, was the view of the revolutionary intellectuals. It is no part of my intention to second guess their analysis and pass judgment on the diagnosis and the cure. I simply record it as the stark reality of the early thirties, the total ambiance and combination of influences that induced me, and certain of my companions, to pursue our inquiry as creative citizens in the direction I have indicated. The center of revolutionary ferment was in small intellectual worlds such as we inhabited. The logic of our lives as intellectuals, our preoccupation with the rights of man, and the dream with which we had studiously kept faith, were strong imperatives to us to pursue any line of inquiry that promised a way out of the absurd circumstance of starvation in the midst of plenty.

For the record, however, this analysis of the intellectuals, which we accepted, was essentially correct. The danger latent in fascism exploded into war. What we had not foreseen was the Nazi-Soviet Pact that strengthened Hitler's hand. We had, however, foreseen that fascism would eventually attempt to destroy its arch enemy, the Soviet Union; we were not surprised when Hitler double-crossed Stalin and invaded Russia in June 1941. Only fools could have been fooled by the Nonaggression Pact. At home, the New Deal, taken in its entirety, was revolutionary *only* if Hoover's political and economic philosophy were taken as the norm. And yet, though it did considerable immediate good, it was not revolutionary enough. Starvation in the midst of plenty could not be eliminated by destroying food and curtailing production as a means of raising prices. The depth of the Great Depression was reached after two years of the New Deal. What eventually brought the depression to an end was not revolutionary change in the economic structure but World War II. Thus, we achieved a temporary, artificial recovery by the destruction occasioned by a World War II. In order to prevent World War III—or to assure victory should it explode upon us—that unhealthy recovery would be extended indefinitely into the future. The end of the depression did not necessarily mean the end of the crisis, for as late as the eve of the 1976 presidential elections, the state of the economy was not very encouraging. There were still about eight million people unemployed, the purchasing value of the dollar was about half what it had been ten years before, and the expert economists had not found a cure for the inflationary spiral. The need for conservation of all nonrenewable resources, including land, was more urgent than it had been years earlier. Protection of the total environment from pollution, the need for which no one denies, presented problems that were but vaguely perceived in the thirties—if at all. With the supply of fossil fuels running critically low, the use of nuclear energy presented grave problems that could not be solved along party lines. Such were some of the economic realities about ten years ago, and they constituted more urgent imperatives for a planned economy than existed in the thirties.

So much for the record. I return now to the revolutionary intellectuals produced by the crisis, with whom we made common cause in pursuing any line of inquiry that promised a way out of the absurdity of starvation in the midst of plenty.

From the crisis of the thirties, there came into being, as if its immediate and necessary cause, a new generation of revolutionary writers. As testimony to the fact that the crisis was worldwide and spiritual as well as political and economic, the three writers who produced works of permanent literary value were a Frenchman, an Italian, and an American—André Malraux, Ignazio Silone, and John Steinbeck. The three were roughly the same age. Malraux published *Man's Fate* in 1933; Silone wrote *Fontamara* in exile in Switzerland in 1930. The two books were published in America in 1934. Steinbeck's *The Grapes of Wrath* was published in 1939.

There is virtual agreement among competent literary critics that, for their revolutionary fervor and excellence as literature, those three books were classic literary achievements of the revolutionary thirties. Of the three, *Fontamara* had an added virtue, for at its conclusion it raised a question that was implicit in the other two and was being asked by an entire generation of men and women who thought seriously about rational ways out of the crisis: *Che dobbiamo fare?* What must we do? And for me it had an added appeal. Its characters were peasants whose misery was an aggravated form of the misery I had known in Casabianca; the narrative dramatized the brutality of fascism, which by now I had come to despise with a passion; and its author had fled the native land for want of freedom as I had fled it for want of bread. My Italian blood warmed to this; for the moment I felt that Silone and I were living in exile, seeking in alien lands what the native land had denied us. Perhaps, after the madness of fascism—it could not possibly last a full generation!—Silone would return to take up the work of reconstruction with the men of the Resistance, and I might go to Italy to see him. I felt certain that this would come to pass. That divinity that shapes our ends had never failed me.

Reading that starkly realistic documentary of what happened to the peasants of Fontamara for having risen against the predators of fascism, I felt a fullness of communion with the author and his characters. The substance of that narrow world I had known as a boy and never forgotten, Silone's creative imagination had forged into a masterpiece of literary art, and he had done it without in any way altering its total integrity. I had not known in Casabianca the brazen cruelty of a dictatorship; that much was shockingly new. But all the rest was there in that deceptively simple narrative: the labor and the misery; the hereditary search for the daily bread on insufficient and exhausted land, rented or perennially mortgaged; the un-Christian church; the isolation of the peasantry from all that constitutes the nation's culture; the patience and the hopelessness inherited and transmitted from one generation to the next; the circumscription of life from birth to death within the few kilometers that could be traversed by foot in a single day. Reading *Fontamara* in the depth of the depression, I blessed once again, as on many occasions past, the day that we left Casabianca forever. America in the depth of the Great Depression was an earthly paradise compared with the many Fontamaras of southern Italy.

Now those tokens of despair that rounded out the lives of the Fontamaresi were aggravated and rendered unbearable by a regime that had justified its seizure of power by the claim that it had saved the country from the savagery of communism. I need not review the various episodes that constitute the novel—the indecencies, indignities, vulgarities, and brutalities inflicted on the peasants by the provincial hierarchs of Mussolini—for I want only to indicate how the question at the end of the novel came to be raised and then press on to other matters. The peasants knew nothing of communism, had never heard of Russia, the proletariat, the class struggle, the rights of man, the various freedoms, or of democracy, monarchy, or dictatorship. These were the concern of the world of the citizens in the flow of history. Being excluded from history and what passes for progress, the peasants were not concerned with what they did not know. Mussolini could have burned all the books and silenced all dissidents by murder, torture, and exile without impinging in any way on the world of the peasants. They had observed the processes of procreation in plants and animals, and they were on intimate terms with the land and had mastered the use of the peasant's tools. Beyond their concern about the ills that mortal flesh is heir to, their entire persistent, perennial preoccupation was with the means necessary to keep bread on the table, and they knew with apodictic certainty the oppression of the landlord and the state when it aggravated their struggle for survival. That was the sum total of their knowledge; all else was myth, superstition, and wild imaginings.

The oppression of the state in the form of taxes and of the landlord in the form of rent, they had known from time immemorial. It had always been severe, but they had borne it with grumbling patience. Their first and only awareness of a new government in Rome was occasioned by an enormous increase in the rate and number of their taxes and by the appearance in their province of a super-landlord, an enterpriser, called the impresario, the provincial political boss, the podesta appointed by Rome. He was now the state made manifest as an insatiable predator, and this is how he brought fascism home to the peasants. We are asked to imagine Fontamara as the poorest and most backward village in a poor region of the Abruzzi in the south of Italy. It is situated on a hillside to the north of the drained bed of lake Fucino, where arable land is scarce, rocky, and arid. As if by a miracle, a small stream flows across that hot, rocky waste. From time immemorial, the scant water of that stream was used by the peasants of Fontamara to irrigate their parched acres. The meager flow of that rivulet, its source in a hillside spring in a land where water was scarce, was their very life's blood; without it, little or nothing would grow on that sunburnt land. Therefore the Fontamaresi regarded the stream with reverence and its flow as being governed by the same law that determined the order of the seasons, a thing of nature, the gift of a merciful God to his poor children of Fontamara.

The impresario, who was rapidly becoming the owner of everything in the region, needed the water of that stream to irrigate land he had recently acquired. Taking advantage of their naïveté and ignorance of the formal language, he tricked the peasants into signing a petition that granted him the right to divert the flow of the stream onto his own land. When they discovered the deceit, the peasants resisted. For insisting on a restoration of what was theirs by a law of nature, they were accused of being communists, anarchists, agitators, and a threat to the state. Armed blackshirts invaded the village, ransacked the houses, raped the women, and thus sought by brutality to purge Fontamara of its arrogance and anarchy. The peasants, however, rebelled, and their village was destroyed. But on the rubble heap of that destruction there came into being an organized resistance to fascism, and a martyr to charge it with moral force. One of their number, who had some notion of the brute realities of the new order, and whose potential for leadership was fully realized in the crisis, gave his life to protect the leader of the underground and publisher of the clandestine press. Thus, by one of the inevitable ironies of history, those who had seized power to destroy a nonexistent communism became the very agents who brought it into being. What professional agitators in Fontamara had never been able to accomplish, fascist brutality accomplished in a few days.

Their village destroyed, their leader slaughtered, their water taken from them, those who had survived the onslaught of the blackshirts were drawn together into a unity, something new in Fontamara. Their common cry became: *Che dobbiamo fare?* "After so much brutality and bloodshed, after so much suffering and so many tears, after so much hatred and despair, *Che dobbiamo fare?*" Thus the book ends.

What must we do? What is to be done? The cry had been raised by Lenin as a rhetorical weapon in urging mass support for the revolution. Tolstoy as Levin, in *Anna Karenina,* had raised substantially the same question, though in a different context, and had it answered by a peasant. What must we do? Why, live for others, for a cause! Sacrifice one's life, if necessary, for the common welfare. At the end of *Fontamara, Che dobbiamo fare?* became a powerful rallying cry. But as a question, it had already been answered by the leader of the peasants who, as Katov in *Man's Fate,* had sacrificed his life for a cause. It was the first time in the chronicles of the peasantry that a simple, unschooled *cafone*—a peasant—had given his life for a cause. And it was the first time in the history of Italian letters that he had been made the hero in a major work of literary art. Can one imagine D'Annunzio or Pirandello, the two best known and most celebrated Italian writers of the first quarter of the twentieth century, writing in the mode of *Fontamara* and about the *cafoni* of southern Italy?

Silone wrote *Fontamara* in exile in 1930. In retrospect it may be regarded as a prelude to the revolutionary literature of the thirties and an inspiration to the new generation of proletarian writers in America—Malcolm Cowley, John Dos Passos, James Farrell, Richard Wright, William Saroyan, Granville Hicks, Sidney Hook, Nelson Algren, Robert Cantwell, Edward Dahlberg, Erskine Caldwell, John Steinbeck, Clifford Odets, and many others. These

writers, uneven in their achievement and most of them now completely forgotten, were born in the first decade of the century and established their literary reputations in the thirties. Nearly all of them came from working class
families and were themselves wage earners and victims of the depression.
Thus their radical militancy was a form of self-expression. Some joined the
Communist party and produced works effective as propaganda but of scant
literary value; others, such as John Steinbeck, served the revolutionary cause
with works of enduring literary merit. All of them found scope for their various talents, their unique opportunity to tell their story in their own way, in
the challenge posed by the crisis. The entrenched Mussolini and the emerg-
ing Hitler were forming an alliance. The Austrian Nazis had crushed the opposition in Austria. Fascism was definitely on the march—toward Poland,
France, Russia. Where would it stop? Could it, indeed, happen here? In the
depth of the depression, a general strike had been called in San Francisco.
There were fifteen million unemployed. *Che dobbiamo fare?*

The question raised so prophetically in *Fontamara* in 1930 became the
rallying cry of the new generation of writers in America. Mussolini and the
other dictators had crushed the opposition and silenced all dissenters; hence
the cry there was muted, a secret cry of the hunted underground. In the
America of the Great Depression there were as yet no repressive measures,
no effective witch hunts. These would come later. But in the confusion and
turbulence and uncertainty of the early thirties, the breadth and depth of dissent was such that a Martin Dies dared not challenge it. The cry was raised in
the noonday brightness of the open forum, and the new generation of revolutionary writers, praised and directed by such influential journals of opinion
as the *New Republic* and the *New Masses* and by such radical critics as John
Chamberlain in the *New York Times,* were united in an unprecedented exercise of all the freedoms granted in the First Amendment. Whereas the writers of the twenties had professed a wistful, modish socialism and remained
cynically aloof from politics and social issues, the writers of the thirties allied
themselves with society and dramatized the cruel realities of the crisis. As
Silone had dramatized the plight of the *cafoni* under fascism, the most
talented of the American novelists of the thirties dramatized the plight of the
Oakies in the Great Depression.

Malcolm Cowley, the most sane, the most balanced, the most perceptive
and influential literary critic of the era, spelled out in his invariably lucid and

forceful manner, the realities that produced the generation of proletarian writers. Their predecessors in the early twenties had fled from America because "the present system could not provide them the needs of the spirit." They lived abroad supported by American dollars, thinking vaguely of returning home, as they began to realize that a change of climate and cultural milieu did not necessarily enable them to mature into literary artists. And "now the depression was forcing them home by cutting off their incomes." Hitherto they had complained that the system had deprived them of spiritual sustenance; now they were compelled to the realization that the present system "could not even provide for men's physical needs, could not even feed and clothe them." Thus they were obliged to readjust their view of society and their relation to it.

The writers of the thirties, never having had the privilege of balancing the needs of the spirit against the needs of the body or of going abroad because they found the gluttony of the twenties offensive, had no need to make such a readjustment. For they achieved their early manhood as wage earners in a society that was "full of contradictions that were daily becoming more self-evident. Here were wages cut and dividends increased; here were speculators fattening on the general misery; here were breadlines in Times Square in the midst of skysigns advertising all the luxuries they could not buy; here were overproduction and underconsumption, machines standing idle and men waiting in the snow without overcoats, men hungry while wheat was being burned on the prairies, fruit rotting unpicked, milk dumped into gutters—and here were social classes in conflict, sinking, rising, struggling to hold power or merely fighting for enough to eat.

"If one seeks for an explanation of the new political climate that followed the depression, there is no use invoking the missionary zeal of the Comintern or the bones of Karl Marx. There is a homelier reason for it. Once a writer had recognized that society contained hostile classes, that the result of their conflict was uncertain and would affect his own fortunes, then he ceased to believe that political action was silly: he became politicalized. If he also decided that the class whose interests lay closest to his own was the working class, that the home he was seeking lay with them, he became a radical."

Written in the spring of 1934, this is a fair summary of the realities of the crisis that turned the electorate well to the left of center, set the stage for the New Deal, and produced the radical intelligentsia and the radical writers of the thirties. Thus, the question "What must we do?" was answered. The log-ic of the current system led to the promotion of property rights over human rights and to starvation in the midst of plenty. Therefore, we must work toward a radical reconstruction of society that would correct these social evils. Furthermore, those who wielded the ultimate power tended to encour-age fascism; we saw fascism as the self-declared enemy of democracy, a bar-barism in the service of the barons of property, a political "philosophy" in which the use of force and the glorification of war were central elements. Therefore, we must cooperate with the most effective party that urged a united front against war and fascism. In these several ways we must promote the general welfare and seek permanently to establish human rights over property rights. Thus we became radical activists.

The "we" I speak of were, of course, many of the intelligentsia and writers mentioned above. The center of the radical movement was in the industrial East, principally in New York, the home of the Village and traditionally the hub of liberalism. But the leftward trend quickly became a nationwide move-ment with considerable support from labor, academia, and the professions, and we were caught up in it. Not, however, as naive victims seduced by in-tellectuals whom we admired and respected. Our participation was histor-ically motivated and we felt the time had come to move forward as prac-titioners. A few years before, the move would have been premature. Now, with the electorate in a mood for radical measures, the move promised re-sults worth striving for. There is a tide in the affairs of men. . . . So it was at about this time that I joined the Communist party.

It was a bold move attended by some danger. For even in the early thirties when the political climate was such that political heresy in the community was more tolerated than at any time in the past, a communist was generally regarded as a traitor. And he was particularly vulnerable if he was employed by the state. This I knew, and I was willing to take the risk. I had been so pro-foundly moved by *Fontamara* that I was disposed to put my own security in jeopardy in behalf of the common welfare. To this extent—if I may be thus charitable to myself—the move involved some sacrifice of self for the cause, a reasoned response to a moral imperative. An individual who honestly and openly espouses unpopular views of a significant social nature is generally so maligned in the community that I must dwell a little on the moral imperative of which he is the agent.

A passion for the public welfare, for the rights of man, for any course of action designed to relieve life from the preventable burden of man-made evils, is frequently as profoundly religious as a passion for heavenly grace and the love of God. I have seen this passion embodied luminously in the most cultivated men and women and in peasants with no formal education whatever. I am thinking at the moment of two such disparate sons of man as John Henry Cardinal Newman and Bartolomeo Vanzetti. The one, as erudite a gentleman as graced nineteenth-century England; the other a humble fish peddler in a foreign land. When I read the *Apologia,* which intellectually I rejected almost in toto, I could not avoid a feeling of communion with a man whose belief in God and His ordinances and in the absolute authority of the Church was so profound, so sincere, and so persuasive. I had never known anything like it in literature or in life. Listen to this: "O that we could take that simple view of things, as to feel that the one thing which lies before us is to please God! What gain is it to please the world, to please the great, nay even to please those whom we love, compared with this? What gain is it to be applauded, admired, courted, followed—compared with this one aim, of not being disobedient to a heavenly vision? What can this world offer comparable with that insight into spiritual things, that keen faith, that heavenly peace, that high sanctity, that everlasting righteousness, that hope of glory, which they have, who in sincerity love and follow our Lord Jesus Christ? Let us beg and pray Him day by day to reveal Himself to our souls more fully, to quicken our senses, to give us sight and hearing, taste and touch of the world to come; so to work within us, that we may sincerely say—Thou shalt guide me with Thy counsel, and after that receive me with glory. Whom have I in heaven but Thee? and there is none upon earth that I desire in comparison of Thee. My flesh and my heart faileth, but God is the strength of my heart, and my portion forever."

How can one help but feel the moral pulse in these eloquent lines, and admire as a kindred spirit one who could eschew the world's vanities and live in obedience to the heavenly vision? Substitute the love of man for the love of God, the natural for the supernatural, the just society for the heavenly vision, and you have the litany of Bartolomeo Vanzetti. And of my tailor and dearest of friends, who declared in a public meeting when Mussolini's air force was dropping bombs on the people of Spain, that he was ashamed of being an Italian and he gave of his savings to the cause of the Spanish republic. "In all my life I have never stolen I have never killed I have never spilled blood." Having thus purged himself of a crime he had not committed, obedient to his vision of a just society, Bartolomeo Vanzetti faced death with the serenity of a Socrates; so had Cardinal Newman, in obedience to the heavenly vision, endured with serenity the obloquy heaped upon him by the tribe of Kingsley after his conversion to Catholicism. Such is the spiritual power of a moral imperative in one who lives in unquestioning obedience to a vision, heavenly or otherwise.

I do not intend to suggest that, when my companions and I joined the Communist party, and accepted the risk entailed by the affiliation, we closed ranks with such heroes of the spirit as these, but we were pleasantly aware that some measure of self-sacrifice ennobled our decision. As for the rest, I have already indicated that our decision was historically motivated. The time had come to listen to the practicing Marxists so that we might learn from the inside what they had to offer that would lead us out of the absurdity of starvation in the midst of plenty. We had enough knowledge of history, particularly of our own political, juridical, and economic history, to know that any given major crisis has its roots in the past. Thus, when we sought to understand the Great Depression in terms of its ultimate causes, we came to the conclusion that it was the necessary consequence of six decades of practically unfettered sway of laissez-faire capitalism. From the presidency of Grant in 1870 to the presidency of Franklin Roosevelt in 1932, the business community, the economic royalists, operated without any effective regulation or restraint by the government. During the administration of President Harrison, and the first term of Grover Cleveland, the Sherman Anti-Trust Act and the Interstate Commerce Act were passed in response to the people's demand for regulation of the growing monopolies. But these were drawn purposely up as a sop to the people and never intended seriously to regulate industry and commerce. Furthermore, the Supreme Court, as I have noted in another chapter, immediately pulled out whatever teeth the Anti-Trust Act may have had. The courts also defanged the liberal, regulatory legislation enacted during the Wilson administration, that affected industry and commerce. The Child Labor Acts were declared unconstitutional, and that portion of the Clayton Anti-Trust Act that favored labor and was hailed by labor as its Magna Carta was substantially weakened by court interpretation. Thus it is fair to say that Hoover's brand of rugged individualism, un-regulated, unrestrained, and culminating in the twenties after the World War years, had sixty years to prove and perfect itself; its soundness, in terms of the general welfare, must be measured by the results achieved after so long a trial.

Consider the salient facts. Viewed historically, there was a certain con-vincing plausibility in regarding the boom of the twenties as the last great hurrah, the last lavish barbecue of the gilded age. After the Civil War, mea-sured in terms of natural resources and what we generally mean by "oppor-tunity," America was in fact the land of promise. The total land area, includ-ing Alaska and Hawaii, was 3,548,974 square miles. Of this, more than one half of the whole area, 1,048,111,608 acres, belonged to the government. It was land rich in minerals, coal, oil, timber—far richer than the land in any other sovereign state. There were thousands of miles of shoreline and vast waterways in the interior. Hordes of cheap labor from poorer countries stood ready to answer the call of the entrepreneur. The stage was set for the greatest surge of material progress—in technology, managerial strategy, and the skills of production—in the history of man. Opportunities beckoned in every direction. America was up for grabs. Expressed in Darwinian terms, the time was at hand for the race that would be won by the fittest. In the new land there were no royal houses, no dukedoms and earldoms, no landed aris-tocracy, and no clerical empires; competitors for possession of the land would begin on even terms.

There is no way of knowing the vast number who entered the race, but the reliable historian C. Beard has listed the eleven great survivors, "as impos-ing in their day as the barons of Magna Carta, rulers of England in the days of King John"—Jay Gould, William H. Vanderbilt, Collis P. Huntington, James J. Hill, Edward H. Harriman, John D. Rockefeller, Andrew Carnegie, Jay Cooke, J. Pierpont Morgan, William A. Clark, Philip D. Armour. Only two of these men built their vast fortunes on an inheritance; the others began as wage earners. They had much else in common: they were "men of heroic audacity and magnificent exploitive talents—shrewd, energetic, aggressive, rapacious, domineering, insatiable." They were men equal to the challenge of industrializing America and converting its resources into all those things that constitute the good life. No one denies the considerable good they did, but they did irreparable damage. They wasted resources on a massive scale.

As empire builders and exploiters, they used whatever means were effective: they exploited workers—remember Boss Johnson?—"bought legislators, bribed congressmen, spied upon competitors, hired private armies, dynamited property, used threats and force and intrigue." As rugged individualists, they did not hesitate to use government to promote their ends, and as rugged individualists they sought to eliminate competition. They succeeded in doing both. They procured high tariffs, ruinous to the consumer, particularly the farmer; the courts sustained them in their opposition to an income tax law until the Sixteenth Amendment was ratified in 1913; with the aid of the courts they turned back repeated efforts to enact child labor laws and laws designed to fix minimum wages and maximum hours; they resisted all legislation designed to strengthen the bargaining position of labor. They also succeeded in eliminating competitors so that, by the end of the century, one or more of the enterprisers listed above controlled one segment of the economic empire: the steel segment by Carnegie, mining by Clark, finance by Cooke and Morgan, and so on. In less than two decades John D. Rockefeller had eliminated all competitors and was "master of the oil business from the well to the pump." Thus, rugged individualism was essentially a myth, for the captains of industry and finance depended heavily on the government and tried to avoid as much as they could—which was a great deal—the free play of competition.

What disturbed us, as young idealists, was the self-righteousness with which these latter day barons pursued their acquisitive ways. They were convinced that they were great industrial architects in the service of the nation, and in this they were right. Who can deny the social value of the network of railways wrought by such great empire builders as Hill and Harriman and Huntington? Or of the oil brought to the lamps of the new nation by Rockefeller? These were great achievements of which they could be justly proud. But they were wrong in their insistence that the ends they sought justified the predatory means they used. Pay whatever bribes are necessary to get what we want, said Collis P. Huntington to one of his agents. "The growth of a large business is merely the survival of the fittest," said Rockefeller, drawing on Darwinian biology to justify his conquest of the oil empire. "The fortunes of the railroad companies are determined by the law of the survival of the fittest," said James J. Hill, confident that he was speaking for the entire generation of empire builders.

In making these claims they were rationalizing the unfettered sway of their acquisitive instincts, and they were using the phrase "the survival of the fittest" most uncritically. The fittest for what? To what end? In what context? As often as not, in the frenzied acquisitive race, the survival of the fittest was, in fact, the surfittal of the vilest. Witness Jay Gould "the sordid wrecker in Wall Street" whose greedy hand "ruined everything it touched"; and Daniel Drew, stock manipulator and cattle-drover, who gave large doses of salt to his cattle and then bloated them with water before they were placed on the market scales. Credit belongs to him for having enriched the language with the phrase "watered stock."

Such were the good and the evil of the gilded age. When we considered the Great Depression in the perspective of recent history, we saw it as the necessary consequence of six decades of unrestrained and unregulated *laissez-faire*. The Yazoo Land Frauds, and all the corrupt acquisitions of which they became the symbol, were the honored precedents of the peculations of the Grant administration and the predatory ways of such spoilsmen as Jay Gould and Daniel Drew. These, in turn, were the precedents for the Teapot Dome scandal and the ruinous stock manipulations of the twenties. And the "policies of the past eight years" which Hoover promised to continue if elected president in 1928, were nothing more than the unrestrained and unregulated rugged individualism that led to starvation in the midst of plenty, the tragic crisis of the early thirties. Therefore, the imperative we felt was clear. There must be a reconstruction of society along such lines as would remove the evils reviewed here. We had all the necessary resources; if the practicing Marxists could in any way instruct us, the time had come to listen to them.

I need not give a detailed account of my membership in the Communist party. It was brief. The activities it entailed were unpleasant and, so it seemed to me, irrelevant to the challenge posed by the depression: What had caused the depression and what could be done to avoid its recurrence? Karl Marx was an economist of the stature of Adam Smith. What was his analysis of capitalism? Were the premises sound? According to his interpreters, the communists, what, if anything, could be done within the framework of the fundamental law that would prevent the periodic slumps? Would the system eventually destroy itself? The search for answers to these probing questions, conducted rationally, dispassionately, in the manner of my great teachers, would have produced something of the enlightenment I sought.

I soon discovered that the party bosses, largely not very learned, were either ignorant of these issues or indifferent to them. Their sincerity I never doubted. However, they had two fixed goals: The end they sought was revolution, and the means to that end was an enlargement and a strengthening of the Communist party. For the first time in its history, conditions were right for making converts to the party, and its leaders were intent on taking advantage of this while the soup lines lengthened. Consequently, the main business of the party was devising recruitment strategies. Members were urged to infiltrate community organizations and persuade whatever members they could to join the party. That was an effective and understandable strategy, but it failed to excite me for I had not joined the party for that purpose. Since the Communist party had not provided the enlightenment I had hoped for, I resigned. The reasons I gave for withdrawing were substantially those here reviewed.

It was not an easy thing to do, for I was abandoning some close friends who were working for a cause. But I did it with a clear conscience, and the separation was amicable. I bore no one ill will, and had absolutely no intention of betraying friends who remained in the fold. Nor did I have the slightest suspicion that I myself would be betrayed, and that the move I had made in the hope of finding a way out of the crisis would, in a dozen years or so, plunge me into the major crisis of my hitherto happy and untroubled life.

In 1917 we entered World War I against Germany and other countries. In 1941 we entered World War II against the Nazi-Fascist Axis. The avowed purpose of World War I was "to make the world safe for democracy," primarily against the threat of the Huns. The avowed purpose of World War II was to prevent the scourge of fascism, spearheaded by the Nazis, from destroying the western democracies and conquering the world. One of the major consequences of World War I was World War II. One of the consequences of World War II was a new kind of war—the Cold War, made hot now and then, as in Korea and Vietnam. By another of the tragic ironies of history, both wars were followed, almost immediately in America, the last great bastion of democracy, by a fresh attack on the very essence of democracy. In 1919 Mitchell Palmer launched his "war on the Reds." The Dies Committee on Un-American Activities, established as a temporary measure in 1938, was made permanent in 1945; its counterpart in the Senate was activated in the early fifties under the leadership of Senator Joseph McCarthy. These various committees pursued their "patriotic" labors in purging the nation of communists and fellow travelers, in flagrant disregard of the democratic liberties guaranteed in the First, Fourth, Fifth, and Fourteenth Amendments. Nor did the voice of such defenders of the Constitution as Justice William O. Douglas prevail against them. Fortunately, those spurts of hysteria, in direct line of descent from the infamous Sedition Acts of 1798, were of short duration; and the American conscience, embodied in the conservative Senator Watkins of Utah, relegated Senator Joseph McCarthy to the oblivion he deserved.

It must not be supposed, however, that those committees acted without mass support, for during their brief reign of terror they were the agents of conservative majorities in Congress and in several state legislatures. The arrogance and defiance of labor soon after the war and the aggressive moves of Russia into Finland and later into the liberated countries of eastern Europe, increased the endemic fear of communism in America—a fear that underlay the enactment of the Smith Act, the Taft-Hartley Act in 1946, and the McCarran Act in 1950. Thus, the hunters of subversives, from 1946 through the early fifties, had mass support. Their intent, of course, was to put an end to "creeping socialism" and to stop "the march of communism" against which attorney Joseph H. Choate had warned in opposing the income tax law in 1895. But once again, by one of the inevitable ironies of history, what they accomplished by their misplaced patriotic zeal was precisely the opposite of what they had intended. The radicalism of the late sixties and early seventies, accompanied by such violence as had been no part of the radical movement of the preceding decades, was the young generation's answer to the excesses of McCarthyism. And the triumph of communism in Italy, France, China, Vietnam, and elsewhere, was, in the long run, aided rather than hindered, by the anticommunist thrust of our foreign policy. Furthermore, because of their sordid history and gross abuse of power as investigative agencies, such un-American activities committees may very well have dug their own graves. When would conservatives and reactionaries learn that true conservatism is as well "an ability to improve as a disposition to preserve?"

In our own state "the communist menace" was met by the Joint Committee on Un-American Activities created by the legislature in 1947. Its chairman was a politician whose qualification as a statesman was a stint as a county sheriff's deputy. He and his associates charged that the main thrust of the communist menace was in the university. On April 23, 1948, the chairman of the committee announced that an investigation would begin immediately, to be followed by a "hearing" soon thereafter. Thus, on July 19, 1948, about twenty of us from the university were ordered to appear before "the high image of authority," pathetically embodied in the ex-deputy sheriff. He was a slight man, blown with political ambition, hallowed with "patriotism"; as chairman of the committee, he wielded the ultimate power—such power as historically descended from the Inquisition and the Star Chamber. His authority was absolute, his judgment final. Under the rules of that political game and the guidelines for such committees, there was no appeal from the order to appear, and the penalty for defiance was imprisonment. Hence there was no hope to balance the wretchedness one would suffer in that slight man's pillory, no legal remedy for the loss one was certain to sustain in the proceedings.

This was the dread reality, the utterly despairing reality, that weighed heavily upon me as I waited to be called to the witness stand. It was, as I remember, on what proved to be the last, or next to the last day of the hearing, when I sat alone in my car during the lunch hour, knowing that I would be called to the stand that afternoon. The day was warm and heavenly clear. In the natural splendor of the Puget Sound country, composed of mountains, wooded hills, and many waters, a land that I now claimed as my native land, the merry life of summer, in its various manifestations, was all around me. But I was alone, in a state of absolute alienation. Cars were speeding by with creatures of another world at the wheel, and people in their light summer wear were moving to and fro in the hurly-burly of the sun-drenched city, as if this day were but another of the yesterdays that had come and gone. None aware of my complete isolation. Strange panorama that in its very familiarity seemed now so unfamiliar! Alone in the gloom of the noonday sun, the burden I must bear was indivisible. None could alleviate it. I had a wife, children, and friends, all dear to me and I dear to them, but none could, by his love and faith in me, alter by so much as an imperceptible quantum the dread reality that I must face alone. The only possible relief was in the nature of a miracle and therefore unreal: the vain wish that the hound of heaven might appear and put an end to the inquisition.

Vain wish! I was parked on a hillside with my bitter bread in a brown bag, and below me a block away was the massive brick bastion, the Armory Building in which the hearings were held. As my eyes turned from the landscape and came to rest on the prison house, I fancied that I saw above its arched entrance, the doom Dante had seen inscribed on Hell Gate:

> Per me si va nella citta dolente;
> Per me si va nell'eterno dolore;
> Per me si va tra la perduta gente . . .
> Lasciate ogni speranza voi ch'entrate.

Do I exaggerate? My life was not at stake. What there was left of tomorrow was not at stake. My bread was not at stake. Regardless of what those inquisitors might do to me, I could manage for myself and my family. But there was no hope of salvaging what was as dear to me as life and family: my good name, the future I had planned as a writer, teacher, lecturer—my own private dream. My first book would be published in two months and its author now disgraced. My application for a Guggenheim fellowship had been sent to New York—and the applicant now disgraced. And I must come to terms with an incredible vulgarity: that what had brought me to the brink of ruin was a passion for the rights of man, a more just society, a concern for the general welfare, a faith in the American Dream that had survived disillusionment, a dedication to learning and the truth! Bess Evans had warned me to resist the pleasures of the flesh that had ruined Tito Melema. She had not warned me that the idealism she had instilled in me might cause me grief.

No! There was no hope whatsoever! Dante was right: Abandon hope all ye who enter here. Within the fatal hour I would be at the mercy of the merciless inquisitors and I knew precisely what they would seek to wrest from me: the loathsome service of an informer. The high image of authority had tried to make a deal with me before the hearing. One of his investigators had told me what I already knew: that an ex-communist had told the committee that I and certain others had been members of the party. And he told me, also, that except for that one "blemish" on my character, my reputation was very good. Thank you very much. And the deal was this: if I promised to be a friendly witness and to give the committee the names of all others whom I knew to be or to have been members of the party, I would be interrogated for only a few minutes and then walk out of the Armory a free man, trailing clouds of glory, praised by the committee, and even by the Hearst newspaper, which was at that time the witch-hunter's bible, for being a true and loyal American. Think it over, young man. If you refuse to cooperate, the penalty will be a citation for contempt of the legislature, and that means a stiff fine and a year in jail.

I had good reason to believe that the university administration and the Board of Regents advised "complete cooperation" with the committee in its effort to purge the faculty of subversives. One of the deans had advised me to "go along with the committee. A year hence all of this will be forgotten." And a member of the Board had urged us all publicly to "stand up like men and be counted." That same loyal American, some time later, under indictment for some such patriotic service as income tax evasion, stood up like a man and took the Fifth over a hundred times. If he lacked a passion for the rights of man, he was not lacking in a passion for acquisition.

However, I had an abundance of the one and none of the other. I would not make a secret of my past. I certainly would stand up like a man and be counted as one who had joined the party for a short time and then left it some twelve years ago. If given the opportunity at the hearing, I would explain what had led me to explore what the communists had to offer toward the achievement of a more just and harmonious society. For I was proud of having made the investigation for worthy reasons and for having pursued the inquiry in a direction that entailed some danger and, therefore, some self-sacrifice. Wasn't that commendable? How else does one learn? What did my inquisitors know about Marxism? Henceforth my rejection of communism as a political party would be based more on knowledge than on ignorance, on rational judgment rather than on prejudice. Could my inquisitors say as much? But I knew that I would be given no opportunity to speak thus; for what was called a "hearing" was, in reality, more akin to an inquisition. If I had the courage of a martyr, or the indifference to consequences of an adventurer, I might suggest to the committee that what they were doing had an ignoble history and was more in harmony with fascist brutality than with the principles of American democracy. Lacking such courage and the opportunity to state my case fully, I would proceed with such tact as I could muster and refuse the deal. That is precisely what I did. Having refused to cooperate, I was dismissed from the witness stand but held as an unfriendly witness and given to understand that I would be returned to the pillory later.

That did not happen. For the hound of heaven, whose intercession I had wistfully hoped for, miraculously appeared and barked the high image of authority into oblivion. It came about thus: The professor whom the committee wanted to ruin above all others was an outspoken liberal and a philosopher with a national reputation. The committee produced a professional informer from New York who testified, under oath, that in the summer of 1938 the professor had been in attendance at a high level communist training school in New York. The professor offered to prove that during that summer he was at a certain mountain lodge writing a book on esthetics. Had the committee attempted to frame the professor? If so, and he could establish his alibi, his inquisitors would be caught in their own trap. Indeed, after a brief recess, the chairman adjourned the infamous committee "until further notice." That was about forty years ago and the end of the committee. It was also the end of the political career of its chairman, for in a bid for a seat in Congress at the next elections he was repudiated by his own constituency. His brief political career and gross abuse of power had been an instance (as Shakespeare wrote) of:

> Man, proud man,
> Dressed in a little brief authority,
> Most ignorant of what he's most assured,
> His glassy essence, like an angry ape,
> Plays such fantastic tricks before high heaven
> As makes the angels weep. . . . "

Years later, hoping that he had learned his lesson, I felt a measure of pity for the man who had failed to realize what to him must have been his private dream.

Thus, for having taken the Declaration and the Constitution seriously; for having been justly concerned with the rights of man and the general welfare; for having steadfastly believed in the reality of social ideals; and for having kept faith with the American Dream, I was brought to the brink. But once again the guardian deity that shapes our ends was at my elbow, and I was saved from the ruin I had feared. There was a heap of future left. Tomorrow—to fresh fields and pastures new.

CHAPTER XI

Runnymede: Journey to the Fountainhead

There were, indeed, fresh fields and pastures new and world enough and time in which to explore their promised bounty. Looking back now, as I write the concluding chapter of my chronicle, I remember the autumn of 1948 as the happiest season of my life. In the pursuit of ends studiously conceived, though occasionally revised, it was a time of joyous realization. Hitherto, and notwithstanding inevitable reverses, my life as an immigrant had been an essentially good life. In the nearly four decades that followed, I have known that serene tranquility that comes with age and congenial labor amply rewarded with bread for the table and such intangibles as the esteem of one's fellows. But for sheer joy of ecstatic intensity, such as one may feel when one is yet relatively young, that season stands apart as the one in which I knew the highest pinnacle of contentment. For I was now well on the way toward the achievement of my private dream—the pursuit of happiness in self-realization.

Chronologically, the year 1948 was, roughly, at once the midpoint in my status as immigrant and the beginning of my career as writer and lecturer on themes inherent in the course I had chosen to follow as an immigrant. It was, in a sense, the end of one and the beginning of another period in a life that continues to be enormously happy. In that autumn I celebrated the thirty-fifth anniversary of my arrival on the western frontier of the new land: November 11, 1913. I was now forty-five years of age, physically and mentally in the prime of life, and I felt with untroubled certainty that I was on the very threshold of productive decades and great expectations—great in the modesty and reasonableness of what I expected.

Hitherto I had been primarily a student. Since I had sought my professional future in history, in speech, in the law, and, finally, in literature and philosophy, I achieved my doctorate some years later than my contemporaries who had pursued an undeviating course. I think I gained rather than lost by the several explorations; but I remained, as this chronicle has shown, primarily a student. After the autumn of 1948, though never ceasing to be a student, I would be primarily a teacher; quite unexpectedly, I would enlarge my academic forum by adding the community to the classroom. I would become, by request, teacher-in-residence to the new land. More on this later.

Before I proceed to relate what happened in the autumn of 1948, let me briefly review my state of mind and general situation, after the "hearing," since these relate to the theme of my narrative. During the preceding decades I had concentrated my efforts on becoming an American, on getting well into the mainstream of its life. I had also wisely decided, early in my career, to learn more about the land where I was born and to try to understand the quality of my ancestral heritage, that I might at least attempt to integrate something of what was excellent in it into my life in the new land. This I had done and would continue to do. After the early stages of the process of becoming an American, and when I was well into my career as student and teacher, I had refused to regard myself as an Italian-American. A plague on such schizophrenic identity! That label was descriptive of nothing to which I could attach any meaning. I wanted to be what in fact I have become: a certain kind of American whose personality, mode of behavior, and general philosophy of life are, in part, determined by ancestry, place of birth, and early training; different from my neighbor who was born in Nebraska and takes milk with his dinner, whereas I was born in Italy and take wine with mine, but no less an indivisible American than he.

This attitude, however, increased rather than decreased my admiration and affection for Italians as people, and my desire to learn as much as possible about the land of my birth. I had cultivated the friendship of certain of the older immigrants whom I could admire and with whom I could speak the language, and followed as closely as I could the political situation in Italy after the advent of Mussolini. I had acquired a small library of Italian books. Thus, by the autumn of 1948, I had read, in Italian, such noted writers as Boccaccio, Petrarch, Dante, Tasso, Ariosto, Machiavelli, Cellini. I had even dared to defile my mind and risk damnation by furtive dips into the obscenities of the nasty Aretino who, with scornful pride, had admitted having spoken ill of everyone except Christ, whom, he said, apologetically, he did not know: *Scusandosi col dir no lon conosco!* I had read, also, some of the works of such noted writers as Verga, Deledda, D'Annunzio, Papini, Pirandello, Manzoni, Carducci, Leopardi, De Sanctis. And in the late thirties and early forties I read the principal works of Ignazio Silone and Carlo Levi. The irony is that, had I not been an American, I would most certainly have never known a single one of those writers.

And what about my political education, my determination to become an American in the spirit of the Declaration, and to come to terms with the ideals and practical realities of twentieth-century America? If this had not been quite completed in the autumn of 1948, its essentials had been firmly established. I would learn nothing thereafter that would require a significant revision of the conclusions I had drawn from my study of American political, economic, and judicial history. One of the most important of these was the disturbing fact that, in the interpretation of that masterpiece of statecraft, the American Constitution, those who wielded the ultimate power had too often sacrificed the rights of man to property rights. But of equal importance was the fact that they had been opposed from the beginning by what I have called the American conscience, variously embodied in certain justices, men of state, of letters, the humble and unheard many. A close observer of the American scene could not leave the American conscience out of account, for it too was a part of the reality. It had kept the dream alive. The imperative in 1948, and no less now than then, was to work effectively toward its ascendancy.

Not by revolution! Of this I was absolutely convinced for reasons I stated in the preceding chapter; nothing has happened in the last four decades to change my mind. On the contrary, having survived the frightening excesses of McCarthyism and the constitutional crisis posed by Watergate, democratic processes within the fundamental laws of the nation have proved equal to the severest challenge. I could see no reason that those same processes would not prove as effective in dealing with similar crises in the future. The revolution that had secured them for us, as the unalienable rights of man, had been fought and won; and that victory had been reconsecrated in another bloodbath just short of a century later. Thus we had the rights, and the continuing challenge, which the electorate must never fail to accept, to make them prevail by whatever means the fundamental law allowed. The duty of every citizen, as I conceived it then and as I conceive it now, was to work for the political eminence of such candidates for public office as were honestly pledged to promote the public welfare in the spirit of the principles and ideals set forth in the Declaration. That could be done and it must be done. Nor did I ever doubt that, in the long run, it would be done.

Such, in brief, was the essence of my political state of mind both before and after the "hearing." As I had been a liberal in the tradition of Jefferson and Sam Adams from the very beginning of my political education, I would continue to be a liberal after I had survived the inquisition. I have felt the need to put myself thus on record, because although certain of my contemporaries felt having been a communist a sin that required apology, expiation, and even retreat into reactionary conservatism, I felt nothing of the sort. I had joined in secrecy because it was not safe to openly exercise one's constitutional rights; when I left in secrecy I merely returned to the status quo ante. Had there been an element for me of self-deception or disturbingly felt self-betrayal, or if joining had been in response to total commitment to an ideology, I might have had to undergo a ritual of mea culpa in order to regain my self-respect after the disillusionment. But such had not been the case. Therefore, the affiliation and subsequent severance had not been a traumatic experience. To be at peace with myself I did not need to purge myself of an adultery I had not committed. As I have made clear, my joining had been no more than an exploratory venture in the finest empirical tradition of the search for knowledge, a decision revocable if found to have been mistaken. The "god that failed" had not failed me simply because I had not put my trust in him. Thus, joining and leaving the party, so long as this remained generally unknown, entailed no more than the inconvenience of retracing my steps once I had discovered that I had taken the wrong road. Specifically, the experience had left my political orientation unchanged.

The suffering that the venture had entailed, and of which I have given an account, was caused not by self-reproach but by the vulgarity of the hearing and fear of the penalty that was threatened. Fortunately, that had been avoided. I was not cited for contempt of the legislature, nor in any way disciplined by the university. It did, however, exact a petty retribution. I was not paid for the two or three days that I had suffered at the hearing, even though no substitute had been hired to conduct my classes. But that bit of grace was the measure of charity in a dean who had the power and insisted on his pound of flesh. Bless him! He might have insisted on two!

As the weeks passed and the committee was not called back into session, it seemed more and more evident that it had dug its own grave. When the professor had so convincingly challenged what we had no doubt was perjured testimony—I myself had driven him to the lodge where he had spent the summer with his family—the committee's informer was spirited out of the city, presumably back to New York. On that very day, immediately after the professor had testified, the committee's investigators rushed to the lodge and confiscated the records that proved the truth of his alibi. For what reason would a committee of the legislature rush its star witness out of the jurisdiction and confiscate evidence that would have proved that the professor had been falsely accused? The reader may draw his own conclusions. We had no doubt that it had conspired with the informer to frame the professor, and that, with its incredibly vulgar abuse of power in grave danger of being exposed, it had simply closed its books and ceased operation. My only cause for anxiety now was the possibility that the Congressional committee might come to the state to continue the inquisition begun by the local committee. But that seemed unlikely; as witches, we were entirely too trivial to engage the attention of the great hunters whose arsenal was the U.S. Congress. Thus, by the autumn of 1948, I had no real cause to worry about further inquisition.

But I did have some cause to worry about one of its unavoidable consequences. After the much-publicized exposure of my past association with the party, I had to come to terms with a somewhat tarnished reputation. I had to live, with whatever peace of mind I could find, in a community that, politically, tended to support the committee and to regard its victims with suspicion and varying degrees of contempt. Nor did it make any difference that the committee had used cruel and indefensible means or that it was more interested in justifying its own prejudices and promoting its political ambitions than in exposing anyone who was a real traitor and whose subversion, past and present, could be established in a fair trial. The press was entirely with the committee, and one of the two dailies supported its contention that there were more than one hundred and fifty subversives on the university faculty — a characteristically irresponsible exaggeration. For it is doubtful that in a faculty of well over a thousand one might find even that many mild liberals. As for communists: After spending hundreds of thousands of dollars, and with all the state's resources at its disposal, the committee exposed three. These were such dedicated communists that their membership in the party was really no deep and dark secret. What comfort could I find in such a political climate? In a community where too many were ready to believe that I had secreted a vicious past? That, while posing as a university professor, I had been engaged with others in a conspiracy to corrupt students and overthrow by force and violence the country that had rescued me from hunger and ignominy? The fact that I had joined the party to learn what it had to offer and abandoned it shortly thereafter because of a fundamental disagreement with its strategy and doctrine, did not entirely exculpate me. The stigma of communism was upon me and I must live with it. I was somewhat in the position of one who had been indicted for a felony, brought to trial, found innocent by a jury of his peers, but whom the verdict had not purged of the fact of the indictment. As a matter of fact, such was precisely the attitude of certain people toward me, and they did not hesitate to make me aware of it. A letter bristling with reproach came to me from where I had not expected such unkindness. A lecture I gave, sponsored by an association whose directors believed in me rather than in the committee, was picketed by the usual patriots. Another, arranged before the hearing, was cancelled thereafter. Whatever I might do, while waiting for time's erasures to take effect, I must continue "in the general censure to take corruption from that particular fault"—of having once been a member of the Communist party.

In such circumstances, how could I possibly convince closed and prejudiced minds that would not be convinced, that neither I nor my companions had ever conspired to overthrow the government by force and violence? Lacking a forum in which I might state my case, how could I persuade even such minds as might be persuaded, that I was temperamentally and philosophically opposed to violence as a means of achieving power or securing rights and socially desirable ends? That I sought ways to avoid, not to make revolutions? From what vantage point might I argue my conviction that, in thinking critically about social problems and in being a dissenter, I was exercising rights so unequivocally stated in the First Amendment to the Constitution? My companions and I were "perplexed inquirers socialistically inclined." We were rather too much than too little in the service of American ideals and aspirations. And so had been our masters similarly perplexed and inclined—Bernard Shaw, H. G. Wells, the Webbs, G. Lowes Dickinson, John Dewey, Charles Eliot and Charles Norton of Harvard, J. Allen Smith, Charles Beard, Vernon Parrington. King Oscar of Sweden had remarked to one of his ministers that "a young man who has not been a socialist before he is five and twenty has no heart; but if he continues to be one after five and twenty he has no head." Was that it? When we had passed five and twenty, had we really lost our heads? One conclusion, however, was inescapable: there was no way of avoiding the general censure for the course we had pursued, from whatever noble motives or commendable ends. The hearing had blemished my reputation, and I must live with it until time healed wounds and erased the stigma.

Had I been a nonentity and completely anonymous, I would have had no reputation to recover, but I did have an identity and something of a reputation in the state. Since the late twenties and throughout the thirties, I had lectured occasionally on such themes as the immigrant experience, judicial review, and contemporary Italy. During the war, as a public service and as a contribution to the war effort, the university had sent me on a lecture tour throughout the state for an entire semester. Those lectures had been, in part, autobiographical, the intent being to dramatize the meaning of America as reflected in what the new land had given me, a living testimonial to American democracy, generosity, and abundance. But the main thrust of those lectures had been an indictment of fascism as a scourge that threatened the entire world. Conceived in Italy, it had spread as a plague to Germany, Spain, and Japan. It deified the state, glorified war, defended the use of violence as a political weapon, and rejected in toto the proposition that all governments derive their just powers from the consent of the governed. As the avowed enemy of democracy, and by a series of brazenly aggressive acts, it had drawn us into a war that must be fought to the bitter end and won in order that a government of the people, by the people, and for the people might long endure.

Such had been the substance of my lectures, delivered in schools, churches, and at meetings of such community organizations as Rotary, Kiwanis, and local Chambers of Commerce. We were in the early years of the war, when the frightening successes of the enemy required of us determined resistance and a will to win, such an indomitable will as was so well expressed in the slogan of the Italian Resistance: *non mollare!* Do not yield. Drawing upon my conviction that fascism was a scourge, a gross evil hiding behind a facade of such euphemisms as the corporate state, I had urged my indictment with all the logic and passion at my command. Could there be any doubt about the virtues of the democracy, the sanctity of those Anglo-Saxon traditions the founding fathers had perfected in the Declaration and the Constitution, that we were now called upon to defend against the brutality of the Rome-Berlin-Tokyo Axis, led by a wallpaper-hanger gone stark, raving mad? In my representative capacity, did I not speak with the authority of the millions who had come here seeking bread, seeking their proper identity as human beings, and who were now the grateful beneficiaries of the spiritual and material bounty of the new land? *Non mollare!* Such had been my plea. And when I had occasionally succeeded in being a fiery Fiorello, I had brought an audience to its feet.

Now that I was unmasked, so to speak, did those people who had applauded me in every county in the state regard me as an imposter? In their endemic fear and contempt of communism, were they saying of me "once a communist always a communist?" These were not unjustified speculations. After the hearing, even certain of my neighbors had been visibly cool toward me, and, as I noted above, a lecture I had been scheduled to give had been cancelled. Would I ever be invited to speak again? What could I do to remove the stigma from my reputation? Nothing that seemed appropriate and available at the time. However, there was a ray of hope. I had feared that some of my students might have withdrawn from my classes in order to avoid further corruption. But no one had abandoned me. And they smiled upon my return to the classroom after I had been "disgraced." It was a prophetic sign, for I recovered my reputation in less than a year.

The new land was, for me, still rich in opportunities. These were many and varied, including a pilgrimage to Runnymede where, in June 1215, the barons of England compelled King John to affix his seal to the Magna Carta, the fountainhead of the rights and liberties celebrated in this chronicle. What remains to be told is what these opportunities were, and what use I made of them in the quest for my private dream of the pursuit of happiness in self-realization.

For the next several months after the hearing, there were two matters in the land of my career that caused me considerable anxiety: my application for a Guggenheim fellowship, and the fate of *The Unprejudiced Palate,* my first book, announced for publication in October 1948. Would the foundation refuse to consider my application because I had been exposed as a "subversive" who had refused to cooperate with the committee? Would the nation's booksellers boycott the book for the same reason? My anxiety was not without cause. The northwest agent of my New York publishers was meeting some resistance from book dealers in planning to promote the sale of the book, notwithstanding his own genuine enthusiasm for it. As to the fellowship: In preparing the application forms, I had not been required to reveal my political views nor to answer the question, "Are you now or have you ever been a member . . . ." Thus, my conscience was clear; for I had not withheld any information that was required. But in 1948 the conservatives were entrenched throughout the establishment; and such foundations as the Guggenheim might very well be wary of bestowing their bounty on anyone who had come under the gun of the hunters. Perhaps they were also of the American conscience and properly contemptuous of witch-hunters. I simply did not know, so I waited for the verdict with unavoidable anxiety. Should it be against me, I would know how to live with it.

But the verdict was not against me. Once again, that divinity that shapes our ends had stood by me and set me on course toward the realization of modest goals carefully planned. When *The Unprejudiced Palate* was published, three months after that unhappy week when the future had seemed so grim, it was an immediate critical success. My publishers and I had had no doubt that the book would receive a good press and that it would do well in the bookstores, but we had not expected that it would be so generously and universally praised as a minor classic. Well! I need not dwell on that fact any further. The book remained in print a quarter of a century; since it opened so many doors to me, I must explain how it came to be written, why it was so well received, and how it related to plans and decisions I had made some years before in plotting my course as an immigrant to the new land. Also, I must explain how it diverted all my creative energies away from traditional research as a professor of English and in a direction I had not foreseen.

The Unprejudiced Palate would never have been written had it not been for a lady friend who had repeatedly urged me to write a book that turned out to be that particular book. The desire to become a writer, generated rather early in my career, had increased in urgency after I had published several essays in the professional journals, and in the middle forties I had made tentative plans to write a book on the Italian immigrant to America. But at no time had I planned to write such a book as would persuade critics to hail me as an authority on gastronomy! For that is precisely what happened. Some people are born great, some achieve greatness, and some have a reputation thrust upon them. My reputation as a sophisticated gourmet and a wizard in the realm of pots and pans was thrust upon me and was wholly undeserved. Nor am I being unduly modest.

I have suggested elsewhere in this narrative that both my parents were good cooks and that father insisted on a daily dinner of excellent quality. Once we were settled in the new land, with its fairyland abundance, and our barn was live with animals destined for the table, our cuisine was uniformly superb. I was aware of that; I never took it for granted nor ceased to marvel that it could be so. In my appreciation of fine cuisine I was very much at one with my father. Perhaps I was born with a predisposition to what in Italian is called *ghiottoneria,* a word for which the only English equivalent, gluttony, is not at all an adequate translation. For it means a fondness for food that is delicious. (Paolo Monelli, a distinguished Italian journalist and gourmet, made a survey of the fine regional cuisines of Italy, not a statistical but a tasting survey, and called his book *Il Ghiottone Errante.*) Thus, when I left home and went to college, I was ill prepared for provincial boardinghouse food. Mother O'Bryan was an austere fundamentalist and had herself grown heavy on bland pot roasts and mashed potatoes and gravy. There was really nothing wrong with the way she managed perfectly good raw materials in the kitchen. The trouble was that there was nothing right about the way she managed these materials. And as soon as I "knew my way around" the university community, I left the boardinghouse—forever!

I left Mother O'Bryan—a search for a better boardinghouse than hers would have been futile—and rented an apartment. I set up bachelor quarters and learned to cook. It really wasn't all that difficult, as the saying goes these days. With the aid of Mother Pellegrini, and by picking the culinary brains of certain Italian ladies in the city who were excellent cooks and who were flattered by my interest in their craft, I soon learned how to do certain basic dishes rather well—pastas, soups, roasts, stews. Thus I lived for several years, keeping my nose to windward of good cooks, trying to make myself worthy of their goodwill and what aid they could give me, to improve and extend my rather severely limited culinary repertoire. In these ways, confirmed in a continuing interest in savory food and its preparation, I became known among my friends, before and after marriage, as a very good cook. Among these was a young lady—this was after I had married and become a father—who had often sat at our table and eaten with Johnsonian relish, spaghetti, ravioli, risotto, minestrone, and the few other dishes I could do rather well. It was she who had urged me to write—a cookbook.

A cookbook? How could I possibly write a cookbook when I had no more to offer than about a dozen rather vague, flexible recipes? But she insisted, confident that I could do it and always reminding me that there was "big money" in such a venture. What finally persuaded me to lend her my ear was the birth of a third child. Very well! I did not need big money but I could certainly use a bit of little money. So why not explore the possibility with care. Proceeding in the spirit of a trained scholar intent on producing a definitive treatise on the subject, I made a survey of the recently published cookbooks. And when that was done I was ready to enter the lists. What spurred me to immediate action was the few "chatty" cookbooks that were quite popular at the time. One was about some mythical Clementine in a mythical French kitchen, who produced culinary miracles, using carefully guarded recipes that the author had somehow miraculously got hold of and was now offering to the American housewife. What preposterous quackery! It must not go unchallenged. What Mother O'Bryan needed was not carefully guarded recipes but some plain talk on how easily she could raise the level of her cuisine and improve pot roasts with the use of a bit of onion and garlic, a drop of wine, a leaf of the bay, and by such other means as she could think of, once she had been persuaded that she could easily do it, had the means to do it, and entered the kitchen remembering Doctor Johnson's advice that one must regard one's belly very carefully and very studiously. Thus, in inspired anger and indignation, I began to write *The Unprejudiced Palate*.

I began late in the fall of 1946, when I hadn't yet paid the bill for the birth of that third child who is now forty. Early the following spring, when I had completed the first three chapters, Cecil Scott, senior editor of the Macmillan

Company, came to the city and was told by one of my colleagues that I was writing a book. We met, he scanned what I had written, and before I had finished the Johnnie Walker he had poured me, there was an offer of a contract and an advance payment of five hundred dollars! By the end of the year, nine other chapters had been written and the manuscript was ready for the publisher. It was not the cookbook I had been urged to write, and could not possibly have written, for reasons already stated; but there was enough culinary lore in it so that it would not be entirely out of place on one's kitchen shelf. Its principal virtues, however, were elsewhere than in the few hints I had given on how Mother O'Bryan might make her pot roasts fit for a king.

The omniscient Doctor Johnson, who attacked a joint of mutton with such concentration that it brought beads of sweat to his brow, had once said: "I could write a better book about cookery than has ever been written: It should be a book upon philosophical principles." Acting upon his assurance that it could be done, and since he had not done it, I grasped the opportunity to write such a book myself. Thus I produced, not a book of recipes, but an extended essay, with reflective overtones, on the importance of bread and wine as elements in the good life and in a people's culture. I tried to do it with a sense of urgency and such zest as might inspire the American housewife—or is it now houseperson?—to approach her kitchen with a fresh and aroused imagination. America was now entering the prime of her life. She had perfected the assembly line and twice made the world safe for democracy; she had made a fetish of quantity, mere bigness and acceleration; she had fed hugely but indifferently on the new land's incredible abundance. The time had come when she must begin to think less about the size of a steak and more about how to prepare it for the table in good taste. She must come, rather belatedly, to her culinary senses.

Such was the general tone of the book. There were notes on the kitchen garden, the use of culinary herbs, the wine cellar. There were touches of heresy in it, such as the ex cathedra declarations that wine was the dinner beverage of the sober and the wise; that children should be introduced to wine as soon as they have progressed from sucking to drinking; and that tripe and other viscera, when properly prepared, are gourmet fare. It was in some ways a bold book, but it was gay and honest, original and earth-centered. And it was timely. It not only answered to a need in the nation's coming of age, it discovered that need, sought to define it, and urged the nation to a culinary renaissance that was to flower in the sixties and seventies. In the middle forties, Julia Child, the Galloping Gourmet, and James Beard, to name only three of the professionals who have instructed America in the art of cookery, via the radio and the tube, may have been sharpening their knives and boning up on culinary lore; but it would be a full quarter of a century before they would appear on the culinary stage. Most of the vast library of "gourmet" books on food and wine have been published during the past three decades. In 1948, Americans were beginning to look on wine with increasing curiosity, but it would be a quarter of a century before wine tastings would be generally regarded as the "in thing"—horrible phrase!

And I myself, who had been a pioneer in urging Americans to accept wine as a dinner beverage, would have to wait a quarter of a century before I would be asked to conduct wine tastings in churches and the YWCA, the last social centers to progress from the Puritan toward the Greek view of temperance. Furthermore, during the three preceding decades, I had noted the gradual change in America's attitude toward bread and wine. In 1914 I had been obliged to sneak into the woods, during the school lunch hour, so that no one would see me eating the "dago" food that is now so generally appreciated; and what was maligned with provincial vulgarity as "dago red" in 1914, was now beginning to be respectfully called Cabernet and Pinot. Thus having noted these trends in the middle forties, I was strategically and auspiciously placed to write *The Unprejudiced Palate.*

As the immigrant who is author and subject of this chronicle, I was uniquely qualified to do the job. For I had both the cultural background and the immigrant experience herein recorded without which such a book could not have been conceived and written. The reader will remember that early in my career, I had to decide whether to melt in the melting pot or retain my ethnic identity. Having decided to pursue the latter course, I had explored my ancestral heritage and learned to know my native land, something of its history and literature and culture, in a way and to an extent that would not have been possible had I not left Casabianca and immigrated to the new land. O happy irony!

The native land was an old and wise civilization, poor in material resources but rich in what the Greeks had called the greatest of the arts, the art of living. That would seem to be a rather self-evident truth; but although it was declared by the ancient Greeks, it was the Italians who grasped it and passed it on to the rest of Europe at the time of the Renaissance. For the revolutionary shift from thinking too precisely on the salvation of the soul to thinking more precisely on the pleasures of the flesh began in Italy in the last half of the fourteenth century. That completely new way of coming to terms with life, not in "a vale of tears," but in a lovely, sun-drenched land, was first announced in the works of Petrarch, Boccacio, and Franco Sacchetti. And these were followed in the next century by Luigi Pulci, the Medicis, Angelo Poliziano, Leon Battista Alberti, Boiardo, and, somewhat later, Castiglione, author of *The Courtier*. Whereas Dante, who died in 1321, and other medieval writers had sought happiness in the world beyond the grave, these writers insisted that it must be sought in this world, in the here and now. Their works, in one way or another, celebrated the enjoyment of this life. Dante unwittingly terminated the old way of life with the *Divine Comedy*, while his successors, perfectly aware of what they were doing, gave literary expression to the new with the *Decameron, The Courtier,* and other works collectively known as the *Human Comedy*. Dante had followed the ethereal Beatrice to paradise, where she appeared to him as "radiant light;" Bocaccio and Petrarch pursued Fiammetta and Laura, seductive women of flesh and blood, one of them married, in their social circles.

Among the pleasures of the flesh that they celebrated daily, were the pleasures of the dinner table, especially these since they were the last to lose their edge while the body drew near the inevitable end. No Puritan ethic nor forbidding Calvinism prevented them from indulging the so-called pleasures of the flesh; while the confessional provided them a means of purging themselves, at no greater cost than the penitent recitation of a few Aves and Paternosters, of whatever sins they may have committed when they had supped too heartily on the pleasures of the flesh. Thus they were free to add the pleasures of the body to the pleasures of the mind, and to extract from life whatever gaiety they could before death's inexorable decree.

So it is now as it was then in that fair and sun-bathed land, where Pope Leo X rewarded good poets with fine wine and bad poets with watered wine, and where Savonarola was burned at the stake for his tirades against its voluptuary tendencies. The Puritan may sit to Mother O'Bryan's pot roast with a muttered grace; the Italian's preprandial ritual is an upraised glass of wine and a *Buon Appetito* to his table companions, to companionship in the unforbidden enjoyment of bread and wine. Companionship! The word itself derived from the Latin *cum panis,* or the Italian *con pane,* suggested the dinner table. The celebration of the Eucharist was but a reflection or two away from bread and wine regarded as symbols for fellowship and hospitality.

Thus, when I wrote *The Unprejudiced Palate,* I was able to incorporate in its various chapters materials drawn from my ancestral heritage and from my own experience as a peasant boy in Casabianca. These were in the form of anecdotes and vignettes intended to elucidate meanings, or to introduce the subject matter of certain chapters, and to make the reading of the book a pleasure, even to such readers as might not be particularly interested in the enhancement of Mother O'Bryan's pot roasts. It was this evocation of my past, as a peasant boy in Casabianca and, later, as immigrant to the new land; these reflections on certain aspects of the way of life of a people who had attended to the art of living for centuries that gave the book its unique character and set it apart from the conventional books on cookery. In that sense, and to that extent, it was philosophical, and it bore the unmistakable mark of a jolly schoolmaster. America had taught me so much and given me so much during the past three decades, and now that I was in my prime and facing westward, I might attempt to reciprocate and teach her a thing or two, were it ever so little as the self-evident truth that a shallot and a clove of garlic will enhance the flavor of a steak. But I had something more in mind: As I have already noted, I had explored the possibility of writing a book on the contribution of the Italian immigrant to the culture of America; it was this project I had submitted to the Guggenheim Foundation in my application for a fellowship. More on this later.

The most gratifying praise of the book came from two college presidents, the dean of a graduate school, a noted librarian, the editor of a scholarly journal, and the well-known writer Henry Miller. These and some others praised the book for its literary merits. In a personal letter, Henry Miller confessed that he lacked words to express his appreciation for what I had written; the editor of *The Pacific Spectator* asked for an essay on a subject suggested by *The Unprejudiced Palate.* I had hoped for some such criticism and was flattered that it came from educators and such a famous author as Henry Miller.

But most of the reviewers hailed the book as a valuable contribution to the literature on gastronomy, notwithstanding my emphatic declaration that I was neither chef nor gourmet. And, indeed, I was not; nor am I one now. That reputation thus thrust upon me, I could not easily escape all its consequences. The editor of a magazine asked me to edit its culinary articles, an offer that I politely refused. The director of a cooking school in Chicago, with no further evidence of my qualifications than he had assumed from reading *The Unprejudiced Palate,* made me an incredible offer by telephone. Would I preside over a television program on cookery, at twice my university salary? The answer was no; I was a professor of English literature and in no way qualified to do what he proposed, much less fake it even for big money. Another offer, congenial to my nature and for which I was amply qualified, I accepted. For a modest retainer on a yearly basis, I consented to give an occasional lecture on wine for the California Wine Institute. These lectures, sometimes as introductions to tastings, were to be delivered to college audiences. And although I had some knowledge of wine and had produced some exceptional vintages in our own cellar, I would not present myself as an authority on wine. My task was to extol the virtues of the "Holy Blood of the Grape" as a dinner beverage and as what Hemingway had called "one of the most beautiful things in life." That I could do with zest and honesty and so accepted the offer. Then there was the request of a newspaper editor that I write a weekly column for the newspaper's food section. That offer, too, I accepted when the editor agreed that I might write generally and as I pleased on bread and wine.

None of these undertakings had I sought; they, and several others I need not mention, had all been proposed to me as a result of the reputation the reviewers of *The Unprejudiced Palate* had thrust upon me. Then came offers of a somewhat different sort, and more in accord with what I had intended to write. At about the time that the reviews of that book began to appear, I was notified by the Guggenheim Foundation that my request for a fellowship had been granted. That, coming a few months after the inquisitors had threatened me with ruin, must have been the happiest day of my life. Only established writers of genius might dream of the Pulitzer and the Nobel prizes, but of all the prizes to which even quite ordinary scholars might aspire, the Guggenheim was the most liberal and the most prestigious. My qualifications for it, in terms of scholarly achievements, were rather slender. The foundation had been given an advance copy of *The Unprejudiced*

Palate; beyond that were the few essays I had published in the professional journals. So I was banking rather heavily on the unique project I had submitted. We were two decades away from the ethnic revival. Would the committee of selection see merit in my proposal? And after they had read my book, would they be persuaded that I could deliver? Such being the imponderables, I must not be too confident. Having invoked the blessings of the deity that had never let me down, I was prepared to receive an adverse verdict without bitterness or disappointment.

Applicants who have been granted the fellowship are normally notified early in the spring following the year when the application was filed. Thus there was a flurry of excitement in our home when a letter came from the foundation, a couple of months before the verdict was expected. When we returned from a weekend "abroad"—Vancouver, B.C., a hundred miles to the north—where we had gone to celebrate the success of the book, we found a note in our mailbox, a notice that a registered, special delivery letter was being held at the central post office. It was late in the evening and the post office was five miles away, but we rushed thither without delay, for I was certain it must be something dreadfully important. Could it be from the foundation? It was! And it was a request that I send immediately an estimate of what funds I would need, for travel and other expenses, over and above the fellowship stipend, in order to do the research for my project. The letter did not say that the fellowship had been granted. But surely I must be among the lucky winners! In my application I had stated that the research would entail a journey to the native land. Could it be possible that granting the fellowship would be contingent on whether the foundation could afford the paltry sum necessary for such a journey? Banish the thought! The Guggenheims did not quibble over a few pennies. That night we did not sleep. I prepared and immediately dispatched the required data, asking for less rather than more funds than I would need. In due time the formal announcement came, with a request that on my way to Italy I should stop in New York and have lunch or dinner with Henry Allen Moe, the executive secretary of the Guggenheim Foundation. I wondered why I should be the recipient of so much grace!

Henry Moe was then wine steward of the Century Club, and when we met he told me he had a favor to ask of me. While I was in Italy would I take a little time to do some tasting for him, and advise him on what special vintages he should order for his club? Bless him! He had read *The Unprejudiced Palate*. Some twenty-five years later I had dinner with Henry at the home of Charles Odegaard, president of the university, and on that occasion I had the pleasure of being wine steward to him. The wine was a twenty-year-old Cabernet, the finest I had produced in our cellar. And Henry Allen Moe proposed a toast to the cellarmaster.

The journey to the native land was my first since I had left it thirty-five years before, and I had looked forward to it with furious excitement. A long-dreamed-of return to Casabianca with my American mate, a grand lady of Nordic ancestry, to tread with me once more the sod of my humble origins! The reality seemed altogether unreal. Do I wake or dream? This time I would travel first class on the finest train to New York and on a luxury liner across the Atlantic. And the new land would pick up the tab! I thought of father. Would he now be persuaded that in America all is different?

The reign of Mussolini was now a remembered nightmare. The feckless House of Savoy had been sent packing. Italy was now a constitutional democracy. After the carnage of two global wars within a single generation, the Furies who make wars were prostrate with exhaustion and peace at long last seemed permanent. I would meet some of the leaders of the Resistance, among them Enzo Agnoletti, editor of *Il Ponte*, Italy's best political and literary monthly, and its publisher, Piero Calamandrei. I would sit in the Chamber of Deputies, seek an audience with De Gasperi, the prime minister, and see democracy at work in the land I had left for want of bread. I would make a survey of the background of the five million Italians who had immigrated to America and return to write a book on their contribution to its culture. It was heady stuff, that unequivocal promise of so much pleasure, and I did much of what I had planned. But I did not write that particular book.

For the journey to the native land turned out to be bittersweet, a profoundly disturbing experience. I hadn't been there more than a few weeks when I realized that I could not write the book I had planned. That caused me a great deal of worry, for it meant that I could not fulfill my moral obligation to my benefactor, the Guggenheim Foundation, an obligation that I felt very deeply. I wrote several letters to Henry Moe, reports on the vintages I was tasting for him, and I included in them something of my troubled state of mind, with hints that, while I felt that such a book as I had promised could be written, my urge to write it was weakening. Thus I was preparing the ground for a request that I had planned to lay before him upon my return to New York.

The reason why I could not deliver what I had promised was that another book was urging itself upon my consciousness. The more I saw of the native land, the more I reflected on what I observed and felt, particularly in Casabianca, the tiny world I had inhabited as a young boy and from which I had been miraculously rescued, the more I felt with commanding urgency that I must write, not a book on the immigrant's contribution to America, but one on what the new land had given the immigrant. When I called on Henry Moe in New York, before I had even hinted at my dilemma, he had sensed it. This, in substance, is what he said: "Mr. Pellegrini, when you are ready to write your book, you must feel absolutely free to do the bidding of your heart and mind. Our confidence in you is on record. We are not censors. Now let's talk about wine."

We are not censors! That was the meaning of the freedom of thought! And as I took his hand in gratitude, I saw in that urbane gentleman, the flawless image of the conscience of America, the embodiment of the First Amendment. He may have been, even as Justice Oliver Wendell Holmes, a patrician and proud conservative. I never knew his political views, nor did he inquire about mine. I did learn, however, that he had nothing but contempt for the Dies Committee and its successors, when their use of absolute power, to implement the political ambitions of its members, made a mockery of the rights and freedoms plainly granted in the First, Fourth, Fifth, and Fourteenth Amendments. The foundation, he assured me, would never yield to such committees. We are not censors! What a world of difference between him and the deputy sheriff who had caused me so much grief!

And yet I was obliged to keep in mind that each represented one of the two realities to which I have frequently referred in this chronicle, one of the two Americas: the one dating from the Declaration, the other, from the infamous Sedition Act of July 14, 1798. Occasionally the one prevailed over the other, depending on whom the electorate returned to eminence in the quadrennial contest for power. Nor must I be discouraged by the historical fact that the latter had too frequently prevailed over the former, as it had in the immediate past, in 1947, when the now celebrated "Hollywood Ten" had been sent to jail for insisting on rights granted in the First Amendment. But the possibility and the means of making the one prevail over the other were undeniable; they were the central reality in the democratic process and they must be treasured with tenacity. Nor must I forget that when the latter triumphed and grossly abused the use of its power, as it had in 1798 and on other occasions thereafter, the rights it had abrogated were frequently restored later. The Sedition Act was in force until March 1801. Small consolation for those who had suffered its severe penalties, but such are the ways of the democratic process. Thus, while I was in the New York office of my benefactor, I felt once again, and with renewed faith, my duty and that of my fellow citizens: *non mollare*! Do not yield! We must labor constantly, with enduring patience, and within the limits of the fundamental law, toward the ultimate realization of the American Dream.

Meanwhile, my own little dream, conceived in the promise of the larger dream, was well in the process of being fulfilled. When I returned from the native land, my extracurricular activities as author, lecturer, amateur chronicler of the Italian immigrant in the new land, and teacher-in-residence to the community on bread and wine as elements in the good life, were about to begin. The book I published as a Guggenheim fellow was *Immigrant's Return*. But before that book was even conceived, I had published the essay requested by the editor of *The Pacific Spectator*. The editor had asked for an essay on my father, a subject suggested to her by *The Unprejudiced Palate*. But when the request came I had just lost my mother, two weeks before the book was published. So I wrote a memorial essay on her and called it "La Bimbina," a name her Italian friends had bestowed upon her because of her enduring youth. I wrote it with ease and in sorrow and sent it to the editor a few weeks before I left for Italy. It was published without delay and I saw it in print in the American library in Rome. Soon thereafter it was condensed in *Reader's Digest* and featured in its several foreign editions. A pleasant and profitable surprise! Nor was that the end of it. On the basis of that memorial to my mother, written in sorrow, I was awarded a medal and a sum of money by Freedoms Foundation of Valley Forge, of which Dwight Eisenhower was then president. The presentation was made by the president of our university at a Chamber of Commerce luncheon in 1950 shortly after I had returned from Italy. The large medal bore the inscription: "for outstanding achievement in bringing about a better understanding of the American way of life." Thus, the immigrant from Casabianca, who two years before had been disgraced as a dangerous "subversive," was now honored for a contribution to a better understanding of the new land to which he had come in search of bread.

I had not sought that prize; I had not labored toward that end. It would never have occurred to me to exploit the death of my mother for money and fame. When I wrote the memorial for publication, as requested, I did it in the spirit of "caring for grief, he cared his grief away." I had no other intention than to produce an honest, truthful portrait of mother, with no other embellishment than such grace of language as I might command, with love and admiration free of sentimentality. When the essay was completed, I had no doubt that I had achieved what I had intended, and my interest in the essay ended there. I certainly had not thought of the possibility that it might interest the editors of *Reader's Digest* and the trustees of Freedoms Foundation. However, reading the essay after it had brought me such unexpected rewards, I perceived in it the larger meaning and conceived the idea for my third book.

When I wrote *Immigrant's Return,* published in 1951, I had come out of the kitchen and the cellar, so to speak, intending to establish myself as an amateur chronicler of the immigrant experience. It was a subject on which I would do considerable writing and lecturing during the next two decades, including this chronicle on a phase of the subject I had not hitherto explored. The book was dealt with kindly by the critics and several times reprinted. It was made available to the blind in braille and on phonograph records; one of its chapters was published in translation in the magazine, *Il Ponte,* in Italy. The local library, in a most gracious gesture, recommended the book to the reading public in a brochure that indicated its merits. Since my first two books had been such a modest success, my publishers suggested a third, on the subject I had proposed to the Guggenheim Foundation.

In planning that book, *Americans by Choice,* I proceeded on the assumption that the chronicle of any immigrant whose story was worth telling, as an immigrant to the new land, must necessarily be also a chronicle of the America in which he had lived his productive years, and this chronicle must be ample proof that the assumption was fairly sound. Accordingly, and in the manner of the essay "La Bimbina," I wrote the story of six Italian immigrants who had come to America in their late teens or early twenties near the turn of the century. I chose some for their virtues and success, others, for their vices and failure. I avoided, as being atypical, the extremes of success and failure; the biographical data, while adhering strictly to the facts, were so presented that the story of each, more by implication than direct statement, reflected the America in which each had lived. One, for example, was a bootlegger, and his story revealed something about the America during the decade of that "noble experiment." Corrupted by the easy money he made in the illicit liquor traffic and by his association with corrupt public officials, he died a failure and in disgrace. Another, and by way of contrast, was a ditchdigger. From first to last he earned his bread with the tools he had learned to use as a child, raised a large family, lived happily, laid the foundation for a sewer construction venture pursued by his sons, and died at seventy with boots on his feet and a pick in his hands. His story reflected the America of westward expansion during the decades when most of the work of railway and road construction was done by pick and shovel and wheelbarrow.

That book, too, was dealt with kindly by the critics, and shortly after it was published, it appeared in translation in Spain, South America, and in India. However, the best evidence that I had achieved what I had intended came from the most unexpected quarters. The State Department asked my publishers for permission to issue an inexpensive edition of the book for distribution abroad through the facilities of the U.S. Information Service. As part of its cold war strategy, the State Department at that time was seeking, in a variety of ways, to bring within the orbit of American influence such countries as seemed in danger of yielding to the promise of communism. Apparently, *Americans by Choice,* for what the several chronicles revealed about the American way of life, was considered by the department an effective contribution toward the success of that strategy. I was pleased that the book could be used to promote the foreign policy of our country.

My next publication was a profile of the state of Washington for young readers done at the request of Coward McCann. Then, in the middle sixties, and once again by request, I returned to the kitchen and the cellar, two sources of what is good in the good life that were always present in my consciousness. Having come to the new land in search of bread and found a prodigal abundance, I had celebrated bread and wine as central blessings whenever it had seemed appropriate in the course of whatever I was writing. Thus, in *Americans by Choice,* in describing a dinner I had with the winegrower, Louis Martini, I had written with such zest about a Zinfandel that the reviewer could not resist the temptation to set the book down, go to his wine merchant, procure a bottle, and return to drink heartily of it while he finished reading the book. If one may judge from the spirited review he produced, the wine had sharpened his perception.

The two books I wrote on that subject, and in the manner of *The Unprejudiced Palate*, were *Wine and the Good Life* (1965) and *The Foodlover's Garden* (1970). These were written at the request of Alfred Knopf, after he had tasted one of my vintages, and Judith Jones, one of his editors, after she had seen my kitchen garden. After these were published, I was asked to write the Italian section for the Time-Life *Melting Pot Cookbook*.

With these commissions completed, I was now ready to continue my work as amateur chronicler of the immigrant. In the spring of 1969 I returned once again to the native land; that experience I recorded in thirty-five brief essays, published by a metropolitan newspaper under the title "The Native Land Revisited." When I returned from that journey, the "ethnic revival" was noisily under way and I wrote ten essays on the Italian immigrant pioneers to the Pacific Northwest. Their lives and labor as one of the several ethnic minorities, I felt, were important data in any complete account of northwest history.

Of the five million Italians who had come to America from 1885 to 1915, only a few thousand had found their way, as had my father, to the far northwest corner of the continent during the early years of the first decade of this century. In that sense they were pioneers in a region that was on the threshold of large scale industrialization and general development. In that great surge of economic activity (also attended by regrettable waste), when forests were cut down, hills mined, and cities built, they had all begun as pick and shovel men. By hard labor, careful husbandry, and patient endurance they had earned their way into the mainstream of American life in less than three decades. Some did rather well, progressing from menial labor to various kinds of business success. Two had sons who attained political eminence. All of this they achieved without marching, breaking windows, or clamoring for rights. They had done it in the manner of the Italian peasant, with a combination of shrewdness and *pazienza*. Their various stories were chronicles of integration, and I felt it was appropriate to record them at that time.

A few years thereafter I had a most welcome and unexpected opportunity to reach a vast television audience as an ameteur historian of the immigrant experience. In celebration of the bicentennial, Thames Television of London produced a number of one-hour documentaries on immigration to America called *Destination America*. I was asked to work with them in planning and executing the documentary that dealt with the Italians. Since the request came from London, the intended audience of the program was so vast, and the intent was to commemorate the bicentennial, I felt that my participation in this production was a climax to my work hitherto as an observer and chronicler of the Italian immigrant in America. What remained for me to do in that capacity was the writing of this chronicle, which is now nearly concluded.

Such were my labors, outside the classroom, from 1948 to the present— these and hundreds of lectures within the state of Washington, in British Columbia, New York, Texas, Arizona, California, Utah, and in several other states. For congenial labor amply rewarded, it was America's rich bounty to the young immigrant who, early in his career, had seen the opportunities in this land of promise and planned to make the most of them. However, in all that I was able to achieve there was an element of luck without which I might not have fared so well. The time of my arrival in the new land, the place where my father had settled, the superb teachers who had guided me, the absence of hardships that could not be overcome, my graduation from the university in the glorious twenties when so many doors were open to me, the writing of that first book at the insistence of a friend and its unforeseen timeliness: These were the gratuities of that divinity that shapes our ends. In retrospect, these made possible the achievements of which I have given an account.

Though good fortune made my achievements possible, they were also the consequence of the course I had chosen to follow early in my career. To be sure, there was premature and unintended wisdom in that choice; but as I grew older, the course I had chosen began to bear fruit and I had the good sense to perceive its wisdom, to pursue it more positively, and to seize the opportunities that were inherent in it. The result was the productive decades I have reviewed.

What I published during those decades was in large measure unique; for no other immigrant to the new land had mined the vein that I discovered in the late forties and continued to explore thereafter. This I was able to do for two reasons: I had prepared myself to write what I did, though again rather unwittingly; and America was ready, not only to respond generously to what I had to offer, but to request it. For when I enlarged my academic forum to include the community, and became a teacher-in-residence to the new land after 1948, it was at the request of publishers and fellow Americans who were beginning to realize that what an immigrant such as myself had to say about improving the quality of life in the new land deserved an attentive ear. Specifically, the nation was becoming increasingly interested in bread and wine as elements in the good life, and I was on hand ready to respond to that interest and to further it. It was because of what I have called the "ethnic revival" that in the late sixties and early seventies I found a receptive audience for my essays on the immigrant experience. Had I come to America two or three decades earlier I would not have written such a book as *The Unprejudiced Palate*; and no publisher would have asked me to write *Wine and the Good Life* and *The Food Lover's Garden*. Nor would I have been asked to lecture in the several states on wine and gourmet cooking, and to conduct wine tastings even in churches. It must be noted that, of the hundreds of organizations that have requested my lectures, not one, after 1948, has asked me to lecture on subjects I have been teaching at the university as a professor of English. After the publication of that first book, whether I liked it or not, I was considered an authority on gastronomy, and the community insisted on being taught what it assumed I knew. Only last week I completed a series of lectures at one of the churches on the kitchen, the garden, and the cellar; I have others scheduled for the next six months. One, incredibly, is on Shakespeare!

Thus we see that while my personal story was also one of American chronicles from the beginning, it became more so, and in a very special way, after 1948. It was to document and emphasize this fact that I have reviewed my extracurricular activities during the past three decades. For what determined the course of my labors after that date, in addition to my work in the classroom was a relatively recent phase of American cultural history: the growing preoccupation with the arts of living and, more recently, a more intelligent approach to the various problems posed by the ethnic revival.

All this places the latter half of this American chronicle in its proper historical context, and explains, rather fully, how the labors of which I have given an account diverted all my creative energies away from traditional research as a professor of English. For after I had published the several scholarly essays mentioned earlier in this narrative, I published nothing such as was required of my colleagues under the threat of "publish or perish." Measured on a purely quantitative scale, my publications are no less than what may be reasonably expected of an ordinary professor in three decades of full-time teaching, and I have no illusions regarding their merit. Nor do I regret having pursued a course that diverted my creative energies away from traditional research. I have enjoyed my labors, particularly the writing of this chronicle; the generous response to all that I have written, by publishers, critics, and others who have read my books and essays, has been most gratifying. I have firmly resisted all temptations urged on me to exploit my talents for mere gain and studiously avoided writing anything that was in any way dishonest. Thus, everything considered, in pursuing the course I have described, and in urging my fellows to explore more studiously the blessings inherent in bread and wine, I have myself lived more fully the good life.

However, the pursuit of that course entailed a price: I had to abandon the opportunities I had seen in the traditional scholarship that I had begun to explore prior to 1948. In order to complete the account of what the new land made available to an immigrant such as myself, I must briefly indicate the alternative course I might have pursued. By "an immigrant such as myself," I mean no more than this: one who came as a young boy, went to school, was blessed by good fortune, chose an academic career, refused to melt in the melting pot, clung to his ancestral heritage, and sought what knowledge he could about his native land while becoming a complete American. It is important to keep this in mind because only an insignificant minority of those early immigrants were so young and so favored; while the vast majority of those who were born here and might have done what I did, chose rather to turn their backs on the land of their parents (for reasons I have detailed earlier in this narrative) and failed to learn their native language beyond the few words they gleaned from their untutored parents. Indeed, so scant is their interest in their antecedents and so little do they know about the land whence their parents came, that not many can even tell you with any precision from what region in Italy they came. It is for these reasons, and not because I am in any significant way exceptional, that immigrants such as myself are rare.

This, it seems to me, is regrettable; what I have written could very well have been written by many others, from a different perspective and in a different way, had the new land urged rather than discouraged them to cling to their ancestral heritage and improve their knowledge of it. Had they been urged to do what I did by way of self-assertion in those early years when I had to come to terms with humiliating discrimination, we might have an interesting variety of immigrant literature. For the Italian nation is composed of culturally diverse regions, each with its dialect, customs, mythology, cuisine, and political and economic problems. Ironically, I knew nothing of this until I came to America, where I met for the first time immigrants from Sicily, Calabria, Piedmont, and other regions, whose language I did not understand and who were in various ways different from us Tuscans. For these reasons it seems to me a regrettable loss that the very young among them, and the children of the older immigrants, were not urged as a matter of national policy to pursue some such course as I did.

The alternative course I might have taken, once I had abandoned the law and chosen an academic career, was suggested to me in the late thirties and early forties when I was doing research for my doctorate. While reading the history of Italian literature for the first time, I noted that what was written in Italy for a century and a half after the Council of Trent, differed significantly from what was produced in England during the same period. What was that difference and what were the reasons for it? What seventeenth-century writers in Italy could compare with Milton, Locke, and Newton? During the fifteenth and sixteenth centuries, Italy had been master to Europe in letters, the arts, and science. Its great innovators in philosophy and natural science were Bernardino Telesio, Galileo Galilei, Giordano Bruno, and Tommaso Campanella. The first two were empirical scientists. Telesio, in the tradition of the thirteenth century Bacon, had done original work toward perfecting the experimental method of inquiry, a method employed by his successor, Galileo, with such striking results. Bruno and Campanella, in the tradition of the early Greeks, were metaphysical philosophers, but in full accord with the inductive method of their contemporaries. On the negative side, their revolutionary approach to the science of man and nature entailed a rejection of the ascetic ideal of the Middle Ages, the authority of Aristotle, the scholastic method of reasoning, and, by implication, the authority of the Church. That was rank heresy; and the Inquisition dealt with the men of the new science without mercy, especially after the Council of Trent. Of the four, Telesio was the least abused; he died in 1588. Bruno was burned at the stake in 1600.

Campanella and Galileo were imprisoned and tortured. One died in 1638, the other, in 1642, the year Sir Isaac Newton was born.

One is tempted to see a benevolent destiny at work here in giving mankind a genius who, with his illustrious contemporaries, would continue in Protestant England what was no longer permitted in Catholic Italy after the Council of Trent. The Council was convened in 1545 and concluded its deliberations in 1563. As the doctrinal and tactical basis of the Counter-Reformation, it defined and codified the doctrines of the Church, reformed its most glaring abuses, which had been condemned by Martin Luther, and condemned the Reformation. The abiding hope of some of the Tridentine Fathers who composed the Council had been that it might effect a reconciliation with the Protestant Congregation, but the intransigent majority only deepened the schism. For what the enlightened reformers insisted on, beyond the elimination of clerical abuses, was freedom of conscience and the use of reason in the interpretation of the Bible and the resolution of theological questions. In substance, and put in more contemporary terms, what the reformers insisted on was the right of the individual to think, to write, and to speak, each in his own way and as his conscience required. They demanded the very basis of what would later be called man's natural rights. The Italian pioneers of the new science had observed that man had been thinking with the brain of others; thenceforward he would think with his own. But the Council of Trent, in asserting the supreme authority of the Church and the infallibility of the Pope, would not permit this; for those who challenged that authority, the penalty was torture and burning at the stake.

Thus after the Council of Trent and the death of Telesio, Bruno, Campanella, and Galileo, Italy lost the primacy in the advancement of learning to England and Europe. This I learned when I read for the first time the history of Italian literature; it was then that I thought seriously of seeking an answer to the questions I raised above: When men of talent were no longer permitted to think, what did they write? How did the literature of seventeenth-century Italy differ from that of England for the same period? Were the men of learning in Italy anywhere near the stature of Milton, Newton, and Locke?

The issues involved in that line of inquiry were especially attractive to me at that time, since they related closely to the theme of this chronicle: my political education. For I had been tracing the course of the rights of man in the new land with increasing interest, and I was a confirmed anticlerical. Never antireligious nor antiCatholic, but always contemptuous of the worldliness of the Church, its secular pretensions, and, above all else, of the curb it had historically sought to impose on the freedom of inquiry. The very suggestion that anyone had the authority—and, pray, whence derived?—to tell me what I must not read and to settle whatever accounts I may have had with the Creator, made me blush with rage. I had read Milton's *Areopagitica* and accepted as an incontrovertible truth his assertion in the opening lines of *Paradise Lost* that the Holy Spirit prefers "before all temples the upright heart and pure"; as a young lion I could never forgive the hierarchs of the Church for what they had done to such profoundly spiritual beings as Giordano Bruno. Thus I was ready to enter the lists on the side of the reformers who insisted that every man is his own priest and entitled to the free exercise of what a later generation would define as man's natural rights.

The opportunity to pursue that course and to deal with those issues in my own way would have required years of careful research, the reading of many books, seclusion in the ivory tower, and a willingness to let the rest of the world go by. That line of inquiry was attractive, and the new land had given me the opportunity to prepare myself to explore it with pleasure if not with distinction. But for reasons already stated, I wrote *The Unprejudiced Palate*, and the consequences of that jolly venture have been told.

However, having taken a course that entailed those consequences in no way diminished my abiding interest in what Bess Evans had called "creative citizenship." In a land such as ours, where fabulous material resources tended to generate a greed commensurate with the opportunity to subsume their bounty, there was always the danger that those who wielded the ultimate power would attempt to sacrifice principles and ideals to rights of property. The duty of creative citizenship has always been to guard against that danger, to keep alive the splendor of the American Dream by elevating to political eminence men who could be trusted to shape national policy in the spirit of the Declaration and of the fundamental law. That duty, conceived early in my career under the tutelage of great teachers, I have always considered antecedent to all other duties incident to citizenship. In seeking to abide by it, particularly as one whom immigration to the new land had salvaged from nonbeing, I became interested in tracing the course of the rights of man from the heroic labors of the founding fathers to the bicentennial.

Thus it was that when I first conceived the idea of writing this chronicle, I felt the need to make a journey to Runnymede, the fountainhead of those rights. Since I was in my seventieth year, required to yield the tools of my trade to steadier, more capable hands, and put to pasture to ruminate on the past, the journey to Runnymede would be that of a pilgrim's pilgrimage to his shrine and a ritual end, both to my labors and to my political education. Not an undistinguished way to come to terms with the crepuscular years, the common lot of every mortal. In such a mood I planned the pilgrimage.

There was another, a purely domestic reason for it, urged on me by the current interest in ethnic origins. Until a few years ago, ethnology had been a branch of anthropology and, as such, only professional anthropologists had been interested in it. But in the late sixties and early seventies, as a consequence of the demand by neglected minorities for rights, equal opportunities, and recognition, what had been the concern of professional anthropologists alone became the concern of the nation. Ethnic cultural centers were established in various universities, and many mainstream Americans became interested in the cultural significance of their ethnic origins. One such was my wife.

She was the issue of Scotch, Irish, and English ancestors, some of whom had come to America as long ago as the late seventeenth century. Quite naturally, she had hitherto felt no need to assert her ethnic identity. Her assertion of it now came about in this way: Our children, now all adults and exemplary in their respect and love for their parents, bore an Italian name. Furthermore, for reasons implicit in this narrative, the "Italian influence" in our home had been considerable. Since they had no cause to regret the name and what their father had accomplished, they tended to exaggerate the value of what they called their Italian heritage. My wife's response to this was both wise and just. She reminded them that they were as much Scotch, Irish, and English as they were Italian, and that she, too, had a heritage that they ought to take into account. But since it had been neither defined nor translated into such palpable terms as *pasta al pesto* and wine as mine had been, I offered to take her on a tour of the British Isles where she might seek her ethnic identity, define it, and, perhaps, match my *pasta al pesto* with haggis and mead. She had gone twice with me to my native land where I had gone to become better acquainted with my heritage. The time had come for me to reciprocate by going with her to the land of her ancestors.

Thus, in the early summer after my retirement, we flew to Shannon whence our tour of the British Isles would begin. I did not reveal to my wife my private reason for the tour. This was her journey and I was along as her companion. Nor did I tell her that I would observe her reactions and, perhaps, record them in an essay for later publication. In Ireland and, later, in Scotland, as we moved from one marvel to another, she was excited, thrilled, reverent. The British Isles in the height of summer—the downs, the emerald green, the hedgerows, the meadows, the wooded hillsides, the highlands—are a lovely land, but now they had an added splendor. This was the land of her ancestors! I admired her intelligent awareness, her discriminating judgments, noted what her painter's eye saw in a landscape, and her reverent attitude in the presence of the various monuments raised by her ancestors. Indeed, I became so absorbed in noting her reactions that I was seeing everything through her eyes. Until we approached Runnymede.

The word itself is quaint and poetic. It derives from Germanic and Middle English roots that mean "meadow on the council island." And that is precisely what it is—no more than a half dozen acres of meadowland on the south bank of the Thames about twenty miles west of London. Its historical importance, to such English speaking people as are aware of it, lies in the fact that on June 15, 1215, "in the meadow which is called Runnymede, between Windsor and Staines," King John affixed his seal to the Great Charter, known as the Magna Carta. That historic meadow is now sacred ground in the care of the British National Trust. The only memorial on that sacred land, which is itself a memorial, is a star-spangled blue dome supported by eight stone columns that bears the inscription "To commemorate Magna Carta Symbol of Freedom Under Law." It was the gift of the American Bar Association in 1957.

It is an appropriately simple memorial, in good taste, on that pastoral landscape that the British National Trust had wisely left unencumbered by monuments. It seemed to me appropriate that America should have raised it and kept it unobtrusive, for it was in the name of the principles derived from the Magna Carta that the colonies declared their independence and established a new nation. That nation has now been made into a "teeming nation of nations" by the millions who came there from other lands and became by choice the beneficiaries of the Magna Carta. One of them was Joseph Kennedy; to the memory of his son John F. Kennedy, the people of England have dedicated one acre of the meadow called Runnymede.

And I am another. Pardon the juxtaposition of my name with that of an illustrious American! I know what I am. Mine is not a name to be remembered and memorialized. But among the millions of my fellows, anonymous or otherwise, who came to America and became the beneficiaries of the Magna Carta, I yield to no one in the degree of reverence I feel for that historic document. There are four extant copies of it that bear the seal of King John. Two are in the British Museum; the others are in the cathedrals at Lincoln and Salisbury. When we left the sacred meadow and arrived in London, I went directly to the museum, anxious to see the historic document itself and to feel its transcendence. I said above that I had vaguely thought of my journey to Runnymede as a pilgrim's pilgrimage to his shrine. And so it was! Hitherto I had a student's knowledge of the Magna Carta and had properly revered it as the "chief cornerstone of the Common Law of England," but never so intensely and with such religious fervor as now when, my eyes fixed on the great seal, the visual and the conceptual faculties merged to reveal the full majesty of that symbol.

Reading with my scant knowledge of Latin the celebrated article thirty-nine, "No freeman shall be taken or imprisoned or disseised . . . ," I groped for the substance of that singular achievement of the Anglo-Saxon genius. And there it was: free man. There was little of the slavish in those Angles and Saxons of towering strength who came down from the shores of the Baltic, drove out the Romans, and took possession of England. The individual, conscious of his worth, was a free man. His relation to the warrior chief was a voluntary arrangement, a contract, a compromise. He must have a voice in the government of the tribe, give or withhold his consent to any course that affected his welfare.

What a flow of memories was occasioned by these reflections! I remembered the fate of Richard II, the last of the Plantagenets, and of the Stuart, Charles I, who had tried to impose the royal will upon their subjects; I recalled Milton's classic defense of freedom of the press, and the glorious revolution that established the primacy of Parliament. I remembered Shakespeare's variously repeated assertion that no man shall ever stand in awe of another, and that, but for ceremony, a king is but another man. I remembered Locke's theory of government, according to which man has a right to life, liberty, and property, and that in England his philosophy had prevailed over that of Hobbes, the apostle of absolutism and exponent of materialism, who had found life "nasty, brutish, and short." I remembered Mill's

Essay on Liberty and Jefferson's substitution of "the pursuit of happiness" for Locke's ownership of property as one of man's natural rights. I remembered, also, Patrick Henry in the Colonial Congress and Lincoln at Gettysburg and the creed that Whitman urged on young poets: "Love the Earth and the Sun and the animals . . . hate tyrants . . . take off your hat to no man. . . ." And I recalled the substance of the American Dream, and the conscience of America as the unyielding guardian of that dream.

Reflecting further on these remembered achievements of some of the best minds of the race as I studied the historic document in the British Museum, I realized that what they had in common was their heretical insistence on the primacy of the human spirit. They were all of the secular fraternity, but they were profoundly religious men. Their heresies would be, or had been, translated into man's unalienable rights. And at this point in my reflections on the meaning of the Magna Carta after I had left the sacred ground, I felt the fullness of something that hitherto I had felt but imperfectly and as an abstraction: the premise, the truth of truths—that those rights were of divine origin; that while *historically* they had been regarded as having issued from that fountainhead, the Great Charter, their ultimate origin was a moral law, immutable, eternal, and not subject to review by human tribunals. For the *legal* rights, which had been declared to all mankind and written into the Declaration and the Constitution, were the Creator's grants to man and unalienable. Thus, life, liberty, and the pursuit of happiness were not merely *constitutional* rights; they were moral rights, God-given and not to be denied. "Congress shall make *no law . . . abridging the freedom of speech. . . .*" As in the Decalogue, there are no conditions imposed. It is an ordinance of the Creator translated into legal terms, in language that is simple and not in the least ambiguous. I have more than once stated, during the course of this chronicle, that we young idealists, in full accord with the conscience of America, took the Declaration and the Constitution and the dream seriously. Were we wrong, naive, dreamers, in so doing? After my journey to Runnymede, I felt that our position had been incontrovertible. The rights with which the Creator had endowed man must be revered and taken seriously, or they should not be declared at all.

Right or wrong, such were my conclusions after my pilgrimage to ground as hallowed as the battleground at Gettysburg. And was it not strange that the gentleman who had been guide to our tour and who had lectured so learnedly on the historic places we had visited has so little to say about Runnymede? And even more strange that my wife, when we stood on that sacred ground, manifested no particular interest in it? She apparently was not aware of the fact that what was most precious in her heritage was there, in that lovely meadow by the Thames. Not being an immigrant herself, did she lack the experience that had fixed it in my consciousness? Had she ever heard of Runnymede? Of the Magna Carta? I kept these reflections to myself and smiled inwardly and, I fear, with a touch of satanic humor, at the ironic turn that our quest had taken: in taking her to the land of her ancestors that she might find and define *her* heritage, I had found and defined my own in hers!

From Runnymede we proceeded to Speaker's Corner in Hyde Park. The progression was a logical one, for there, on a fair Sunday afternoon, we saw free men in the uninhibited exercise of one of their moral rights. There were dozens of speakers and thousands of listeners, and but two unarmed officers in the entire area. Freedom under law. Passions were at a fever pitch, voices were eloquent, verbal challenges were hurled and accepted. But there was order. And the spirit of John Stuart Mill, the most cogent advocate of the freedom there exercised, presided over the whole.

When we left London, I felt that we were leaving a land that, in many ways, is the center of good sense; and I was aware that we were returning to another which in very significant ways became an extension of it. The English dissidents who had made America their home, building on the foundations struck at Runnymede, had established a society more fluid, less burdened with regressive traditions than that of the Old World, not always loyal to its declared high imperatives, but a blessed land, rich in material and spiritual resources, where man has been relatively free to work, play, and enjoy the fruits of his labor. Years ago, in another book, I had stated that, although I had issued from my mother's womb in Casabianca, I was actually born on the western frontier of the new land. For one may properly maintain that he was born on the day on which he actually began to live, earning his bread in the sweat of his brow, but with purpose, with dignity, and a sense of direction, rooted in the confident awareness that he was free to order his life to the requirements of his heart and mind. The course of my life in the decades that followed strengthened that conviction.

Seventy years ago, having arrived on that western frontier by the miracle of immigration, I had begun my general and political education, guided by wise, kind, and generous teachers. The starting point in that high adventure when I was a young boy learning the English language and knowing nothing of the traditions, customs, and mythology of America, had been what I learned from one of those kind teachers about the Pilgrim fathers at Plymouth and the meaning of the Thanksgiving holiday. Proceeding thence to what has been recorded in the early chapters of this chronicle, I became passionately interested in tracing the course of the rights of man in the new land, rejoicing where they had been granted and indignant where they had been denied. That education had now come full circle and at a ritual end with my reflections at Runnymede, the historical fountainhead of those rights.

Now in retirement, facing westward into the twilight, I was free to ruminate on the past and to write this chronicle. In good health, husband of a lady of exceptional virtues, father of exemplary children, I am still at my workbench, adding day by day to that which by its very nature is coextensive with life, the happiness that inheres in labor the goal of which is self-realization.

Now that what was my story is your story, you and I are one. Let us remember the human family, and so revitalize our faith in the American conscience that its ascendancy will be assured. Let us cooperate in promoting the general welfare and in conserving the cornucopia of this blessed land so that, by virtue of our enlightened stewardship, tomorrow's children of fecund America, each in his own way, may seek happiness in the pursuit of the American Dream.

Design by David Bullen
Typeset in Mergenthaler Sabon
by Harrington-Young
Printed by Maple-Vail
on acid-free paper